Praise for *More Effective*

"Shining a bright light into many of the dark corners of C# 3.0, this book not only covers the 'how,' but also the 'why,' arming the reader with many field-tested methods for wringing the most from the new language features, such as LINQ, generics, and multithreading. If you are serious about developing with the C# language, you need this book."

—Bill Craun, Principal Consultant, Ambassador Solutions, Inc.

"*More Effective C#* is an opportunity to work beside Bill Wagner. Bill leverages his knowledge of C# and distills his expertise down to some very real advice about programming and designing applications that every serious Visual C# user should know. *More Effective C#* is one of those rare books that doesn't just regurgitate syntax, but teaches you *how* to use the C# language."

—Peter Ritchie, Microsoft MVP: Visual C#

"*More Effective C#* is a great follow-up to Bill Wagner's previous book. The extensive C# 3.0 and LINQ coverage is extremely timely!"

—Tomas Restrepo, Microsoft MVP: Visual C++, .NET, and Biztalk Server

"As one of the current designers of C#, it is rare that I learn something new about the language by reading a book. *More Effective C#* is a notable exception. Gently blending concrete code and deep insights, Bill Wagner frequently makes me look at C# in a fresh light—one that really makes it shine. *More Effective C#* is at the surface a collection of very useful guidelines. Look again. As you read through it, you'll find that you acquire more than just the individual pieces of advice; gradually you'll pick up on an approach to programming in C# that is thoughtful, beautiful, and deeply pleasant. While you can make your way willy-nilly through the individual guidelines, I do recommend reading the whole book—or at least not skipping over the chapter introductions before you dive into specific nuggets of advice. There's perspective and insight to be found there that in itself can be an important guide and inspiration for your future adventures in C#."

—Mads Torgersen, Program Manager, Visual C#, Microsoft

"Bill Wagner has written an excellent book outlining the best practices for developers who work with the C# language. By authoring *More Effective C#*, he has again established himself as one of the most important voices in the C# community. Many of us already know how to use C#. What we need is advice on how to hone our skills so that we can become wiser programmers. There is no more sophisticated source of information on how to become a first-class C# developer than Bill Wagner's book. Bill is intelligent, thoughtful, experienced, and skillful. By applying the lessons from this book to your own code, you will find many ways to polish and improve the work that you produce."

—Charlie Calvert, Community Program Manager, Visual C#, Microsoft

More Effective C#

Effective SOFTWARE DEVELOPMENT SERIES ⋏⋎
Scott Meyers, Consulting Editor

The **Effective Software Development Series** provides expert advice on all aspects of modern software development. Books in the series are well written, technically sound, of lasting value, and tractable length. Each describes the critical things the experts almost always do—or almost always avoid doing—to produce outstanding software.

Scott Meyers (author of the *Effective C++* books and CD) conceived of the series and acts as its consulting editor. Authors in the series work with Meyers and with Addison-Wesley Professional's editorial staff to create essential reading for software developers of every stripe.

TITLES IN THE SERIES

Elliotte Rusty Harold, *Effective XML: 50 Specific Ways to Improve Your XML*
0321150406

Ted Neward, *Effective Enterprise Java* 0321130006

Diomidis Spinellis, *Code Reading: The Open Source Perspective* 0201799405

Diomidis Spinellis, *Code Quality: The Open Source Perspective* 0321166078

Bill Wagner, *Effective C#: 50 Specific Ways to Improve Your C#*
0321245660

For more information on books in this series please see www.awprofessional.com/esds

More Effective C#

50 Specific Ways to Improve Your C#

Bill Wagner

✦✦ Addison-Wesley

Upper Saddle River, NJ • Boston • Indianapolis • San Francisco
New York • Toronto • Montreal • London • Munich • Paris • Madrid
Capetown • Sydney • Tokyo • Singapore • Mexico City

Many of the designations used by manufacturers and sellers to distinguish their products are claimed as trademarks. Where those designations appear in this book, and the publisher was aware of a trademark claim, the designations have been printed with initial capital letters or in all capitals.

The author and publisher have taken care in the preparation of this book, but make no expressed or implied warranty of any kind and assume no responsibility for errors or omissions. No liability is assumed for incidental or consequential damages in connection with or arising out of the use of the information or programs contained herein.

The publisher offers excellent discounts on this book when ordered in quantity for bulk purchases or special sales, which may include electronic versions and/or custom covers and content particular to your business, training goals, marketing focus, and branding interests. For more information, please contact:

U.S. Corporate and Government Sales
(800) 382-3419
corpsales@pearsontechgroup.com

For sales outside the United States please contact:

International Sales
international@pearson.com

Visit us on the Web: informit.com/aw

Library of Congress Cataloging-in-Publication Data

Wagner, Bill.
  More effective C# : 50 specific ways to improve your C# / Bill Wagner.
     p.   cm.
  Includes bibliographical references and index.
  ISBN 978-0-321-48589-2 (pbk. : alk. paper)
  1. C# (Computer program language) 2. Database management. 3.
Microsoft .NET. I. Title.

  QA76.73.C154W343 2008
  005.13'3—dc22

                                                        2008030878

ISBN-13: 978-0-321-48589-2
ISBN-10:   0-321-48589-0
Text printed in the United States on recycled paper at Donnelley in Crawfordsville, IN.
First printing, October 2008

For Marlene, who puts up with me writing,
time and time again.

Contents at a Glance

Contents

Introduction

When Anders Hejlsberg first showed Language-Integrated Query (LINQ) to the world at the 2005 Professional Developers Conference (PDC), the C# programming world changed. LINQ justified several new features in the C# language: extension methods, local variable type inference, lambda expressions, anonymous types, object initializers, and collection initializers. C# 2.0 set the stage for LINQ by adding generics, iterators, static classes, nullable types, property accessor accessibility, and anonymous delegates. But all these features are useful outside LINQ: They are handy for many programming tasks that have nothing to do with querying data sources.

This book provides practical advice about the features added to the C# programming language in the 2.0 and 3.0 releases, along with advanced features that were not covered in my earlier *Effective C#: 50 Specific Ways to Improve Your C#* (Addison-Wesley, 2004). The items in *More Effective C#* reflect the advice I give developers who are adopting C# 3.0 in their professional work. There's a heavy emphasis on generics, an enabling technology for everything in C# 2.0 and 3.0. I discuss the new features in C# 3.0; rather than organize the topics by language feature, I present these tips from the perspective of recommendations about the programming problems that developers can best solve by using these new features.

Consistent with the other books in the Effective Software Development Series, this book contains self-contained items detailing specific advice about how to use C#. The items are organized to guide you from using C# 1.x to using C# 3.0 in the best way.

Generics are an enabling technology for all new idioms that are part of C# 3.0. Although only the first chapter specifically addresses generics, you'll find that they are an integral part of almost every item. After reading this book, you'll be much more comfortable with generics and metaprogramming.

Of course, much of the book discusses how to use C# 3.0 and the LINQ query syntax in your code. The features added in C# 3.0 are very useful in their own right, whether or not you are querying data sources. These changes in the language are so extensive, and LINQ is such a large part of the justification for those changes, that each warrants its own chapter. LINQ and C# 3.0 will have a profound impact on how you write code in C#. This book will make that transition easier.

Who Should Read This Book?

This book was written for professional software developers who use C#. It assumes that you have some familiarity with C# 2.0 and C# 3.0. Scott Meyers counseled me that an *Effective* book should be a developer's second book on a subject. This book does not include tutorial information on the new language features added as the language has evolved. Instead, I explain how you can integrate these features into your ongoing development activities. You'll learn when to leverage the new language features in your development activities, and when to avoid certain practices that will lead to brittle code.

In addition to some familiarity with the newer features of the C# language, you should have an understanding of the major components that make up the .NET Framework: the .NET CLR (Common Language Runtime), the .NET BCL (Base Class Library), and the JIT (Just In Time) compiler. This book doesn't cover .NET 3.0 components, such as WCF (Windows Communication Foundation), WPF (Windows Presentation Foundation), and WF (Windows Workflow Foundation). However, all the idioms presented apply to those components as well as any other .NET Framework components you happen to prefer.

About the Content

Generics are the enabling technology for everything else added to the C# language since C# 1.1. Chapter 1 covers generics as a replacement for `System.Object` and casts and then moves on to discuss advanced techniques such as constraints, generic specialization, method constraints, and backward compatibility. You'll learn several techniques in which generics will make it easier to express your design intent.

Multicore processors are already ubiquitous, with more cores being added seemingly every day. This means that every C# developer needs to have a solid understanding of the support provided by the C# language for multithreaded programming. Although one chapter can't cover everything you need to be an expert, Chapter 2 discusses the techniques you'll need every day when you write multithreaded applications.

Chapter 3 explains how to express modern design idioms in C#. You'll learn the best way to express your intent using the rich palette of C# language features. You'll see how to leverage lazy evaluation, create composable interfaces, and avoid confusion among the various language elements in your public interfaces.

Chapter 4 discusses how to use the enhancements in C# 3.0 to solve the programming challenges you face every day. You'll see when to use extension methods to separate contracts from implementation, how to use C# closures effectively, and how to program with anonymous types.

Chapter 5 explains LINQ and query syntax. You'll learn how the compiler maps query keywords to method calls, how to distinguish between delegates and expression trees (and convert between them when needed), and how to escape queries when you're looking for scalar results.

Chapter 6 covers those items that defy classification. You'll learn how to define partial classes, work with nullable types, and avoid covariance and contravariance problems with array parameters.

Regarding the Sample Code

The samples in this book are not complete programs. They are the smallest snippets of code possible that illustrate the point. In several samples the method names substitute for a concept, such as `AllocateExpensiveResource()`. Rather than read pages of code, you can grasp the concept and quickly apply it to your professional development. Where methods are elided, the name implies what's important about the missing method.

In all cases, you can assume that the following namespaces are specified:

```
using System;
using System.Collections.Generic;
using System.Linq;
using System.Text;
```

Where types are used from other namespaces, I've explicitly included the namespace in the type.

In the first three chapters, I often show C# 2.0 and C# 3.0 syntax where newer syntax is preferred but not required. In Chapters 4 and 5 I assume that you would use the 3.0 syntax.

Making Suggestions and Providing Feedback

I've made every effort to remove all errors from this book, but if you believe you have found an error, please contact me at bill.wagner@srtsolutions.com. Errata will be posted to http://srtsolutions.com/blogs/MoreEffectiveCSharp.

Acknowledgments

A colleague recently asked me to describe what it feels like to finish a book. I replied that it gives you that same feeling of satisfaction and relief that shipping a software product gives you. It's very satisfying, and yet it's an incredible amount of work. Like shipping a software product, completing a book requires collaboration among many people, and all those people deserve thanks.

I was honored to be part of the Effective Software Development Series when I wrote *Effective C#* in 2004. To follow that up with *More Effective C#* and cover the numerous and far-reaching changes in the language since then is an even greater honor. The genesis of this book was a dinner I shared with Curt Johnson and Joan Murray at PDC 2005, when I expressed my excitement about the direction Hejlsberg and the rest of the C# team were presenting there. I was already taking notes about the changes and learning how they would affect the daily lives of C# developers.

Of course, it was some time before I felt comfortable in offering advice on all these new features. I needed to spend time using them and discussing different idioms with coworkers, customers, and other developers in the community. Once I felt comfortable with the new features, I began working on the new manuscript.

I was lucky enough to have an excellent team of technical reviewers. These people suggested new topics, modified the recommendations, and found scores of technical errors in earlier drafts. Bill Craun, Wes Dyer, Nick Paldino, Tomas Restrepo, and Peter Ritchie provided detailed technical feedback that made this book as useful as it is now. Pavin Podila reviewed those areas that mention WPF to ensure correctness.

Throughout the writing process, I discussed many ideas with members of the community and the C# team. The regulars at the Ann Arbor .NET Developers Group, the Great Lakes Area .NET User Group, the Greater Lansing User Group, the West Michigan .NET User Group, and the Toledo .NET User Group acted as prototype audiences for much of the advice presented here. In addition, CodeMash attendees helped me decide what to leave in and what to leave out. In particular, I want to single out Dustin Campbell, Jay Wren, and Mike Woelmer for letting me discuss ideas with them. In addition, Mads Torgersen, Charlie Calvert, and Eric Lippert joined me in several conversations that helped clarify the advice detailed here. In particular, Charlie Calvert has the great skill of mixing an engineer's understanding with a writer's gift of clarity. Without all those discussions, this manuscript would be far less clear, and it would be missing a number of key concepts.

Having been through Scott Meyers's thorough review process twice now, I'd recommend any book in his series sight unseen. Although he's not a C# expert, he's highly gifted and clearly cares about the books in his series. Responding to his comments takes quite a bit of time, but it results in a much better book.

Throughout the whole process, Joan Murray has been an incredible asset. As editor, she's always on top of everything. She prodded me when I needed prodding, she provided a great team of reviewers, and she helped shepherd the book from inception through outlines, manuscript drafts, and finally into the version you hold now. Along with Curt Johnson, she makes working with Addison-Wesley a joy.

The last step is working with a copy editor. Betsy Hardinger was somehow able to translate an engineer's jargon into English without sacrificing technical correctness. The book you're holding is much easier to read after her edits.

Of course, writing a book takes a large investment of time. During that time, Dianne Marsh, the other owner of SRT Solutions, kept the company moving forward. The greatest sacrifice was from my family, who saw much less of me than they'd like while I was writing this book. The biggest thanks go to Marlene, Lara, Sarah, and Scott, who put up with me as I did this again.

1 | Working with Generics

Without a doubt, C# 2.0 added a feature that continues to have a big impact on how you write C# code: generics. Many articles and papers have been written about the advantages of using generics over the previous versions of the C# collections classes, and those articles are correct. You gain compile-time type safety and improve your applications' performance by using generic types rather than weakly typed collections that rely on `System.Object`.

Some articles and papers might lead you to believe that generics are useful only in the context of collections. That's not true. There are many other ways to use generics. You can use them to create interfaces, event handlers, common algorithms, and more.

Many other discussions compare C# generics to C++ templates, usually to advocate one as better than the other. Comparing C# generics to C++ templates is useful to help you understand the syntax, but that's where the comparison should end. Certain idioms are more natural to C++ templates, and others are more natural to C# generics. But, as you'll see in Item 2 a bit later in this chapter, trying to decide which is "better" will only hurt your understanding of both of them. Adding generics required changes to the C# compiler, the Just In Time (JIT) compiler, and the Common Language Runtime (CLR). The C# compiler takes your C# code and creates the Microsoft Intermediate Language (MSIL, or IL) definition for the generic type. In contrast, the JIT compiler combines a generic type definition with a set of type parameters to create a closed generic type. The CLR supports both those concepts at runtime.

There are costs and benefits associated with generic type definitions. Sometimes, replacing specific code with a generic equivalent makes your program smaller. At other times, it makes it larger. Whether or not you encounter this generic code bloat depends on the specific type parameters you use and the number of closed generic types you create.

Generic class definitions are fully compiled MSIL types. The code they contain must be completely valid for any type parameters that satisfy the constraints. The generic definition is called a **generic type definition.** A specific instance of a generic type, in which all the type parameters have been specified, is called a **closed generic type.** (If only some of the parameters are specified, it's called an **open generic type.**)

Generics in IL are a partial definition of a real type. The IL contains the placeholder for an instantiation of a specific completed generic type. The JIT compiler completes that definition when it creates the machine code to instantiate a closed generic type at runtime. This practice introduces a tradeoff between paying the increased code cost for multiple closed generic types and gaining the decreased time and space required in order to store data.

Different closed generic types may or may not produce different runtime representations of the code. When you create multiple closed generic types, the JIT compiler and the CLR perform some optimizations to minimize the memory pressure. Assemblies, in IL form, are loaded into data pages. As the JIT compiler translates the IL into machine instructions, the resulting machine code is stored in read-only code pages.

This process happens for every type you create, generic or not. With non-generic types, there is a 1:1 correspondence between the IL for a class and the machine code created. Generics introduce some new wrinkles to that translation. When a generic class is JIT-compiled, the JIT compiler examines the type parameters and emits specific instructions depending on the type parameters. The JIT compiler performs a number of optimizations to fold different type parameters into the same machine code. First and foremost, the JIT compiler creates one machine version of a generic class for all reference types.

All these instantiations share the same code at runtime:

```
List <string> stringList = new List<string>();
List<Stream> OpenFiles = new List<Stream>();
List<MyClassType> anotherList = new List<MyClassType>();
```

The C# compiler enforces type safety at compile time, and the JIT compiler can produce a more optimized version of the machine code by assuming that the types are correct.

Different rules apply to closed generic types that have at least one value type used as a type parameter. The JIT compiler creates a different set of machine instructions for different type parameters. Therefore, the following three closed generic types have different machine code pages:

```
List<double> doubleList = new List<double>();
List<int> markers = new List<int>();
List<MyStruct> values = new List<MyStruct>();
```

This may be interesting, but why should you care? Generic types that will be used with multiple different reference types do not affect the memory footprint. All JIT-compiled code is shared. However, when closed generic types contain value types as parameters, that JIT-compiled code is not shared. Let's dig a little deeper into that process to see how it will be affected.

When the runtime needs to JIT-compile a generic definition (either a method or a class) and at least one of the type parameters is a value type, it goes through a two-step process. First, it creates a new IL class that represents the closed generic type. I'm simplifying, but essentially the runtime replaces T with int, or the appropriate value type, in all locations in the generic definition. After that replacement, it JIT-compiles the necessary code into x86 instructions. This two-step process is necessary because the JIT compiler does not create the x86 code for an entire class when loaded; instead, each method is JIT-compiled only when first called. Therefore, it makes sense to do a block substitution in the IL and then JIT-compile the resulting IL on demand, as is done with normal class definitions.

This means that the runtime costs of memory footprint add up in this way: one extra copy of the IL definition for each closed generic type that uses a value type, and a second extra copy of machine code for each method called in each different value type parameter used in a closed generic type.

There is, however, a plus side to using generics with value type parameters: You avoid all boxing and unboxing of value types, thereby reducing the size of both code and data for value types. Furthermore, type safety is ensured by the compiler; thus, fewer runtime checks are needed, and that reduces the size of the codebase and improves performance. Furthermore, as discussed in Item 8, creating generic methods instead of generic classes can limit the amount of extra IL code created for each separate instantiation. Only those methods actually referenced will be instantiated. Generic methods defined in a nongeneric class are not JIT-compiled.

This chapter discusses many of the ways you can use generics and explains how to create generic types and methods that will save you time and help you create usable components. I also cover when and how to migrate .NET 1.x types (in which you use System.Object) to .NET 2.0 types, in which you specify type parameters.

Item 1: Use Generic Replacements of 1.x Framework API Classes

The first two releases of the .NET platform did not support generics. Your only choice was to code against System.Object and add appropriate runtime checks to ensure that the runtime type of the object was what you expected, usually a specific type derived from System.Object. This practice was even more widespread in the .NET Framework, because the framework designers were creating a library of lower-level components that would be used by everyone.

System.Object is the ultimate base class for every type you or anyone else creates. That led to the obvious decision to use System.Object as a substitute for "whatever type you want to use in this space." Unfortunately, that's all the compiler knows about your types. This means that you must code everything very defensively—and so must everyone who uses your types. Whenever you have System.Object as a parameter or a return type, you have the potential to substitute the wrong type. That's a cause for runtime errors in your code.

With the addition of generics, those days are gone. If you've been using .NET for any period of time, you've probably adopted the habit of using many classes and interfaces that now should be cast aside in favor of an updated generic version. You can improve the quality of your code by replacing System.Object with generic type parameters. Why? It's because it's much harder to misuse generic types by supplying arguments of the wrong type.

If correctness isn't enough to motivate you to replace your old System.Object code with generic equivalents, maybe performance will get you interested. .NET 1.1 forced you to use the ultimate base class of System.Object and dynamically cast objects to the expected type before using them. The 1.1 versions of any class or interface require that you box and unbox value types every time you coerce between the value type and the System.Object type. Depending on your usage, that requirement may have a significant impact on performance. Of course, it applies only with value types. But, as I said earlier, the weakly typed systems from the 1.1 days require both you and your users to author defensive code to test the runtime type of your parameters and return types. Even when that code functions correctly, it adds runtime performance costs. And it's worse when it fails; the runtime costs probably include stack walks and unwinding when casts throw exceptions and the runtime searches for the proper catch clause. You run the risk of everything from costly application slowdown to abnormal application termination.

A good look at the .NET Framework 2.0 shows you how much you can transform your code by using generics. The obvious starting point is the `System.Collections.Generics` namespace, followed by the `System.Collections.ObjectModel` namespace. Every class that is part of the `System.Collections` namespace has a new, improved counterpart in `System.Collections.Generics`. For example, `ArrayList` has been superseded by `List<T>`, `Stack` has been replaced by `Stack<T>`, `Hashtable` has been replaced by `Dictionary<K,V>`, and `Queue` has been replaced by `Queue<T>`. In addition, there are a few new collections, such as `SortedList<T>` and `LinkedList<T>`.

The addition of these classes meant the addition of generic interfaces. Again, the `System.Collections.Generics` namespace points to the obvious examples. The original `IList` interface has been extended with `IList<T>`. All the collections-based interfaces have been similarly upgraded: `IDictionary<K,V>` replaces `IDictionary`, `IEnumerable<T>` extends `IEnumerable`, `IComparer<T>` replaces `IComparer`, and `ICollection<T>` replaces `ICollection`.

I say "extends" and "replaces" deliberately. Many of the generic interfaces derive from their nongeneric counterparts, extending the classic capability with upgraded, type-specific versions. Other classic interfaces are not part of the signature of the newer interfaces. For a variety of reasons, the newer interface method signatures aren't consistent with the classic interfaces. When that happened, the framework designers chose not to tie the new interface definitions to an outdated interface.

The .NET 2.0 Framework has added an `IEquatable<T>` interface to minimize the potential errors involved in overriding `System.Object.Equals`:

```
public interface IEquatable<T>
{
    bool Equals(T other);
}
```

You should add support for this interface wherever you would have overwritten `System.Object.Equals`.

If you need to perform comparisons on a type defined in another library, the .NET 2.0 Framework has also added a new equality interface in the generic collections namespace: `IEqualityComparer<T>`. This interface has two methods: `Equals` and `GetHashCode`.

```
public interface IEqualityComparer<T>
{
    int Equals( T x, T y);
    int GetHashCode(T obj);
}
```

You can create a helper class that implements `IEqualityComparer<T>` for any third-party type you use today. This class works like any class that implements the 1.1 version of `IHashCodeProvider`. It enables you to create type-safe equality comparisons for your types, deprecating the old versions based on `System.Object`. You'll almost never need to write a full implementation of `IEqualityComparer<T>` yourself. Instead, you can use the `EqualityComparer<T>` class and its `Default` property. For example, you would write the following `EmployeeComparer` class, derived from `EqualityComparer<T>`, to test the equality of `Employee` objects created in another library:

```
public class EmployeeComparer : EqualityComparer<Employee>
{
    public override bool Equals(Employee x, Employee y)
    {
        return EqualityComparer<Employee>.Default.Equals(x, y);
    }

    public override int GetHashCode(Employee obj)
    {
        return EqualityComparer<Employee>.Default.
            GetHashCode(obj);
    }
}
```

The `Default` property examines the type argument, `T`. If the type implements `IEquatable<T>`, then `Default` returns an `IEqualityComparer<T>` that uses the generic interface. If not, `Default` returns an `IEqualityComparer<T>` that uses the `System.Object` virtual methods `Equals()` and `GetHashCode()`. In this way, `EqualityComparer<T>` guarantees the best implementation for you.

These methods illustrate one essential fact to remember about generic types: The more fundamental the algorithm, such as equality, the more likely it is that you will want a generic type definition. When you create fundamental algorithms that have several variations, you'll want the compile-time checking you get with generic type definitions.

To show you what I mean, let's browse through the `System` namespace to learn from the other generic classes that are available in the .NET 2.0 Framework. I'm taking you on this tour for two reasons. First, if you've been using C# for a while, you've already developed 1.1 habits that don't include these classes. You should change those habits to incorporate the improvements offered by the generic versions. Second, the framework classes provide a great set of examples for the kinds of problems you can solve using generics.

I mentioned that the `System.Collections.Generic` namespace contains an `IComparer<T>` interface to improve on the classic `IComparer` interface. Well, the `System` namespace also contains a generic compare interface: `IComparable<T>`.

```
public interface IComparable<T>
{
    int CompareTo(T other);
}
```

The obvious analog is the old-style `IComparable` interface:

```
// 1.1 Comparable signature
public interface IComparable
{
    int CompareTo(object other);
}
```

The gains provided by the typical implementation show exactly when the generic version is superior. Here's a snippet of code from Item 9 in my earlier book *Effective C#: 50 Specific Ways to Improve Your C#* (Addison-Wesley, 2004):

```
// Code from the Customer struct (a value type)
public int CompareTo(object right)
{
    if (!(right is Customer))
        throw new ArgumentException("Argument not a customer",
            "right");
    Customer rightCustomer = (Customer)right;
    return Name.CompareTo(rightCustomer.Name);
}
```

The `IComparable<T>` version is much simpler than the `IComparable` version, which relies on `System.Object`:

```
public int CompareTo(Customer right)
{
    return Name.CompareTo(right.Name);
}
```

You gain four advantages by creating and using generic interfaces, because generic interfaces are type-safe. Notice the difference between the implementation of IComparable and IComparable<T>. The IComparable<T> version is much smaller, because the runtime type checking needed for the IComparable version is enforced by the compiler when you implement IComparable<T>. Therefore, you create less code, and that code does the same work. The generic version is also faster; you've removed some error checking. In addition, the generic version avoids any boxing and unboxing, along with the type conversions. Finally, the generic version does not emit any runtime errors. All those runtime errors that are generated by the nongeneric version are caught by the compiler in the generic version.

Of course, there are times when using System.Object makes sense. Your design may include comparing objects that are not related by type (or by inheritance) but may have similar properties. In that situation, you should implement the classic interfaces in addition to the newer generic versions (see Item 10 later in this chapter). Suppose you have used a third-party e-commerce system that must integrate with your own legacy shipping system. Both systems have the concept of an Order. Those two concepts are not related in any way by inheritance:

```
namespace ThirdPartyECommerceSystem
{
    public class Order
    {
        // details elided
    }
}
```

You would modify your own order system to include the classic interfaces so that it would support equality for both kinds of Order objects:

```
namespace InternalShippingSystem
{
    public class Order : IEquatable<Order>,
        IComparable<Order>
    {
```

```
#region IEquatable<Order> Members
public bool Equals(Order other)
{
    // elided
    return true;
}
#endregion

#region IComparable<Order> Members
public int CompareTo(Order other)
{
    // elided
    return 0;
}
#endregion

public override bool Equals(object obj)
{
    if (obj is Order)
        return this.Equals((Order)obj);
    else if (obj is ThirdPartyECommerceSystem.Order)
        return this.Equals
            ((ThirdPartyECommerceSystem.Order)obj);
        throw new ArgumentException(
            "Object type not supported", "obj");
}
public bool Equals(ThirdPartyECommerceSystem.Order
    other)
{
    bool equal = true;
    // tests elided
    return equal;
}
    }
}
```

The classic interfaces can support this kind of relationship between unrelated types that represent the same concept. This isn't a design I would intentionally add to my system, but when you must get libraries from different vendors to work together with similar concepts, it is the best option.

Examine the code carefully, and notice that the code overriding `System.Object.Equals()` reports problems using runtime errors instead of compile-time errors.

Whenever you can replace `System.Object` with the correct type, you'll get compile-time type safety, along with some performance gains. Clearly, `IComparable<T>` is preferred to `IComparable` in almost all cases. In fact, almost any 1.x interface that used `System.Object` has been updated and replaced with a generic equivalent. The only obvious counterexample is `ICloneable`, which has not been updated with a generic equivalent. Implementing `ICloneable` is discouraged. See Krzysztof Cwalina and Brad Abrams, *Framework Design Guidelines: Conventions, Idioms, and Patterns for Reusable .NET Libraries* (Addison-Wesley, 2005), pp. 221–222.

One of the most commonly used generic additions in the .NET 2.0 Framework is the **nullable generic type.** Nullable types are implemented using two complementary type definitions: the `Nullable<T>` struct, and the static `Nullable` class. The `Nullable<T>` struct is the wrapper for any value type that needs to also represent a null value (see Item 45, Chapter 6). For the moment, it's enough to know that one generic type handles the relationship between a nullable type and the underlying value type instance that it should represent.

To support nullable value types, the base class library added a static `Nullable` class and a `Nullable<T>` generic structure. The static `Nullable` class contains some generic methods that you can use to work with nullable types. `Nullable.GetUnderlyingType(Type t)` returns the type of the underlying object in a `Nullable<T>`; in other words, the following actual runtime type compares two nullables of the same type and determines whether they are equal:

```
Nullable.Compare<T> (Nullable<T> left, Nullable<T> right);
```

Together, these classes provide the functionality that the C# compiler uses to implement your requests for nullable types.

The .NET Framework designers also added some utility delegates using generics that you can use (and they use) to handle common patterns. For example, suppose you want to create a callback that visits every element of a generic collection. Using `IEnumerable<T>`, you could visit each element using a simple `foreach` loop:

```
List<MyType> theList = new List<MyType>();
foreach (MyType thing in theList)
    thing.DoSomething();
```

You can replace DoSomething with any function that matches the System.Action delegate:

```
public delegate void Action<T>(T obj);
```

A simple generic function can now visit every item in a collection and perform some action on each element:

```
public static void EnumerateAll<T>(IEnumerable<T>
theCollection,
    Action<T> doIt)
{
    foreach (T thing in theCollection)
        doIt(thing);
}
```

Of course, in C# 3.0, you should prefer to create this as an extension method:

```
public static void EnumerateAll<T>(this IEnumerable<T>
theCollection,
    Action<T> doIt)
{
    foreach (T thing in theCollection)
        doIt(thing);
}
```

When you want to sort an array of objects that doesn't implement IComparable<T>, you can supply a delegate that matches the System.Comparison delegate:

```
delegate int Comparison<T>( T x, T y);
```

This delegate is used in List.Sort<T>(Comparison<T> comparison), an overload of Sort() that allows you to specify your own comparison method.

There are also a couple of delegates that you can use to transform objects contained in a collection in a type-safe manner. The System.Converter delegate converts one input object into a corresponding output:

```
public delegate TOutput Converter<TInput, TOutput>(TInput
    input);
```

This delegate lets you write a generic method that transforms a sequence of one type into a sequence of another type:

```
public IEnumerable<TOutput> Transform<TInput, TOutput>(
    IEnumerable<TInput> theCollection,
    Converter<TInput, TOutput> transformer)
{
    foreach (TInput source in theCollection)
        yield return transformer(source);
}
```

Transform contains two type parameters: TInput and TOutput. They represent the input and output types for the transform. System.Converter uses the same convention to describe the two types.

Sometimes you want to perform a test on every object of a collection. To do that, you create a method that uses the System.Predicate delegate:

```
delegate bool Predicate<T>(T obj)
```

Another simple modification lets you create a sequence of all the elements of a sequence that pass a test:

```
public IEnumerable<T> Test<T> (IEnumerable<T> theCollection,
Predicate<T> test)
{
    foreach (T source in theCollection)
        if ( test( source ) )
            yield return source;
}
```

Generics also can help you implement events with a lot less hand-written code. In .NET 1.1, you had to create a class derived from EventArgs, then create the delegate definition, and then create an event definition to match the delegate. It's not difficult, but it's terribly repetitive. Instead, the .NET 2.0 Framework includes a generic definition for an event handler:

```
public delegate void EventHandler<TEventArgs>(
    object sender, TEventArgs args)
    where TEventArgs: EventArgs
```

This replaces the most repetitive of the custom code you needed to create the delegate. The separate delegate and event definitions might look like this:

```
public delegate void MyEventHandler(object sender,
    MyEventArgs args);
public event MyEventHandler OnRaiseMyEvent;
```

Instead, you now have this:

```
public event EventHandler<MyEventArgs> OnRaiseMyEvent;
```

It's a small saving, but it adds up when you're defining numerous events.

That covers the major generic additions to the `System` namespace, but there is one more important addition to mention: `System.Component-Model.BindingList<T>`. Creating a type that implemented `IBind-ingList` in the .NET 1.x Framework was a boring and painful task. Also, most of that code was very similar, and it had little to do with the actual type being placed in the list. But `IBindingList`, `ICancelAddNew`, and `CurrencyManager` work together, so there were many opportunities to make mistakes. For example, if you wanted to create a class that implemented `IBindingList` for a typical employee class, it would take you several pages of code. In .NET 2.0, it's simply this:

```
System.ComponentModel.BindingList<Employee>
```

What could be easier?

That concludes the tour of the major generic classes in the .NET 2.0 Framework. You can see that using generics means that you write less error-checking code, because now the compiler validates the types of parameters and return values in those places where you had to do it before. Generics are a big win, so get to know the generic definitions in the framework, and use them.

The final question is what to do with your current 1.1 code assets that have better generic equivalents. I recommend that you replace that code with its generic equivalent at your earliest convenience, but don't create a separate task simply to use generics. Code that already works is fine as it is. But as soon as you update or modify it, you encounter new opportunities to create bugs that the compiler would find for you. When you undertake a large task on any nongeneric class, start by replacing the pertinent definitions with the generic equivalent, and let the compiler help you find the remaining issues.

This item presents the case for changing any habits you have of building code using the classic nongeneric application programming interface (API) in favor of using the newer generic versions. It will be easier to use your libraries correctly, and harder to use them incorrectly. You'll leverage the compiler to do more type checking for you. By using the generic delegate definitions, you'll be better able to leverage the C# 3.0 enhancements that let the compiler infer types, freeing you to think about algorithms and logic. The sooner your code uses generics instead of nongeneric counterparts wherever possible, the sooner you'll be able to leverage the newest language features.

Item 2: Define Constraints That Are Minimal and Sufficient

The constraints you declare on your type parameters specify the must-have behaviors your class needs in order to accomplish its work. A type that doesn't satisfy all your constraints simply won't work. Balance that against the fact that every constraint you impose could mean more work for developers who want to use your type. The right choice varies from task to task, but either extreme is wrong. If you don't specify any constraints, you must perform more checks at runtime: You'll perform more casts, possibly using reflection and generating more runtime errors if your users misuse your type. Specifying unneeded constraints means making too much work for the users of your class. Your goal is to find the middle ground, where you specify what you need but not everything you want.

Constraints enable the compiler to expect capabilities in a type parameter beyond those in the public interface defined in `System.Object`. When you create a generic type, the C# compiler must generate valid IL for the generic type definition. While doing so, the compiler must create a valid assembly even though the compiler has only limited knowledge of the actual type that may be used to substitute for any type parameters. Without any guidance from you, the compiler can only assume the most basic capabilities about those types: the methods exposed by `System.Object`. The compiler cannot enforce any assumptions you have made about your types. All the compiler knows is that your types must derive from `System.Object`. (This means that you cannot create unsafe generics using pointers as type parameters.) Assuming only the capabilities of `System.Object` is very limiting. The compiler will emit errors on anything not defined in `System.Object`. This includes even such fundamental operations as `new T()`, which is hidden if you define a constructor that has parameters.

You use constraints to communicate (to both the compiler and users) any assumptions you've made about the generic types. Constraints communicate to the compiler that your generic type expects functionality not included in `System.Object`'s public interface. This communication helps the compiler in two ways. First, it helps when you create your generic type:

The compiler asserts that any generic type parameter contains the capabilities you specified in your constraints. Second, the compiler ensures that anyone using your generic type defines type parameters that meet your specifications.

The alternative is for you to perform a lot of casting and runtime testing. For example, the following generic method does not declare any constraints on T, so therefore it must check for the presence of the IComparable<T> interface before using those methods.

```
// Without constraints
public bool AreEqual<T>(T left, T right)
{
    if (left == null)
        return right == null;

    if (left is IComparable<T>)
    {
        IComparable<T> lval = left as IComparable<T>;
        return lval.CompareTo(right) == 0;
    }
    else // failure
    {
        throw new ArgumentException(
            "Type does not implement IComparable<T>",
            "left");
    }
}
```

The equivalent method is much simpler if you specify that T must implement IComparable<T>:

```
public bool AreEqual<T>(T left, T right)
    where T : IComparable<T>
{
    return left.CompareTo(right) == 0;
}
```

This second version trades runtime errors for compile-time errors. You write less code, and the compiler prevents those runtime errors that you must code against in the first version. Without the constraint, you don't have good options for reporting an obvious programmer error. You need to specify the necessary constraints on your generic types. Not doing so would mean that your class could easily be misused, producing exceptions or other runtime errors when client programmers guess wrong. They'll guess wrong often, because the only way client programmers can determine how to use your class is to read your documentation. Being a developer yourself, you know how likely that is. Using constraints helps the compiler enforce the assumptions you've already made. It minimizes the number of runtime errors and the likelihood of misuse.

But it's easy to go too far in defining constraints. The more constraints you place on the generic type parameters, the less often your generic class can be used by the client programmers you're trying to help. Although you need to specify the necessary constraints, you also need to minimize the number of constraints you place on your generic parameters.

There are a number of ways that you can minimize the constraints you specify. One of the most common ways is to ensure that your generic types don't require functionality that they can do without. For example, let's look at `IEquatable<T>`. It's a common interface, and certainly one that many developers would implement when creating new types. You could rewrite the `AreEqual` method using `Equals`:

```
public static AreEqual<T>(T left, T right)
{
    return left.Equals(right);
}
```

What's interesting about this version of `AreEqual` is that if `AreEqual<T>()` is defined in a generic class declaring the `IEquatable<T>` constraint, it will call `IEquatable<T>.Equals`. Otherwise, the C# compiler cannot assume that `IEquatable<T>` is present. The only `Equals()` method in scope is `System.Object.Equals()`.

This example illustrates the major difference between C# generics and C++ templates. In C#, the compiler must generate IL using only the information specified in constraints. Even if the type specified for a specific instantiation has a better method, it won't be used unless it was specified when the generic type was compiled.

`IEquatable<T>` is certainly a more efficient way to test equality when it is implemented on the type. You avoid the runtime tests necessary to implement a proper override of `System.Object.Equals()`. You avoid the boxing and unboxing that would be necessary if the type used as your generic type were a value type. If you are highly performance conscious, `IEquatable<T>` also avoids the small overhead of a virtual method call.

So asking your client developers to support IEquatable<T> is a good thing. But does it rise to the level of a constraint? Must everyone using your class implement IEquatable<T> when there is a perfectly good System.Object.Equals method that works correctly, if somewhat less efficiently? I recommend that you use the preferred method (IEquatable<T>) if available, but transparently downgrade to the less preferred API method (Equals()) if the preferred method is not available. You can do that by creating your own internal methods that are overloaded based on the capabilities you support. Essentially, this is the original AreEqual() method I show at the beginning of this item. This approach takes more work, but we'll look at how to query a type for capabilities and use the best interface available in the type parameter, without mandating extra work on the part of client developers.

Sometimes mandating a constraint is too limiting for the use of a class, and you should instead view the presence or absence of a particular interface or base class as an upside rather than a mandate. In those cases, you should code your methods to consider the case when the type parameter may provide extra benefits, but those enhanced functions may not always be available. This is the design implemented in Equatable<T> and Comparable<T>.

You can extend this technique to other constraints when there are generic and nongeneric interfaces—for example, IEnumerable and IEnumerable<T>.

The other location you need to carefully consider is the default constructor constraint. Some of the time, you can replace the new() constraint by replacing new calls with a call to default(). The latter is a new operator in C# that initializes a variable to its default value. This operator creates the default 0 bit pattern for value types and returns null for reference types. So replacing new() with default() may often mean introducing either the class or value constraints. Notice that the semantics of default() are very different from the semantics for new() when you're working with reference types.

You'll often see code that uses default() in generic classes that need default values for objects of the type parameters. Following is a method that searches for the first occurrence of an object that satisfies a predicate. If the sought object exists, it is returned. Otherwise, a default value is returned.

```
public static T FirstOrDefault<T>(this IEnumerable<T> sequence,
    Predicate<T> test)
{
```

```
    foreach (T value in sequence)
        if (test(value))
            return value;


    return default(T);
}
```

Contrast that with this method. It wraps a factory method to create an object of type T. If the factory method returns null, then the method returns the value returned by the default constructor.

```
public delegate T FactoryFunc<T>();
public static T Factory<T>(FactoryFunc<T> makeANewT)
    where T : new()
{
    T rVal = makeANewT();
    if (rVal == null)
        return new T();
    else
        return rVal;
}
```

The method that uses default() needs no constraints. The method that calls new T() must specify the new() constraint. Also, because of the test for null, the behavior is very different for value types, as compared with reference types. Value types cannot be null. Therefore, the clause under the if statement will never be executed. Factory<T> can still be used with value types, even though it checks for a null value internally. The JIT compiler (which replaces T with the specific type) will remove the null test if T is a value type.

You should pay careful attention to constraints for new(), struct, and class. The foregoing example shows you that adding any of those constraints creates assumptions about how an object will be constructed, whether or not the default value for an object is all zeros or a null reference, and whether or not instances of your generic type parameter can be constructed inside the generic class. Ideally, you should avoid any of these three constraints whenever you can. Think carefully about whether you must have those assumptions for your generic types. Often, you've merely created an assumption in your own mind ("Of course I can call new T()") when there is a suitable alternative (such as default(T)). Pay careful attention to the assumptions you've implicitly made. Remove those that aren't truly necessary.

To communicate your assumptions to your client programmers, you need to specify constraints. However, the more constraints you specify, the less often your class can be used. The whole point of creating a generic type is to create a type definition that can be used efficiently in as many scenarios as possible. You need to balance the safety of specifying constraints against the extra work required by client programmers to deal with every extra constraint. Strive for the minimal set of assumptions you need, but specify all the assumptions you make as constraints.

Item 3: Specialize Generic Algorithms Using Runtime Type Checking

You can easily reuse generics by simply specifying new type parameters. A new instantiation with new type parameters means a new type having similar functionality.

All this is great, because you write less code. However, sometimes being more generic means not taking advantage of a more specific, but clearly superior, algorithm. The C# language rules take this into account. All it takes is for you to recognize that your algorithm can be more efficient when the type parameters have greater capabilities, and then to write that specific code. Furthermore, creating a second generic type that specifies different constraints doesn't always work. Generic instantiations are based on the compile-time type of an object, and not the runtime type. If you fail to take that into account, you can miss possible efficiencies.

For example, suppose you write a class that provides a reverse-order enumeration on a sequence of items:

```csharp
public sealed class ReverseEnumerable<T> : IEnumerable<T>
{
    private class ReverseEnumerator : IEnumerator<T>
    {
        int currentIndex;
        IList<T> collection;

        public ReverseEnumerator(IList<T> srcCollection)
        {
            collection = srcCollection;
            currentIndex = collection.Count;
        }
```

```csharp
        #region IEnumerator<T> Members
        public T Current
        {
            get { return collection[currentIndex]; }
        }
        #endregion

        #region IDisposable Members
        public void Dispose()
        {
            // No implementation needed.
            // No protected Dispose() needed
            // because this class is sealed.
        }
        #endregion

        #region IEnumerator Members
        object System.Collections.IEnumerator.Current
        {
            get { return this.Current; }
        }

        public bool MoveNext()
        {
            return --currentIndex >= 0;

        }

        public void Reset()
        {
            currentIndex = collection.Count;
        }
        #endregion
    }

    IEnumerable<T> sourceSequence;
    IList<T> originalSequence;

    public ReverseEnumerable(IEnumerable<T> sequence)
    {
        sourceSequence = sequence;
    }
```

```
#region IEnumerable<T> Members
public IEnumerator<T> GetEnumerator()
{
    // Create a copy of the original sequence,
    // so it can be reversed.
    if (originalSequence == null)
    {
        originalSequence = new List<T>();
        foreach (T item in sourceSequence)
            originalSequence.Add(item);
    }
    return new ReverseEnumerator(originalSequence);
}
#endregion

#region IEnumerable Members
System.Collections.IEnumerator
    System.Collections.IEnumerable.GetEnumerator()
{
    return this.GetEnumerator();
}
#endregion
}
```

This implementation assumes the least amount of information from its arguments. The ReverseEnumerable constructor assumes that its input parameter supports IEnumerable<T>, and that's it. IEnumerable<T> does not provide any random access to its elements. Therefore, the only way to reverse the list is shown in the body of ReverseEnumerator<T>.GetEnumerator(). Here, if the constructor is being called for the first time, it walks the entire input sequence and creates a copy. Then the nested class can walk the list of items backward.

It works, and when the actual input collection does not support random access of the sequence, that's the only way to create a reverse enumeration of a sequence. In practice, though, this code is ugly. Many collections you work with support random access, and this code is highly inefficient in those cases. When the input sequence supports IList<T>, you've created an extra copy of the entire sequence for no good reason. Let's make use of the fact that many of the types that implement IEnumerable<T> also implement IList<T> and improve the efficiency of this code.

The only change is in the constructor of the `ReverseEnumerable<T>` class:

```
public ReverseEnumerable(IEnumerable<T> sequence)
{
    sourceSequence = sequence;
    // If sequence doesn't implement IList<T>,
    // originalSequence is null, so this works
    // fine.
    originalSequence = sequence as IList<T>;
}
```

Why don't we simply create a second constructor using `IList<T>`? That helps when the compile-time type of the parameter is `IList<T>`. But it doesn't work in some cases—for example, when the compile-time type of a parameter is `IEnumerable<T>` but the runtime type implements `IList<T>`. To catch those cases, you should provide both the runtime check and the compile-time overload.

```
public ReverseEnumerable(IEnumerable<T> sequence)
{
    sourceSequence = sequence;
    // If sequence doesn't implement IList<T>,
    // originalSequence is null, so this works
    // fine.
    originalSequence = sequence as IList<T>;
}

public ReverseEnumerable(IList<T> sequence)
{
    sourceSequence = sequence;
    originalSequence = sequence;
}
```

`IList<T>` enables a more efficient algorithm than does `IEnumerable<T>`. You haven't forced consumers of this class to provide more functionality, but you have made use of greater capabilities when they have provided it.

That change handles the vast majority of cases, but there are collections that implement `ICollection<T>` without implementing `IList<T>`. In those cases, there are still inefficiencies. Look again at the `ReverseEnumerable<T>.GetEnumerator()` method.

```
public IEnumerator<T> GetEnumerator()
{
    // Create a copy of the original sequence,
    // so it can be reversed.
    if (originalSequence == null)
    {
        originalSequence = new List<T>();
        foreach (T item in sourceSequence)
            originalSequence.Add(item);
    }
    return new ReverseEnumerator(originalSequence);
}
```

The code that creates the copy of the input sequence will execute more slowly than needed if the source collection implements ICollection<T>. The following method adds a Count property that you can use to initialize the final storage:

```
public IEnumerator<T> GetEnumerator()
{
    // Create a copy of the original sequence,
    // so it can be reversed.
    if (originalSequence == null)
    {
        if (sourceSequence is ICollection<T>)
        {
            ICollection<T> source = sourceSequence
                as ICollection<T>;
            originalSequence = new List<T>(source.Count);
        }
        else
            originalSequence = new List<T>();
        foreach (T item in sourceSequence)
            originalSequence.Add(item);
    }
    return new ReverseEnumerator(originalSequence);
}
```

The code I've shown here is similar to the code in the List<T> constructor that creates a list from an input sequence:

```
List<T>(IEnumerable<T> inputSequence);
```

There's one side point I want to cover before we leave this item. You'll notice that all the tests I make in the ReverseEnumerable<T> are runtime tests on the runtime parameter. This means that you assume a runtime cost to query for the extra capabilities. In almost all cases, the cost of the runtime test is much less than the cost of copying the elements.

You may be thinking that we've looked at all the possible uses of the ReverseEnumerable<T> class. But there is still one variation: the string class. string provides methods that have random access to the characters, such as IList<char>, but string does not implement IList<char>. Using the more-specific methods requires writing more-specific code inside your generic class. The ReverseStringEnumerator class (shown next), which is nested inside the ReverseEnumerable<T>, is straightforward. Notice that the constructor uses the string's Length parameter, and the other methods are almost the same as in the ReverseEnumerator<T> class.

```
private class ReverseStringEnumerator : IEnumerator<char>
{
    private string sourceSequence;
    private int currentIndex;

    public ReverseStringEnumerator(string source)
    {
        sourceSequence = source;
        currentIndex = source.Length;
    }

    #region IEnumerator<char> Members
    public char Current
    {
        get { return sourceSequence[currentIndex]; }
    }
    #endregion

    #region IDisposable Members
    public void Dispose()
    {
        // no implementation
    }
    #endregion
```

```
#region IEnumerator Members
object System.Collections.IEnumerator.Current
{
    get { return sourceSequence[currentIndex]; }
}

public bool MoveNext()
{
    return --currentIndex >= 0;
}

public void Reset()
{
    currentIndex = sourceSequence.Length;
}
#endregion
}
```

To complete the specific implementation, the `ReverseEnumer-
able<T>.GetEnumerator()` needs to look at the proper type and create
the right enumerator type:

```
public IEnumerator<T> GetEnumerator()
{
    // String is a special case:
    if (sourceSequence is string)
    {
        // Note the cast because T may not be a
        // char at compile time
        return new ReverseStringEnumerator
            (sourceSequence as string)
            as IEnumerator<T>;
    }

    // Create a copy of the original sequence,
    // so it can be reversed.
    if (originalSequence == null)
    {
        if (sourceSequence is ICollection<T>)
        {
            ICollection<T> source = sourceSequence
                as ICollection<T>;
```

```
            originalSequence = new List<T>(source.Count);
        } else
            originalSequence = new List<T>();
        foreach (T item in sourceSequence)
            originalSequence.Add(item);
    }
    return new ReverseEnumerator(originalSequence);
}
```

As before, the goal is to hide any specialized implementations inside the generic class. This is a bit more work, because the string class specialization requires a completely separate implementation of the inner class.

You'll also note that the implementation of GetEnumerator() requires a cast when the ReverseStringEnumerator is used. At compile time, T could be anything, and therefore it might not be a char. The cast is safe; the only path through the code ensures that T is a char, because the sequence is a string. That's OK, because it is safely hidden inside the class and won't pollute the public interface. As you can see, the existence of generics does not completely remove the need to occasionally convince the compiler that you know more than it does.

This small sample shows how you can create generic classes that work with the fewest formal constraints and still use specific constraints that will provide a better implementation when the type parameter supports enhanced functionality. That provides the best compromise between maximum reuse and the best implementation you can write for a particular algorithm.

Item 4: Use Generics to Force Compile-Time Type Inference

Patterns are a way to standardize the implementation of common algorithms that are not directly supported by the language or the framework. A pattern is a recipe you can follow when solving a well-known problem. The purpose of a pattern is to provide some level of thought reuse when there is limited code reuse. When pattern reuse isn't optimal, it's because it's hard to abstract away all the specific parts of a pattern in code.

Creating generic classes can help you write reusable code that implements many common patterns. The essence of a pattern is that there are common algorithms and code that are supported by and used by types that are specific to each application. You can't use generics for every possible pattern, but generics can give you a great way to minimize the amount of code needed to create and support a given pattern.

The collection classes in the .NET Framework demonstrate this capability in a number of methods that implement a form of the enumerator pattern. `List<T>.Find (Predicate<T> match)` finds the first element in which a given condition has been met. The `List` class also contains similar methods for `FindAll`, `TrueForAll`, `ForEach`, and others. These particular methods may not represent the kind of earth-shattering brilliance you'd expect me to cover. But the design idiom is instructive, because it shows you when the same pattern can apply to you. The collection class now contains the common algorithm to enumerate all nodes in the collection. Client code need only supply the logic that is to be applied on each item in the collection.

Following this pattern means that the .NET Framework designers did not need to anticipate all the use cases for examining or modifying each of the elements in your collection. Instead, they provided the generic method to visit each element and call a function you define with each element. You examine all the elements for a variety of reasons: searching for something, testing the values of the elements, or transforming the values of the elements.

The .NET designers provided you with the mechanisms to define your own tests, or **predicates,** for each of those actions. In fact, you can write those predicates inline as anonymous methods, the subject of Item 18 (Chapter 3).

In the same way, you can create implementations of many design patterns by defining the proper delegates or events in the form of predicates. Those generic implementations of patterns can be reused whenever you need to implement that same pattern.

Let's look at two patterns that are good examples of creating implementations that are easy to reuse and hard to misuse. The simplest is a class that supports serialization using the XML Serializer. A nongeneric version of a class that serializes any arbitrary type works like this:

```
public static class XmlPersistenceManager
{
    public static object LoadFromFile(Type typeToLoad,
        string filePath)
    {
        XmlSerializer factory = new XmlSerializer(typeToLoad);
```

```
        if (File.Exists(filePath))
        {
            using (TextReader r = new StreamReader(filePath))
            {
                object rVal = factory.Deserialize(r);
                return rVal;
            }
        }
        return default(object);
    }

    public static void SaveToFile(string filePath, object obj)
    {
        Type theType = obj.GetType();
        XmlSerializer factory = new XmlSerializer(theType);

        using (TextWriter w = new StreamWriter(filePath,
            false))
        {
            factory.Serialize(w, obj);
        }
    }
}
```

This works, but it's not an easy type to use. Developers who use your class must specify the Type parameters. They can't be inferred.

Well, time passes and you need to serialize another type. There are quite a few locations that call these two methods—sometimes with the same type, at other times with different types. That's probably OK, but there are several shortcomings in this code. The first is type safety: Every time you call the LoadFromFile method, you must cast or convert the return value. At some point, you'll need the cast, but you certainly want to limit the number of locations as best you can.

There's also a hidden inefficiency in this code. Every call to either of these methods creates a new XmlSerializer. Depending on the application, this action creates quite a few more XmlSerializer objects than you need. It's true that the framework designers worked to minimize the cost of creating these objects, but it still creates and destroys more temporary objects than necessary. You might think of making this change:

```
// Don't use. There's a bug in caching
// the XmlSerializer.
public static class XmlPersistenceManager
{
    // cache the serializer once it's created:
    private static XmlSerializer factory;

    public static object LoadFromFile(Type typeToLoad,
        string filePath)
    {
        if (factory == null)
            factory = new XmlSerializer(typeToLoad);
        if (File.Exists(filePath))
        {
            using (TextReader r = new StreamReader(filePath))
            {
                object rVal = factory.Deserialize(r);
                return rVal;
            }
        }
        return null;
    }

    public static void SaveToFile(string filePath, object obj)
    {
        Type theType = obj.GetType();
        if (factory == null)
            factory = new XmlSerializer(theType);

        using (TextWriter w = new StreamWriter(filePath,
            false))
        {
            factory.Serialize(w, obj);
        }
    }
}
```

It looks simple: Create the XmlSerializer once, and cache it for the rest of time. It may even pass your unit tests. But that's a false sense of security. The first application that uses the XmlPersistenceManager with more than one class will have problems. Each XmlSerializer is tied to a specific

Type class. It knows how to serialize only that type. Using it with another Type instance causes an exception.

You could modify the class by storing a hashtable of XmlSerializer objects mapped to the Type instance they use. But that means writing more code, work that the compiler and JIT engine can do for you. (Yes, you can add multiple types to the XmlSerializer instance, but that's not the correct answer in this case.)

It shouldn't take you long to see that you've essentially copied an algorithm and have made a couple of substitutions. Well, that's exactly what the compiler does with generics. So you write this:

```
// Caching works, because a new
// generic instance is created for each distinct T
public static class GenericXmlPersistenceManager<T>
{
    // cache the serializer once it's created:
    private static XmlSerializer factory;

    public static T LoadFromFile(string filePath)
    {
        if (factory == null)
            factory = new XmlSerializer(typeof (T));
        if (File.Exists(filePath))
        {
            using (TextReader r = new StreamReader(filePath))
            {
                T rVal = (T)factory.Deserialize(r);
                return rVal;
            }
        }
        return default(T);
    }

    public static void SaveToFile(string filePath, T data)
    {
        if (factory == null)
            factory = new XmlSerializer(typeof(T));

        using (TextWriter w = new StreamWriter(filePath,
            false))
```

```
        {
            factory.Serialize(w, data);
        }
    }
}
```

Next, you get the requirement to stream XML nodes to an open output stream. You can make a few small changes to your generic class, and everyone benefits:

```
public static class GenericXmlPersistenceManager<T>
{
    // cache the serializer once it's created:
    private static XmlSerializer factory;

    public static T LoadFromFile(string filePath)
    {
        if (File.Exists(filePath))
        {
            using (XmlReader inputStream = XmlReader.Create(
                filePath))
            {
                return ReadFromStream(inputStream);
            }
        }
        return default(T);
    }

    public static void SaveToFile(string filePath, T data)
    {
        using (XmlWriter writer = XmlWriter.Create(filePath))
        {
            AddToStream(writer, data);
        }
    }

    public static void AddToStream(
        System.Xml.XmlWriter outputStream,  T data)
    {
        if (factory == null)
            factory = new XmlSerializer(typeof(T));
        factory.Serialize(outputStream, data);
    }
```

```
    public static T ReadFromStream(
        System.Xml.XmlReader inputStream)
    {
        if (factory == null)
            factory = new XmlSerializer(typeof(T));
        T rVal = (T)factory.Deserialize(inputStream);
        return rVal;
    }
}
```

Another advantage of this version is that the compiler can infer the type parameter for the save methods. The load methods use the type parameter only as a return type, so the load methods still require that developers specify the type parameters. The final lesson from the generic XML serializer is that any fixes or enhancements are immediately available to all implementations that use this implementation.

Many times you'll find that you create algorithms that use the type of an object to implement the algorithm. In that case, you can often create a single generic version of the algorithm by abstracting away the type parameters into generic parameters. Then the compiler can create the specific versions for you.

Item 5: Ensure That Your Generic Classes Support Disposable Type Parameters

Constraints do two things for you and users of your class. First, using constraints transforms runtime errors into compiler errors. Second, constraints provide a clear set of documentation for users of your class as to what is expected when they create an instantiation of your parameterized type. But you can't use constraints to specify what a type parameter *can't* do. In almost all cases, you don't care what capabilities a type parameter has beyond those your type expects and uses. But in the special case of a type parameter that implements IDisposable, you have some extra work on your hands.

Real-world examples that demonstrate this issue become complicated rather quickly, so I've fabricated a simple example to show how this issue occurs and how to rectify it in your code. The problem occurs when you have a generic method that needs to create and use an instance of the type parameter in one of its methods:

```
public interface IEngine
{
    void DoWork();
}

public class EngineDriver<T> where T : IEngine, new()
{
    public void GetThingsDone()
    {
        T driver = new T();
        driver.DoWork();
    }
}
```

You may have introduced a resource leak if T implements IDisposable. In every case where you create a local variable of type T, you need to check whether T implements IDisposable, and, if so, dispose of it correctly:

```
public void GetThingsDone()
{
    T driver = new T();
    using (driver as IDisposable)
    {
        driver.DoWork();
    }
}
```

This may look a bit confusing if you've never seen that sort of cast in a using statement, but it works. The compiler creates a hidden local variable that stores a reference to the driver cast as an IDisposable. If T does not implement IDisposable, then the value of this local variable is null. In those cases, the compiler does not call Dispose(), because it checks against null before doing this extra work. However, in all cases where T implements IDisposable, the compiler generates a call to the Dispose() method upon exiting the using block.

That's a fairly simple idiom: Wrap local instances of type parameters in a using statement. You need to use the cast I've shown here, because T may or may not implement IDisposable.

Your life gets more complicated when your generic class needs to create and use an instance of the type parameters as member variables. Your generic class now owns a reference to a type that may implement IDisposable.

This means that your generic class must implement IDisposable. You need to have your class check whether the resource implements IDisposable, and, if so, it must dispose of that resource:

```
public sealed class EngineDriver<T> : IDisposable
    where T : IEngine, new()
{
    // It's expensive to create, so initialize to null
    private T driver;
    public void GetThingsDone()
    {
        if (driver == null)
            driver = new T();
        driver.DoWork();
    }


    #region IDisposable Members
    public void Dispose()
    {
        IDisposable resource = driver as IDisposable;

        if (resource != null)
        {
            resource.Dispose();
        }
        // Calling Dispose multiple times is OK.
    }
    #endregion
}
```

Your class picked up quite a bit of baggage on this round. You have the added work of implementing IDisposable. Second, you've added the sealed keyword to the class. It's either that or implement the full IDisposable pattern to allow derived classes to also use your Dispose() method. (See Cwalina and Abrams, *Framework Design Guidelines*, pp. 248–261.) Sealing the class means that you don't need that extra work. However, it does limit the users of your class, who can no longer derive a new type from your class.

Finally, notice that this class, as coded, can't guarantee that you don't call Dispose() on the driver more than once. That's allowed, and any type that implements `IDisposable` must support multiple calls to `Dispose()`. That's because there isn't a class constraint on `T`, so you can't set `driver` to null before exiting the `Dispose` method. (Remember that value types cannot be set to null.)

In practice, you often can avoid this design by changing the interface of the generic class somewhat. You can move the `Dispose` responsibility outside the generic class and remove the `new()` constraint by moving the owner-ship outside this generic class:

```
public class EngineDriver<T> where T : IEngine
{
    private T driver;
    public EngineDriver(T driver)
    {
        this.driver = driver;
    }

    public void GetThingsDone()
    {
        driver.DoWork();
    }
}
```

Of course, the comment in the earlier listing implies that creating a `T` object might be very expensive. This latest version ignores that concern. In the end, how you solve this problem depends on many other factors in your application design. But one thing is certain: If you create instances of any of the types described by your generic class's type parameters, you must consider that those types may implement `IDisposable`. You must code defensively and ensure that you don't leak resources when those objects go out of scope.

Sometimes you can do that by refactoring the code so that it does not create those instances. At other times the best design is to create and use local variables, writing the code to dispose of them if needed. Finally, the design may call for lazy creation of instances of the type parameters and implementing `IDisposable` in the generic class. It's a bit more work, but it is necessary work if you want to create a class that is useful.

Item 6: Use Delegates to Define Method Constraints on Type Parameters

At first glance, the constraint mechanism in C# seems too restrictive: You can specify only a single base class, interfaces, class or struct, and a parameterless constructor. That leaves a lot out. You can't specify static methods (which include any operators), and you can't specify any other constructors. From one perspective, the constraints defined by the language can satisfy every contract. You could use parameters to define an `IFactory<T>` interface that creates `T` objects. You can define `IAdd<T>` to add `T` objects and use the static operator + defined on `T` (or use some other method that adds `T` objects). But that's not a good way to solve this problem. It's a lot of extra work, and it obscures your basic design.

Let's consider the `Add()` example. If your generic class needed an `Add()` method on `T`, you'd need to perform several tasks: You would create an `IAdd<T>` interface. You'd code against that interface. So far, that's not too bad. But every developer who wants to use your generic class would need to do even more work. They'd need to create a class that implements `IAdd<T>`, define the methods needed for `IAdd<T>`, and then specify the closed generic class for your generic class definition. To call one method, you've made developers create a class simply to match an API signature. That introduces quite a bit of friction and confusion for developers who want to use your class.

But it doesn't have to be that way. You can specify a delegate signature that matches the method your generic class needs to call. It doesn't mean any more work for you, the author of the generic class. But it saves a great deal of work for the developers who are using your generic class.

Here's how you would define a generic class that needs some method that adds two objects of type `T`. You don't even need to define your own delegate definition; the `System.Func<T1, T2, TOutput>` delegate matches the signature you need. Here is a generic method that adds two objects, using a supplied method that implements `Add`:

```
public static class Example
{
    public static T Add<T>(T left, T right,
        Func<T, T, T> AddFunc)
    {
        return AddFunc(left, right);
    }
}
```

Developers using your class can use type inference and lambda expressions to define the method that should be called when your generic class needs to call `AddFunc()`. You would call the `Add` generic method using a lambda expression like this:

```
int a = 6;
int b = 7;
int sum = Example.Add(a, b, (x, y) => x + y);
```

The C# compiler infers the types and return values from the lambda expression as equivalent to an anonymous delegate. If your users are not familiar with lambda syntax, they could use an anonymous delegate to call `Add()` in this way:

```
int sum2 = Example.Add(a,b, delegate(int x, int y)
{
    return x + y;
});
```

In both cases, in the class containing this code snippet, the C# compiler creates a private static method that returns the sum of the two integers. The name of the method is generated by the compiler. The compiler also creates a `Func<T,T,T>` delegate object and assigns the method pointer to that compiler-generated method. Finally, the compiler passes that delegate to the generic `Example.Add()` method.

I've used the lambda syntax to specify the method that defines the delegate to show why you should create delegate-based interface contracts. The code is a contrived example, but the concept is what's important. When it's unwieldy to use an interface to define a constraint, you can define a method signature and a delegate type that suits your needs. Then you add an instance of that delegate to the list of the parameters of the generic method. The developers using your class can use a lambda expression to define that method, writing much less code, in a much clearer fashion. Developers using your class need to create the lambda expression that defines the method functionality they need. There's no extra code to support the syntax of interface-based constraints.

More often, you'll want to use delegate-based contracts to create algorithms that operate on sequences. Imagine you need to write code that combines samples taken from various mechanical probes and turns these two sequences into a single sequence of points.

Your point class might look like this:

```
public class Point
{
    public double X
    {
        get;
        private set;
    }
    public double Y
    {
        get;
        private set;
    }
    public Point(double x, double y)
    {
        this.X = x;
        this.Y = y;
    }
}
```

The values you've read from your device are List<double> sequences. You need a way to create a sequence by repeatedly calling the Point(double,double) constructor with each successive X,Y pair. Point is an immutable type. You can't call the default constructor and then set the X and Y properties. But neither can you create a constraint that specifies parameters on a constructor. The solution is to define a delegate that takes two parameters and returns a point. Again, it's already in the .NET Framework 3.5:

```
delegate TOutput Func<T1, T2, TOutput>(T1 arg1, T2 arg2);
```

In this example, T1 and T2 are the same type: double. A generic method that creates an output sequence looks like this:

```
public static IEnumerable<TOutput> Merge<T1, T2, TOutput>
    (IEnumerable<T1> left, IEnumerable<T2> right,
    Func<T1, T2, TOutput> generator)
{
    IEnumerator<T1> leftSequence = left.GetEnumerator();
    IEnumerator<T2> rightSequence = right.GetEnumerator();
    while (leftSequence.MoveNext() && rightSequence.MoveNext())
    {
```

```
        yield return generator(leftSequence.Current,
            rightSequence.Current);
    }
}
```

`Merge` enumerates both input sequences, and for each pair of items in the input sequence, it calls the generator delegate, returning the newly constructed `Point` object. (See Item 19, Chapter 3.) The delegate contract specifies that you need a method that constructs the output type from two different inputs. Notice that `Merge` is defined so that the two input types don't need to be the same type. You could create key/value pairs of disparate types using this same method. You'd just need a different delegate.

You would call `Merge` this way:

```
double[] xValues = { 0, 1, 2, 3, 4, 5, 6, 7, 8, 9,
    0, 1, 2, 3, 4, 5, 6, 7, 8, 9 };
double[] yValues = { 0, 1, 2, 3, 4, 5, 6, 7, 8, 9,
    0, 1, 2, 3, 4, 5, 6, 7, 8, 9 };

List<Point> values = new List<Point>(
    Utilities.Merge(xValues, yValues,
    (x, y) => new Point(x, y)));
```

Again, I've used the lambda expression syntax. It's equivalent to the same call with an anonymous delegate:

```
List<Point> values2 = new List<Point>(
    Utilities.Merge(xValues, yValues,
    delegate(double x, double y)
    {
        return new Point(x, y);
    }));
```

As before, the compiler generates a private static method, instantiates a delegate object using a reference to that method, and passes that delegate object to the `Merge()` method.

In the general case, any method your generic class needs to call can be replaced by a specific delegate. These first two examples contain a delegate that is called for a generic method. This practice works even if your type needs the delegate method in many locations. You can create a generic class in which one of the class type parameters is a delegate. Then, when you create an instance of the class, you assign a member of the class to a delegate of that type.

The following simple example caches a delegate that reads a point from a stream and calls that delegate to convert the text input to a `Point`. The first step is to add a constructor to the `Point` class that reads a point from a file:

```
public Point(System.IO.TextReader reader)
{
    string line = reader.ReadLine();
    string[] fields = line.Split(',');
    if (fields.Length != 2)
        throw new InvalidOperationException(
            "Input format incorrect");
    double value;
    if (!double.TryParse(fields[0], out value))
        throw new InvalidOperationException(
            "Could not parse X value");
    else
        X = value;

    if (!double.TryParse(fields[1], out value))
        throw new InvalidOperationException(
            "Could not parse Y value");
    else
        Y = value;
}
```

Creating the collection class requires some indirection. You can't enforce a constraint that your generic type includes a constructor that takes parameters. However, you can mandate a method that does what you want. You define a delegate type that constructs a T from a file:

```
public delegate T CreateFromStream<T>(TextReader reader);
```

Next, you create the container class, and the constructor of that container takes an instance of the delegate type as a parameter:

```
public class InputCollection<T>
{
    private List<T> thingsRead = new List<T>();
    private readonly CreateFromStream<T> readFunc;
```

```
    public InputCollection(CreateFromStream<T> readFunc)
    {
        this.readFunc = readFunc;
    }

    public void ReadFromStream(TextReader reader)
    {
        thingsRead.Add(readFunc(reader));
    }

    public IEnumerable<T> Values
    {
        get { return thingsRead; }
    }
}
```

When you instantiate an `InputCollection`, you supply the delegate:

```
InputCollection<Point> readValues = new
    InputCollection<Point>(
    (inputStream) => new Point(inputStream));
```

This sample is simple enough that you'd probably create the nongeneric class instead. However, this technique will help you build generic types that rely on behavior that cannot be specified by a normal constraint.

Often, the best way to express your design is to use class constraints or interface constraints to specify your constraints. The .NET Base Class Library (BCL) does that in many places, expecting your types to implement `IComparable<T>`, or `IEquatable<T>`, or `IEnumerable<T>`. That's the right design choice, because those interfaces are common and are used by many algorithms. Also, they are clearly expressed as interfaces: A type implementing `IComparable<T>` declares that it supports an ordering relation. A type implementing `IEquatable<T>` declares that it supports equality.

However, if you need to create a custom interface contract to support only a particular generic method or class, you may find that it's much easier for your users to use delegates to specify that contract as a method constraint. Your generic type will be easy to use, and the code calling it will be easy to understand. Whether it's the presence of an operator, another static method, a delegate type, or some other construction idiom, you can define some generic interfaces for the constraint, and you can create a helper type that implements that interface so that you can satisfy the constraints. Don't let a semantic contract that's not directly compatible with constraints stop you from enforcing your design.

Item 7: Do Not Create Generic Specialization on Base Classes or Interfaces

Introducing generic methods can make it highly complicated for the compiler to resolve method overloads. Each generic method can match any possible substitute for each type parameter. Depending on how careful you are (or aren't), your application will behave very strangely. When you create generic classes or methods, you are responsible for creating a set of methods that will enable developers using that class to safely use your code with minimal confusion. This means that you must pay careful attention to overload resolution, and you must determine when generic methods will create better matches than the methods developers might reasonably expect.

Examine this code, and try to guess the output:

```
public class MyBase
{
}

public interface IMessageWriter
{
    void WriteMessage();
}

public class MyDerived : MyBase, IMessageWriter
{
    #region IMessageWriter Members
    void IMessageWriter.WriteMessage()
    {
        Console.WriteLine("Inside MyDerived.WriteMessage");
    }
    #endregion
}

public class AnotherType : IMessageWriter
{
```

```csharp
    #region IMessageWriter Members
    public void WriteMessage()
    {
        Console.WriteLine("Inside AnotherType.WriteMessage");
    }
    #endregion
}

class Program
{
    static void WriteMessage(MyBase b)
    {
        Console.WriteLine("Inside WriteMessage(MyBase)");
    }

    static void WriteMessage<T>(T obj)
    {
        Console.Write("Inside WriteMessage<T>(T):  ");
        Console.WriteLine(obj.ToString());
    }

    static void WriteMessage(IMessageWriter obj)
    {
        Console.Write(
            "Inside WriteMessage(IMessageWriter):  ");
        obj.WriteMessage();
    }

    static void Main(string[] args)
    {
        MyDerived d = new MyDerived();
        Console.WriteLine("Calling Program.WriteMessage");
        WriteMessage(d);
        Console.WriteLine();

        Console.WriteLine(
            "Calling through IMessageWriter interface");
        WriteMessage((IMessageWriter)d);
        Console.WriteLine();
```

```
                Console.WriteLine("Cast to base object");
                WriteMessage((MyBase)d);
                Console.WriteLine();

                Console.WriteLine("Another Type test:");
                AnotherType anObject = new AnotherType();
                WriteMessage(anObject);
                Console.WriteLine();

                Console.WriteLine("Cast to IMessageWriter:");
                WriteMessage((IMessageWriter)anObject);
        }
}
```

Some of the comments might make it a giveaway, but make your best guess before looking at the output. It's important to understand how the existence of generic methods affects the method resolution rules. Generics are almost always a good match, and they wreak havoc with our assumptions about which methods get called. Here's the output:

```
Calling Program.WriteMessage
Inside WriteMessage<T>(T):   Item14.MyDerived

Calling through IMessageWriter interface
Inside WriteMessage(IMessageWriter):
    Inside MyDerived.WriteMessage

Cast to base object
Inside WriteMessage(MyBase)

Another Type test:
Inside WriteMessage<T>(T):   Item14.AnotherType

Cast to IMessageWriter:
Inside WriteMessage(IMessageWriter):
    Inside AnotherType.WriteMessage
```

The first test shows one of the more important concepts to remember: `WriteMessage<T>(T obj)` is a better match than `WriteMessage(MyBase b)` for an object that is derived from `MyBase`. That's because the compiler can make an exact match by substituting `MyDerived` for `T` in that message, and `WriteMessage(MyBase)` requires an implicit conversion. The generic method is better. This concept will become even more important when you see the extension methods defined in the `Queryable` and `Enumerable` classes added in C# 3.0. Generic methods are always perfect matches, so they win over base class methods.

The next two tests show how you can control this behavior by explicitly invoking the conversion (either to `MyBase` or to an `IMessageWriter` type). And the last two tests show that the same type of behavior is present for interface implementations even without class inheritance.

Name resolution rules are interesting, and you can show off your arcane knowledge about them at geek cocktail parties. But what you really need is a strategy to create code that ensures that your concept of "best match" agrees with the compiler's concept. After all, the compiler always wins this battle.

It's not a good idea to create generic specializations for base classes when you intend to support the class and all its descendents. It's equally error prone to create generic specializations for interfaces. But numeric types do not present those pitfalls. There is no inheritance chain between integral and floating-point numeric types. As Item 2 explains, often there are good reasons to provide specific versions of a method for different value types. Specifically, the .NET Framework includes specialization on all numeric types for `Enumerable.Max<T>`, `Enumerable.Min<T>`, and similar methods. But it's best to use the compiler instead of adding runtime checks to determine the type. That's what you're trying to avoid by using generics in the first place, right?

```
// Not the best solution
// this uses runtime type checking
static void WriteMessage<T>(T obj)
{
    if (obj is MyBase)
        WriteMessage(obj as MyBase);
    else if (obj is IMessageWriter)
        WriteMessage((IMessageWriter)obj);
    else
    {
        Console.Write("Inside WriteMessage<T>(T):  ");
        Console.WriteLine(obj.ToString());
    }
}
```

This code might be fine, but only if there are only a few conditions to check. It does hide all the ugly behavior from your customers, but notice that it introduces some runtime overhead. Your generic method is now checking specific types to determine whether they are (in your mind) a better match than the one the compiler would choose if left to its own devices. Use this technique only when it's clear that a better match is quite a bit better, and measure the performance to see whether there are better ways to write your library to avoid the problem altogether.

Of course, this is not to say that you should never create more-specific methods for a given implementation. Item 3 shows how to create a better implementation when advanced capabilities are available. The code in Item 3 creates a reverse iterator that adapts itself correctly when advanced capabilities are created. Notice that the Item 3 code does not rely on generic types for any name resolution. Each constructor expresses the various capabilities correctly to ensure that the proper method can be called at each location. However, if you want to create a specific instantiation of a generic method for a given type, you need to create that instantiation for that type and all its descendents. If you want to create a generic specialization for an interface, you need to create a version for all types that implement that interface.

Item 8: Prefer Generic Methods Unless Type Parameters Are Instance Fields

It's easy to fall into the habit of limiting yourself to generic class definitions. But often, you can more clearly express utility classes by using a nongeneric class that contains numerous generic methods. The reason, again, is that the C# compiler must generate valid IL for an entire generic class based on the constraints specified. One set of constraints must be valid for the entire class. A utility class that contains generic methods can specify different constraints for each method. Those different constraints can make it much easier for the compiler to find the best match and therefore much easier for your clients to use your algorithms.

Also, each type parameter need satisfy the constraints only for the methods in which it is used. With generic classes, in contrast, the type parameters must satisfy all the constraints defined for the complete class. As you expand a class over time, it becomes much more constraining if the type parameters are specified on the class level rather than at the method level. After two releases you'll wish you'd specified your generic methods at the method level. Here's one simple guideline: If a type needs type-level data members, especially data members involving the type parameter, make it a generic class. Otherwise, use generic methods.

Let's consider a simple example that contains generic Min and Max methods:

```
public static class Utils<T>
{
    public static T Max(T left, T right)
    {
        return Comparer<T>.Default.Compare(left, right) < 0 ?
            right : left;
    }

    public static T Min(T left, T right)
    {
        return Comparer<T>.Default.Compare(left, right) < 0 ?
            left : right;
    }
}
```

At first review, it seems to work perfectly. You can compare numbers:

```
double d1 = 4;
double d2 = 5;
double max = Utils<double>.Max(d1, d2);
```

You can compare strings:

```
string foo = "foo";
string bar = "bar";
string sMax = Utils<string>.Max(foo, bar);
```

You're happy, and you head home. But folks who are using your class aren't so happy. You'll notice that every call in the preceding code snippets needs to explicitly specify the type parameter. That's because you've created a generic class instead of a set of generic methods. The extra work is an annoyance, but there are deeper problems here. Many of the built-in types already have accessible Max and Min methods defined. Math.Max() and Math.Min() are defined for all the numeric types. Instead of using those, your generic class always picks up the version you've created using Comparer<T>. That works, but it forces extra runtime checks to determine whether a type implements IComparer<T>, followed by a call to the correct method.

Naturally, you'd like to have your users automatically pick up the best method possible. That's much easier if you create generic methods in a nongeneric class.

```
public static class Utils
{
    public static T Max<T>(T left, T right)
    {
        return Comparer<T>.Default.Compare(left, right) < 0 ?
            right : left;
    }

    public static double Max(double left, double right)
    {
        return Math.Max(left, right);
    }
    // versions for other numeric types elided

    public static T Min<T>(T left, T right)
    {
        return Comparer<T>.Default.Compare(left, right) < 0 ?
            left : right;
    }
    public static double Min(double left, double right)
    {
        return Math.Min(left, right);
    }
    // versions for other numeric types elided
}
```

This `Utils` class is no longer a generic class. Instead, it has several overloads of both `Min` and `Max`. Those specific methods are more efficient than the generic version (see Item 3). Better still, users no longer need to specify which version they call:

```
double d1 = 4;
double d2 = 5;
double max = Utils.Max(d1, d2);

string foo = "foo";
string bar = "bar";
string sMax = Utils.Max(foo, bar);
```

```
double? d3 = 12;
double? d4 = null;
double? Max2 = Utils.Max(d3, d4).Value;
```

If there is a specific version of the parameter type, the compiler calls that version. If there isn't a specific version, the compiler calls the generic version. Furthermore, if you later extend the Utils class with more versions for different specific types, the compiler will immediately pick them up.

It's not only static utility classes that should use generic methods instead of a generic class. Consider this simple class, which builds a comma-separated list of items:

```
public class CommaSeparatedListBuilder
{
    private StringBuilder storage = new StringBuilder();

    public void Add<T>(IEnumerable<T> items)
    {
        foreach (T item in items)
        {
            if (storage.Length > 0)
                storage.Append(", ");
            storage.Append("\"");
            storage.Append(item.ToString());
            storage.Append("\"");
        }
    }

    public override string ToString()
    {
        return storage.ToString();
    }
}
```

As coded, this lets you create any number of disparate types in the list. Whenever you use a new type, a new version of Add<T> is generated by the compiler. If you had instead applied the type parameter to the class declaration, every CommaSeparatedListBuilder would be forced to hold only one type. Either approach is valid, but the semantics are very different.

This sample is simple enough that you could replace the type parameter with System.Object. But the concept is one you can apply often. You can use a catchall generic method in a nongeneric class to create different specialized methods in the class. This class does not use T in its fields but uses it only as a parameter to methods in the public API. Using different types in place of the parameters to that method doesn't mean that you need a different instantiation.

Obviously, not every generic algorithm is suited for generic methods instead of a generic class. Some simple guidelines can help you determine which to use. In two cases you must make a generic class: The first occurs when your class stores a value of one of the Type parameters as part of its internal state. (Collections are an obvious example.) The second occurs when your class implements a generic interface. Except for those two cases, you can usually create a nongeneric class and use generic methods. You'll end up with more granularity in your options for updating the algorithms in the future.

Look again at the code for the preceding sample. You'll see that the second Utils class does not force the callers to explicitly declare each type in each call to one of the generic methods. When possible, the second version is a better API solution, for a number of reasons. First, it's simpler for callers. When you don't specify the Type parameter, the compiler picks the best possible method. That practice gives you, the library developer, many options moving forward. If you find that a specific implementation is better, your callers automatically get the specific method you created. If, on the other hand, your methods force callers to specify all the Type parameters, they will continue to use the generic methods even though you have provided a better alternative.

Item 9: Prefer Generic Tuples to Output and Ref Parameters

One common problem for many developers is how to create a method signature for methods that logically return more than one item. Many developers turn to ref or out parameters in those cases. But it's better to define generic tuples that can return multiple discrete values. A **tuple** is nothing more than a composite with *n* elements.

There are many reasons this is a better plan. Let's begin with immutability. Ref parameters make it harder to create immutable objects.

Here is a simplified class that represents an employee as an immutable type:

```
public class Employee
{
    private readonly string firstName;
    private readonly string lastName;
    private readonly decimal salary;
    public string FirstName
    {
        get { return firstName; }
    }
    public string LastName
    {
        get { return lastName; }
    }
    public decimal Salary
    {
        get { return salary; }
    }
    public Employee(string firstName, string lastName,
        decimal salary)
    {
        this.firstName = firstName;
        this.lastName = lastName;
        this.salary = salary;
    }
    public override string ToString()
    {
        return string.Format("{1}, {0} salary: {2}",
            lastName, firstName, salary);
    }
}
```

You could read an employee definition from the console like this:

```
string last = Console.ReadLine();
string first = Console.ReadLine();
string salary = Console.ReadLine();
Employee emp = new Employee(first, last,
    decimal.Parse(salary));
```

Of course, decimal.Parse could throw an exception if the input string for salary does not parse correctly. That leads us down the path of TryParse:

```
string last = Console.ReadLine();
string first = Console.ReadLine();
string salaryString  = Console.ReadLine();
decimal salary = 0;
bool okSalary = decimal.TryParse(salaryString, out salary);
if (okSalary)
{
    Employee emp = new Employee(first, last, salary);
    Console.WriteLine(emp);
}
```

For the most trivial of examples, we've added quite a bit of code. This problem gets worse as programs get larger.

Also, ref and out parameters make polymorphism much more difficult. Consider this simple definition of a Person and Employee hierarchy:

```
public class Person
{
    private readonly string firstName;
    private readonly string lastName;
    public string FirstName
    {
        get { return firstName; }
    }
    public string LastName
    {
        get { return lastName; }
    }
    public Person(string firstName, string lastName)
    {
        this.firstName = firstName;
        this.lastName = lastName;
    }
}
public class Employee : Person
{
    private readonly decimal salary;
    public decimal Salary
    {
        get { return salary; }
    }
```

```
public Employee(string firstName, string lastName,
    decimal salary) :
    base (firstName, lastName)
{
    this.salary = salary;
}
public override string ToString()
{
    return string.Format("{1}, {0} salary: {2}",
        LastName, FirstName, salary);
}
}
```

Later, someone makes this method to support changing a person's last name:

```
static void ChangeName(ref Person p, string newLastName)
{
    p = new Person(p.FirstName, newLastName);
}
```

ChangeName() cannot be called with an employee object. That's a good thing, because it wouldn't work. This method would transform an Employee (or any other derived object) into a Person. You're losing information. Of course, you also can't write a single method to take an Employee object. That won't compile for any of the base classes. Using ref parameters means you must create a different overload for every type that you intend to support. That's because ref parameters are not covariant or contravariant. When you're using the ref modifier, you cannot use a derived class (or a base class) object when a base class object is expected. However, return values are covariant: A method can create a type derived from the type declared in the method signature. Mix in a little local variable type inference, and developers can make use of types up or down an inheritance hierarchy much more easily.

The effect is similar to the problems outlined in Item 47 (Chapter 6) on array parameters and covariance. The only difference is that in the case of ref parameters, the compiler does a little better job of type checking.

Both of our samples use single ref parameters and void return types. In those cases, you can simply change the method declarations to return a new object of the proper type:

```
static Person ChangeName(Person p, string newLastName)
    { // elided}
static Employee ChangeName(Employee p, string newLastName)
    { // elided}
```

It's more complicated when you have two logical return values. In those cases, you can use generics to define a tuple to return a type that contains all the fields you wish to support. Here is a simple generic definition that supports two return values:

```
public struct Tuple<T1, T2> : IEquatable<Tuple<T1, T2>>
{
    private readonly T1 first;
    public T1 First
    {
        get { return first; }
    }

    private readonly T2 second;
    public T2 Second
    {
        get { return second; }
    }

    public Tuple(T1 f, T2 s)
    {
        first = f;
        second = s;
    }
    // Implementation of IEquatable<Tuple<T1, T2>> elided
}
```

You may recognize that this class definition looks very similar to the `System.Collections.Generic.KeyValuePair` generic type. However, its purpose is very different, so I prefer making a new type. Next, this class is a specific tuple—a pair—that contains two elements. Obviously you can extend this technique for any general tuple you need: three, four, five, or more fields.

This tuple can be the return type for any method that has two logical return values. It's an obvious extension to create a tuple having more than two values. By creating and using tuple classes, you avoid the need to create `ref` and `out` parameters for multiple logical methods. That will make it easier to compose method calls that work with these tuples.

For example, the following method shows how you would use the tuple structure to return the nearest city and its temperature in a `Tuple`:

```
public static Tuple<string, decimal> FindTempForNearestCity
    (string soughtCity)
{
    string city = "algorithmElided";
    decimal temp = decimal.MinValue; // really cold.
    return new Tuple<string, decimal>(city, temp);
}
```

To call it you would use a similar structure:

```
Tuple<string, decimal> weather =
    FindTempForNearestCity("NearHere");
```

You probably don't like the way the `Tuple` definition obscures the real meaning of the type. I don't, either. Thankfully, neither did the C# language designers. They created an extension to the `using` declaration that enables you to specify an alias for any closed generic type:

```
using CityTemperature = Tuple<string, decimal>;
```

The method implementation now reads much more clearly:

```
public static CityTemperature FindTempForNearestCity
    (string soughtCity)
{
    string city = "algorithmElided";
    decimal temp = decimal.MinValue; // really cold.
    return new CityTemperature(city, temp);
}
```

The assignment statement when the method gets called also becomes clearer:

```
CityTemperature weather = FindTempForNearestCity("NearHere");
```

Some of this may look as if I'm simply rearranging method signatures. However, as you get further into C# 3.0 and you begin using increasingly functional programming constructs, you'll find that this technique becomes much more important. Methods that take `out` and `ref` parameters do not support composition very well. Methods returning a single value (however complex that value might be) compose better.

`Ref` and `out` parameters imply that a method can create an object that matches the declared type. Polymorphism implies that more-derived types can always be substituted when a base type is expected. However, the opposite is true when a method creates that object for you. It must create a more-derived type when your calling code expects a base type. These two rules mean that, by and large, `out` and `ref` parameters cannot use polymorphism in any real way. Your algorithms will be much easier to use when you restructure them to return multiple values in a generic tuple.

Item 10: Implement Classic Interfaces in Addition to Generic Interfaces

So far, the items in this chapter have explored all the wonderful benefits of generics. It would be great if we could just ignore everything that predated generics support in .NET and C#. But a developer's life isn't that simple, for a variety of reasons. Your classes will be much more useful if you support the classic nongeneric interfaces in addition to the generic interfaces you'll want to support in new libraries. This recommendation applies to (1) your classes and the interfaces they support, (2) public properties, and even (3) the elements you choose to serialize.

Let's examine why you need to consider support for these nongeneric interfaces, and let's look at how to support these classic interfaces while still encouraging the users of your class to use the newer generic versions. Let's start with a simple implementation of a `Name` class that stores the names of people in an application:

```
public class Name :
    IComparable<Name>,
    IEquatable<Name>
{
    public string First
    {
        get;
        set;
    }

    public string Last
    {
        get;
        set;
    }
```

```csharp
public string Middle
{
    get;
    set;
}

#region IComparable<Name> Members
public int CompareTo(Name other)
{
    if (other == null)
        return 1; // Any non-null object > null.
    int rVal = Comparer<string>.Default.Compare
        (Last, other.Last);
    if (rVal != 0)
        return rVal;
    rVal = Comparer<string>.Default.Compare
        (First, other.First);
    if (rVal != 0)
        return rVal;
    return Comparer<string>.Default.Compare(Middle,
        other.Middle);
}
#endregion

#region IEquatable<Name> Members
public bool Equals(Name other)
{
    if (Object.ReferenceEquals(other, null))
        return false;
    // Semantically equivalent to using
    // EqualityComparer<string>.Default
    return Last == other.Last &&
        First == other.First &&
        Middle == other.Middle;
}
#endregion

// other details elided
}
```

All the core capabilities of the equality and ordering are implemented in terms of the generic (and type-safe) versions. Also, you can see that I've deferred the null checks in `CompareTo()` to the default string comparer. That saves quite a bit of code and provides the same semantics.

But a generic implementation does not play well with any code written using the .NET 1.x methods. What's more, you may need to integrate types from various systems that represent the same logical type. Suppose you purchase an e-commerce system from one vendor and a fulfillment system from a different vendor. Both systems have the concept of an order: `Store.Order` and `Shipping.Order`. You need an equality relationship between those two types. Generics don't do that very well. You'll need a cross-type comparer. Further, you may need to store both types of `Order` in a single collection. Again, a generic type won't do.

Instead, you need a method that checks for equality using `System.Object`, perhaps something like this:

```
public static bool CheckEquality(object left, object right)
{
    if (left == null)
        return right == null;
    return left.Equals(right);
}
```

Calling the `CheckEquality()` method using two `person` objects would yield unexpected results. Instead of calling the `IEquatable<Name>.Equals()` method, `CheckEquality()` would call `System.Object.Equals()`! You'll get the wrong answer, because `System.Object.Equals()` will use reference semantics, and you've overridden `IEquatable<T>.Equals` to follow value semantics.

If the `CheckEquality()` method is in your code, you can create a generic version of `CheckEquality` that calls the right method:

```
public static bool CheckEquality<T>(T left, T right)
    where T : IEquatable<T>
{
    if (left == null)
        return right == null;

    return left.Equals(right);
}
```

Of course, that solution isn't available to you if `CheckEquality()` isn't in your codebase but is in a third-party library or even the .NET BCL. You must override the classic `Equals` method to call the `IEquatable<T>.Equals` method you've written:

```
public override bool Equals(object obj)
{
    if (obj.GetType() == typeof(Name))
        return this.Equals(obj as Name);
    else return false;
}
```

After this modification, almost any method that checks for equality on `Name` types works correctly. Notice that I'm checking the type of the `obj` parameter against the type of `Name` before using the `as` operator to convert to a `Name`. You might think that this check is redundant, because the `as` operator returns `null` if `obj` is not a type that's convertible to `Name`. That assumption misses some conditions: The `as` operator will call user-defined conversions, and that is not the behavior you want. Also, if a class is derived from `Name`, the `as` operator will return a `Name` pointer to the object. The objects aren't equal, even if their `Name` portions are.

Next, overriding `Equals` means overriding `GetHashCode`:

```
public override int GetHashCode()
{
    int hashCode = 0;
    if (Last != null)
        hashCode ^= Last.GetHashCode();
    if (First != null)
        hashCode ^= First.GetHashCode();
    if (Middle != null)
        hashCode ^= Middle.GetHashCode();
    return hashCode;
}
```

Again, this simply expands the public API to ensure that your type plays well with version 1.x code.

If you want to completely ensure that you have covered all your bases, you need to handle a few operators. Implementing `IEquality<T>` means implementing `operator ==`, and that also means implementing `operator !=`.

```
public static bool operator ==(Name left, Name right)
{
    if (left == null)
        return right == null;
    return left.Equals(right);
}
public static bool operator !=(Name left, Name right)
{
    if (left == null)
        return right != null;
    return !left.Equals(right);
}
```

That's enough of equality. The Name class also implements IComparable<T>. You're going to run into the same conditions with ordering relations as you do with equality relations. There's a lot of code out there that expects you to implement the class IComparable interface. You've already written the algorithm, so you should just go ahead and add the IComparable interface to the list of implemented interfaces and create the proper method:

```
public class Name :
    IComparable<Name>,
    IEquatable<Name>,
    IComparable
{
    #region IComparable Members
    int IComparable.CompareTo(object obj)
    {
        if (obj.GetType() != typeof(Name))
            throw new ArgumentException(
                "Argument is not a Name object");
        return this.CompareTo(obj as Name);
    }
    #endregion
    // other details elided
}
```

Notice that the classic interface is defined using explicit interface implementation. This practice ensures that no one accidentally gets the classic interface instead of the preferred generic interface. In normal use, the compiler will choose the generic method over the explicit interface method.

Only when the called method has been typed to the classic interface (`IComparable`) will the compiler generate a call to that interface member.

Of course, implementing `IComparable<T>` implies that there is an ordering relation. You should implement the less-than (<) and greater-than (>) operators:

```
public static bool operator <(Name left, Name right)
{
    if (left == null)
        return right != null;
    return left.CompareTo(right) < 0;
}
public static bool operator >(Name left, Name right)
{
    if (left == null)
        return false;
    return left.CompareTo(right) < 0;
}
```

In the case of the `Name` type, because it both defines an ordering relation and defines equality, you should implement the <= and >= operators:

```
public static bool operator <=(Name left, Name right)
{
    if (left == null)
        return true;
    return left.CompareTo(right) <= 0;
}
public static bool operator >=(Name left, Name right)
{
    if (left == null)
        return right == null;
    return left.CompareTo(right) >= 0;
}
```

You must understand that the ordering relations are independent of the equality relations. You can define types in which equality is defined but ordering relations are not defined. And you can define types that implement an ordering relation and do not define equality relations.

The preceding code more or less implements the semantics provided by the `Equatable<T>` and `Comparer<T>`. The `Default` property of each of those classes contains code that determines whether the type parameter, `T`, implements a type-specific equality or comparison test. If it does, those type-specific versions are used. If it does not, the `System.Object` overrides are used.

I've concentrated on the comparison and ordering relations to demonstrate the incompatibilities between the old and the new (generic) style of interfaces. These incompatibilities can catch you in other ways, too. `IEnumerable<T>` inherits from `IEnumerable`. But full-featured collection interfaces do not: `ICollection<T>` does not inherit from `ICollection`, and `IList<T>` does not inherit from `IList`. However, because `IList<T>` and `ICollection<T>` both inherit from `IEnumerable<T>`, both of those interfaces include classic `IEnumerable` support.

In most cases, adding classic interface support is a simple matter of adding methods having the correct signature to your class. As with the `IComparable<T>` and `IComparable`, you should explicitly implement the classic interface `IComparable` to encourage calling code to use the new versions. Visual Studio and other tools provide wizards that create stubs for the interface methods.

There are many new interfaces and types available in .NET Framework 2.0. They are great additions, and they improve the type safety of the code in your applications and libraries. You should embrace them, but you also should realize that not everyone in the entire world has yet moved there. You should continue to support the analogous classic interfaces, although you should implement them using explicit interface implementation to avoid accidental misuse.

2 Multithreading in C#

Moore's law has changed. Our computers continue to get faster, but not by increasing clock speed. Instead, computers are getting faster by adding cores. As this trend continues, your daily life will include more multithreaded programs than it currently does.

Multithreaded programming is difficult, and it's easy to get it wrong. Subtle bugs occur when threads switch in a particular location. Unless you examine every line of code in your program and consider what happens if a task is switched, something likely will go wrong later. Somewhere, someday, a task switch will happen at a different location from one you reproduced in your testing, and your program will break. That makes it hard to code your programs correctly and even harder to verify them. So even as multithreaded programs become more prevalent, they continue to be more difficult than equivalent single-threaded applications.

This short chapter won't make you an expert in multithreaded programs, but these items contain the most common recommendations you should follow when writing .NET multithreaded programs. For comprehensive coverage of multithreaded techniques, I recommend Joe Duffy's book *Concurrent Programming on Windows Vista: Architecture, Principles, and Patterns* (Addison-Wesley, 2008). With that important disclaimer, let's look at the challenges that make multithreaded programming more complicated than sequential programming.

Running a sequential program in parallel can introduce a great many problems. Let's start with this simple definition of a bank account:

```
public class BankAccount
{
    public string AccountNumber
    {
        get;
        private set;
    }
}
```

```
public decimal Balance
{
    get;
    private set;
}


public BankAccount(string accountNumber)
{
    AccountNumber = accountNumber;
}


public void MakeDeposit(decimal amount)
{
    Balance += amount;
}
public decimal MakeWithdrawal(decimal amount)
{
    if (Balance > amount)
    {
        Balance -= amount;
        return amount;
    }
    return 0M;
}
}
```

This code is so simple that you can almost validate it by inspection. But it will fail miserably in a multithreaded environment. Why? It's because this code contains many possible race conditions. The deposit and withdrawal methods are actually several operations. The += operation involves retrieving the current balance from memory and placing it in the register. Then the CPU performs the addition operation. After that, the new value is stored back into the proper memory location.

The problem is that having multiple cores means that different threads in your application may be running on different cores at the same time. Timing issues among multiple threads means that different threads may interleave their reads and writes to the same memory location, causing data errors. Consider this scenario:

1. Thread A starts the operation for depositing $10,000.
2. Thread A retrieves the current balance of $2,000.

3. Thread B starts the operation for depositing $4,000.
4. Thread B retrieves the current balance of $2,000.
5. Thread B computes the new balance of $6,000.
6. Thread A computes the new balance of $12,000.
7. Thread A stores the result of $12,000.
8. Thread B stores the new balance of $6,000.
9. In this way, the interleaved operations cause errors in previously correct (for a single-threaded world) code.

These **race conditions** occur because this class does not have any synchronization primitives for any of the operations that produce side effects. Both the `Deposit()` and the `Withdrawal()` methods produce side effects: They change observable state in addition to returning any new value. Those methods depend on the current state of the system when the method is called; for example, a withdrawal fails if the account doesn't have sufficient funds. Methods that don't have side effects have less need for synchronization. They don't depend on the current state, so having state change during the execution of a method doesn't change the results.

The fix for our bank account sample seems simple: Add some locking primitives.

```
public void MakeDeposit(decimal amount)
{
    lock (syncHandle)
    {
        Balance += amount;
    }
}
public decimal MakeWithdrawal(decimal amount)
{
    lock (syncHandle)
    {
        if (Balance > amount)
        {
            Balance -= amount;
            return amount;
        }
    }
    return 0M;
}
```

That's better, but now we've introduced a situation in which deadlocks are possible. Suppose a customer has more than one bank account: a savings account and a checking account. Customers will want to make transfers—withdraw from one account and put the money into another account. Logically, that's a single operation. But at the machine level, it's many operations. You make a withdrawal from one account (itself a multistep operation) and then make a deposit into the other account (also a multistep operation). You'd think this would work: Your code would make the withdrawal while holding the lock on one account. Then it would acquire a second lock on the second account and make the deposit.

But if multiple threads are trying to make multiple transfers, a deadlock can occur. **Deadlocks** happen when each of, say, two threads holds a lock that the other thread needs to do its work. Each thread holds on to its lock indefinitely. Neither can get the lock it needs. Time passes, and nothing happens. Your application looks as if it has crashed. It hasn't, but it's waiting for something that will never happen.

A lesser problem than deadlocks is livelocks. **Livelocks** involve a complicated locking mechanism that creates a distinction between reading and writing shared data. It's safe to let multiple readers examine a piece of data. However, only one writer may modify the data at one time. Furthermore, when that one writer is modifying the data, no readers may examine the data. In a livelock, there are so many readers examining the data that no writers can ever get in. The data effectively becomes read-only.

There's no way around it: Multithreaded programming is hard. It adds complexity to everything you do. But multithreaded programs are the future, so every C# developer needs at least a rudimentary knowledge of multithreaded techniques.

The .NET Framework creates multiple threads in a number of places: In Web applications and Web services, for example, ASP.NET worker threads are created for each new request. The remoting libraries do the same thing for incoming calls to a service. Some timer event handlers are called on new threads, and Windows Communication Foundation (WCF) libraries use more than one thread. You can also call asynchronous versions of Web service calls.

You will use at least some of these techniques. You need to understand something about multithreaded techniques if you are going to be successful in .NET.

Item 11: Use the Thread Pool Instead of Creating Threads

You can't know the optimum number of threads that should be created for your application. Your application may run on a machine with multiple cores now, but it's almost certain that whatever number of cores you assume today will be wrong six months from now. Furthermore, you can't control for the number of threads that the CLR will create for its own tasks, such as the garbage collector. On a server application, such as ASP.NET or WCF services, each new request is handled by a different thread. That makes it very hard for you, as an application or class library developer, to optimize for the proper number of threads on the target system. However, the .NET **thread pool** has all the knowledge necessary to optimize the number of active threads on the target system. Furthermore, if you have created too many tasks and threads for the target machine, the thread pool queues up additional requests until a new background thread is available.

The .NET thread pool performs much of the work to handle thread resource management for you. It manages those resources in such a way that you get better performance when your application starts background tasks repeatedly and doesn't interact with those tasks very closely.

`QueueUserWorkItem` uses the thread pool to manage resources for you. When you add an item, it is executed when a thread is available. Depending on the number of running tasks and the size of the thread pool, execution may be immediate or it may wait for a new thread resource to become available. The thread pool starts with a number of ready threads per processer and a second set of read I/O completion threads. The exact number is version dependent. If you start queuing additional tasks, the thread pool starts creating additional threads in the pool, depending on available memory and other resources.

I don't cover the thread pool implementation in exhaustive detail, because the purpose of using the thread pool is to off-load much of that work and make it the framework's problem. In short, the number of threads in the thread pool grows to provide you the best mix of available threads and the minimum amount of allocated and unused resources. You queue up a worker item, and when a thread is available, it executes your thread procedure. The thread pool's job is to make sure that a thread becomes available quickly. Essentially, you fire the request and forget it.

The thread pool also manages the end-of-task cycle automatically. When a task finishes, the thread is not destroyed; instead, it is returned to a ready state so that it is available for another task. The thread is again available for other work, as needed by the thread pool. This next task need not be the same task; the thread can execute any other long-running method your application has in mind. You simply call `QueueUserWorkItem` with another target method, and your thread pool will manage the work for that method as well.

There's one other important way that the thread pool helps you manage your tasks running in other threads. All threads belonging to the thread pool used by `QueueUserWorkItem` are **background threads.** This means that you don't need to clean up those threads before your application exits. If your application exits while these background threads are running, the system stops those tasks and unloads everything related to your application. You need to ensure that you stop all non-background threads in your application before the system will unload your application. If you don't, you can easily end up with an application that no longer does anything and yet consumes resources.

On the other hand, because background threads are killed without warning, you need to be careful how you access system resources to ensure that application termination at the wrong time doesn't leave the system in an unstable state. In many cases, when a thread is terminated, the runtime raises a `ThreadAbortException` on that thread. When an application terminates with background threads running, those background threads receive no notification that the application is terminating. They are simply stopped. If your threads may leave system resources in an unstable state, you should not use background threads. Thankfully, those cases are the minority.

The system manages the number of tasks that are active in a thread pool. The thread pool starts tasks based on the amount of system resources available. If the system is currently operating at close to capacity, the thread pool waits to start new tasks. However, if the system is lightly loaded, the thread pool launches additional tasks immediately. You don't need to write your own load-balancing logic. The thread pool manages that for you.

You might think that the optimal number of tasks would be equal to the number of cores in the target machine. That's not the worst strategy to take, but it's simplistic in its analysis, and it's almost certainly not the best answer. Wait time, contention for resources other than the CPU, and other processes outside your control all have an effect on the optimal number of threads for your application. If you create too few threads, you'll end up not getting the best performance for your application as cores sit idle. Having way too many threads means that your target machine will spend too much time scheduling threads and too little time executing the work performed by them.

To give you some general guidance, I wrote a small application that uses the Hero of Alexandria algorithm to calculate square roots. It's general guidance, because each algorithm has unique characteristics. In this case, the core algorithm is simple and does not communicate with other threads to perform its work.

You start by making a guess at the square root of a number. A simple starting guess is 1. To find the next approximation, you find the average of (1) the current guess and (2) the original number divided by the current guess. For example, to find the square root of 10, you'd make a guess of 1. The next guess is $(1 + (10/1)) / 2$, or 5.5. You continue to repeat the steps until the guess converges at the answer. Here's the code:

```
public static class Hero
{
    private const double TOLERANCE = 1.0E-8;
    public static double FindRoot(double number)
    {
        double guess = 1;
        double error = Math.Abs(guess * guess - number);

        while (error > TOLERANCE)
        {
            guess = (number / guess + guess) / 2.0;
            error = Math.Abs(guess * guess - number);
        }
        return guess;
    }
}
```

To examine the performance characteristics of the thread pool against manually created threads and against a single-threaded version of the application, I wrote test harnesses that perform repeated calculations against this algorithm:

```
private static double OneThread()
{
    Stopwatch start = new Stopwatch();
```

```csharp
        start.Start();
        for (int i = LowerBound; i < UpperBound; i++)
        {
            double answer = Hero.FindRoot(i);
        }
        start.Stop();
        return start.ElapsedMilliseconds;
    }

    private static double ThreadPoolThreads(int numThreads)
    {
        Stopwatch start = new Stopwatch();
        using (AutoResetEvent e = new AutoResetEvent(false))
        {
            int workerThreads = numThreads;

            start.Start();
            for (int thread = 0; thread < numThreads; thread++ )
                System.Threading.ThreadPool.QueueUserWorkItem(
                    (x) =>
                    {
                        for (int i = LowerBound;
                            i < UpperBound; i++)
                        {
                            // Call the calculation.
                            if (i % numThreads == thread)
                            {
                                double answer = Hero.FindRoot(i);
                            }

                        }

                        // Decrement the count.
                        if (Interlocked.Decrement(
                            ref workerThreads) == 0)
                        {
                            // Set the event.
                            e.Set();
                        }
                    });
```

```
            // Wait for the signal.
            e.WaitOne();

            // Get out.
            start.Stop();
            return start.ElapsedMilliseconds;
        }
    }


private static double ManualThreads(int numThreads)
{
    Stopwatch start = new Stopwatch();
    using (AutoResetEvent e = new AutoResetEvent(false))
    {
        int workerThreads = numThreads;

        start.Start();
        for (int thread = 0; thread < numThreads; thread++)
        {
            System.Threading.Thread t = new Thread(
                () =>
                {
                    for (int i = LowerBound;
                        i < UpperBound; i++)
                    {
                        // Call the calculation.
                        if (i % numThreads == thread)
                        {
                            double answer = Hero.FindRoot(i);
                        }
                    }
                    // Decrement the count.
                    if (Interlocked.Decrement(
                        ref workerThreads) == 0)
                    {
                        // Set the event.
                        e.Set();
                    }
                });
            t.Start();
        }
```

```
    // Wait for the signal.
    e.WaitOne();

    // Get out.
    start.Stop();
    return start.ElapsedMilliseconds;
    }
}
```

The single-threaded version is straightforward. Both of the multithreaded versions use lambda syntax (see Item 6 in Chapter 1) to define the actions performed in the background threads. As I say in Item 6, you could replace the lambda expressions with anonymous delegates:

```
System.Threading.ThreadPool.QueueUserWorkItem(
    delegate(object x)
    {
        for (int i = LowerBound; i < UpperBound; i++)
        {
            // Call the calculation.
            if (i % numThreads == thread)
            {
                double answer = Hero.FindRoot(i);
            }
        }

        // Decrement the count.
        if (Interlocked.Decrement(
            ref workerThreads) == 0)
        {
            // Set the event.
            e.Set();
        }
    });
```

Changing to using an explicit method and explicitly creating the delegate requires quite a bit of reorganization. A number of local method variables (the reset event, the number of threads, and the current thread index) are defined in the outer method and used inside the background thread. The C# compiler creates a closure (see Item 33, in Chapter 4, and Item 41, in Chapter 5) when you use the lambda syntax for inline methods. In addition, notice that you can specify lambda syntax even for multiple-statement methods, and not only single expressions.

This main program produces timing for the single-threaded version and both multithreaded versions so that you can see the effect of adding threads using both algorithms. Figure 2.1 shows the resulting graph. There are a few things to learn from this example. First, the manually created threads have much more overhead compared with the thread pool threads. If you create more than ten threads, threading overhead becomes the main performance bottleneck. Even with this algorithm, in which there isn't much wait time, that's not good.

Using the thread pool, you must queue more than 40 items before the overhead dominates the work time. And that's on a dual-core laptop. Server-class machines with more cores would be efficient with more threads. Having more threads than cores is often the smart choice. However, that choice is highly dependent on the application and on the amount of time the application's threads spend waiting for resources.

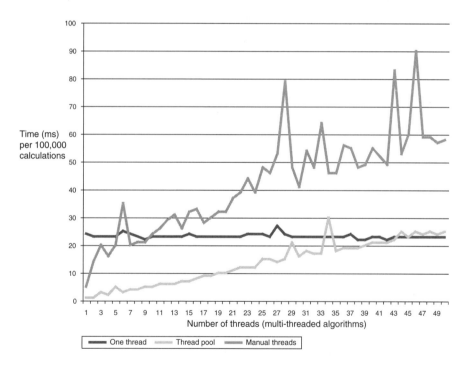

Figure 2.1 The effects of calculation time for the single-threaded and multi-threaded versions using `System.Threading.Thread` versus `System.Threading.ThreadPool.QueueUserWorkItem`. The Y axis shows the time (in milliseconds) per 100,000 calculations on a dual-core laptop.

Two important factors result in the higher performance of the thread pool compared with creating your own threads manually. First, the thread pool reuses threads as they become available for work. When you manually create new threads, you must create a new thread for each new task. The creation and destruction of those threads take more time than the .NET thread pool management.

Second, the thread pool manages the active number of threads for you. If you create too many threads, the system queues them up, and they wait to execute until enough resources are available. QueueUserWorkItem hands work to the next available thread in the thread pool and does some thread resource management for you. If all the threads in the application's thread pool are busy, it queues tasks to wait for the next available thread.

The farther you move down the road into a world with increasing numbers of cores, the more likely it is that you'll be creating multithreaded applications. If you're creating server-side applications in .NET with WCF, ASP.NET, or .NET remoting, you're already creating multithreaded applications. Those .NET subsystems use the thread pool to manage thread resources, and you should, too. You'll find that the thread pool introduces less overhead, and that leads to better performance. Also, the .NET thread pool does a better job of managing the number of active threads that should be performing work than you can manage at the application level.

Item 12: Use BackgroundWorker for Cross-Thread Communication

Item 11 shows a sample that started various numbers of background tasks using ThreadPool.QueueUserWorkItem. Using this API method is simple, because you have off-loaded most of the thread management issues to the framework and the underlying operating system (OS). There's a lot of functionality you can simply reuse, so QueueUserWorkItem should be your default tool of choice when you need to create background threads that execute tasks in your application. QueueUserWorkItem makes several assumptions about how you should be performing your work. When your design doesn't match those assumptions, you'll have more work to do. Instead of creating your own threads using System.Threading.Thread, you should use System.ComponentModel.BackgroundWorker. The BackgroundWorker class is built on top of ThreadPool and adds many features for interthread communication.

The single most important issue you must deal with is exceptions in your `WaitCallback`, the method that does the work in the background thread. If any exceptions are thrown from that method, the system will terminate your application. It doesn't simply terminate that one background thread; it terminates the entire application. This behavior is consistent with other background thread API methods, but the difference is that `QueueUser-WorkItem` doesn't have any built-in capability to handle reporting errors.

In addition, `QueueUserWorkItem` does not give you any built-in methods to communicate between the background threads and the foreground thread. It doesn't provide any built-in means for you to detect completion, track progress, pause tasks, or cancel tasks. When you need those capabilities, you can turn to the `BackgroundWorker` component, which is built on top of the `QueueUserWorkItem` functionality.

The `BackgroundWorker` component was built on top of the `System.ComponentModel.Component` class to facilitate design-level support. However, `BackgroundWorker` is quite useful in code that doesn't include the designer support. In fact, most of the time when I use `Background-Worker`, it is not in a form class.

The simplest use of `BackgroundWorker` is to create a method that matches the delegate signature, attach that method to `BackgroundWorker`'s `DoWork` event, and then call the `RunWorkerAsync()` method of `BackgroundWorker`:

```
BackgroundWorker backgroundWorkerExample =
    new BackgroundWorker();
backgroundWorkerExample.DoWork += new
    DoWorkEventHandler(backgroundWorkerExample_DoWork);
backgroundWorkerExample.RunWorkerAsync();


// elsewhere:
void backgroundWorkerExample_DoWork(object sender,
    DoWorkEventArgs e)
{
    // body of the work elided
}
```

In this pattern, `BackgroundWorker` performs exactly the same function as `ThreadPool.QueueUserWorkItem`. The `BackgroundWorker` class performs its background tasks using `ThreadPool` and by using `QueueUserWorkItem` internally.

The power of `BackgroundWorker` comes with the framework that is already built in for these other common scenarios. `BackgroundWorker` uses events to communicate between the foreground and background threads. When the foreground thread launches a request, `Background-Worker` raises the `DoWork` event on the background thread. The `DoWork` event handler reads any parameters and begins doing the work.

When the background thread procedure has finished (as defined by the exit of the `DoWork` event handler), `BackgroundWorker` raises the `Run-WorkerCompleted` event on the foreground thread, as shown in Figure 2.2. The foreground thread can now do any necessary postprocessing after the background thread has completed.

In addition to the events raised by `BackgroundWorker`, properties can be manipulated to control how the foreground and background thread interact. The `WorkerSupportsCancellation` property lets `Background-Worker` know that the background thread knows how to interrupt an operation and exit. The `WorkerReportsProgress` property informs

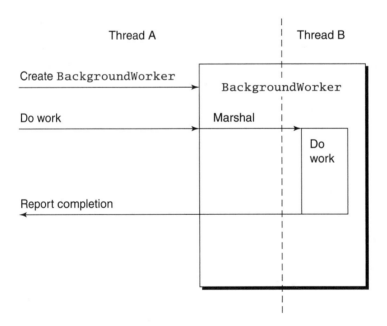

Figure 2.2 The `BackgroundWorker` class can report completion to an event handler defined in the foreground thread. You register the event handler for the completion event, and `BackgroundWorker` raises that event when your `DoWork` delegate has completed execution.

`BackgroundWorker` that the worker procedure will report progress to the foreground thread at regular intervals, as shown in Figure 2.3. In addition, `BackgroundWorker` forwards cancellation requests from the foreground thread to the background thread. The background thread procedure can check the `CancellationPending` flag and stop processing if necessary.

Finally, `BackgroundWorker` has a built-in protocol to report errors that occur in the background thread. In Item 11 (earlier in this chapter) I explain that exceptions cannot be thrown from one thread to another. If an exception is generated in the background thread and is not caught by the thread procedure, the thread will be terminated. Worse, the foreground thread does not receive any notification that the background thread has stopped processing. `BackgroundWorker` solves this problem by adding an `Error` property to `DoWorkEventArgs` and propagating that property to the `Error` property in the result arguments. Your worker procedure catches all exceptions and sets them to the error property. (Note that this is one of the rare occasions when catching all exceptions is recommended.)

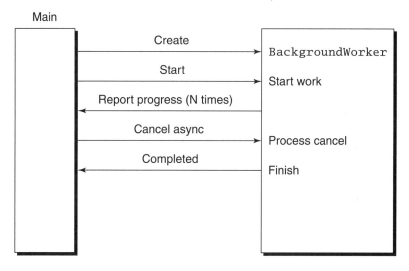

Figure 2.3 The `BackgroundWorker` class supports multiple events to request cancellation of the current task, reporting of progress to the foreground task, completion, and error reporting. `BackgroundWorker` defines the protocol and raises the events necessary to support any of these communication mechanisms. To report progress, your background procedure must raise an event defined on `BackgroundWorker`. Your foreground task code must request that these extra events be raised and must register handlers on these events.

Simply return from the background thread procedure, and handle the error in the event handler for the foreground results.

Earlier I said that I often use `BackgroundWorker` in classes that aren't the `Form` class, and even in non-Windows Forms applications, such as services or Web services. This works fine, but it does have some caveats. When `BackgroundWorker` determines that it is running in a Windows Forms application and the form is visible, the `ProgressChanged` and `RunWorkerCompleted` events are marshaled to the graphical user interface (GUI) thread via a marshaling control and `Control.BeginInvoke` (see Item 16 later in this chapter). In other scenarios, those delegates are simply called on a free thread pool thread. As you will see in Item 16, that behavior may affect the order in which events are received.

Finally, because `BackgroundWorker` is built on `QueueUserWorkItem`, you can reuse `BackgroundWorker` for multiple background requests. You need to check the `IsBusy` property of `BackgroundWorker` to see whether `BackgroundWorker` is currently running a task. When you need to have multiple background tasks running, you can create multiple `BackgroundWorker` objects. Each will share the same thread pool, so you have multiple tasks running just as you would with `QueueUserWorkItem`. You need to make sure that your event handlers use the correct sender property. This practice ensures that the background threads and foreground threads are communicating correctly.

`BackgroundWorker` supports many of the common patterns that you will use when you create background tasks. By using it you can reuse that implementation in your code, adding any of those patterns as needed. You don't have to design your own communication protocols between foreground and background threads.

Item 13: Use lock() as Your First Choice for Synchronization

Threads need to communicate with each other. Somehow, you need to provide a safe way for various threads in your application to send and receive data. However, sharing data between threads introduces the potential for data integrity errors in the form of synchronization issues. Therefore, you need to be certain that the current state of every shared data item is consistent. You achieve this safety by using **synchronization primitives** to protect access to the shared data. Synchronization primitives ensure that the current thread is not interrupted until a critical set of operations is completed.

There are many primitives available in the .NET BCL that you can use to safely ensure that access to shared data is synchronized. Only one pair of them—`Monitor.Enter()` and `Monitor.Exit()`—was given special status in the C# language. `Monitor.Enter()` and `Monitor.Exit()` implement a **critical section** block. Critical sections are such a common synchronization technique that the language designers added support for them using the `lock()` statement. You should follow that example and make `lock()` your primary tool for synchronization.

The reason is simple: The compiler generates consistent code, but you may make mistakes some of the time. The C# language introduces the *lock* keyword to control synchronization for multithreaded programs. The lock statement generates exactly the same code as if you used `Monitor.Enter()` and `Monitor.Exit()` correctly. Furthermore, it's easier and it automatically generates all the exception-safe code you need.

However, under two conditions `Monitor` gives you necessary control that you can't get when you use `lock()`. First, be aware that `lock` is lexically scoped. This means that you can't enter a `Monitor` in one lexical scope and exit it in another when using the `lock` statement. Thus, you can't enter a `Monitor` in a method and exit it inside a lambda expression defined in that method (see Item 41, Chapter 5). The second reason is that `Monitor.Enter` supports a time-out, which I cover later in this item.

You can lock any reference type by using the `lock` statement:

```
public int TotalValue
{
    get
    {
        lock(syncHandle)
        {
            return total;
        }
    }
}

public void IncrementTotal()
{
    lock (syncHandle)
    {
        total++;
    }
}
```

The `lock` statement gets the exclusive monitor for an object and ensures that no other thread can access the object until the lock is released. The preceding sample code, using `lock()`, generates the same IL as the following version, using `Monitor.Enter()` and `Monitor.Exit()`:

```
public void IncrementTotal()
{
    object tmpObject = syncHandle;
    System.Threading.Monitor.Enter(tmpObject);
    try
    {
        total++;
    }
    finally
    {
        System.Threading.Monitor.Exit(tmpObject);
    }
}
```

The `lock` statement provides many checks that help you avoid common mistakes. It checks that the type being locked is a reference type, as opposed to a value type. The `Monitor.Enter` method does not include such safeguards. This routine, using `lock()`, doesn't compile:

```
public void IncrementTotal()
{
    lock (total) // compiler error: can't lock value type
    {
        total++;
    }
}
```

But this does:

```
public void IncrementTotal()
{
    // really doesn't lock total.
    // locks a box containing total.
    Monitor.Enter(total);
    try
    {
        total++;
    }
```

```
    finally
    {
        // Might throw exception
        // unlocks a different box containing total
        Monitor.Exit(total);
    }
}
```

`Monitor.Enter()` compiles because its official signature takes a `System.Object`. You can coerce `total` into an object by boxing it. `Monitor.Enter()` actually locks the box containing `total`. That's where the first bug lurks. Imagine that thread 1 enters `IncrementTotal()` and acquires a lock. Then, while incrementing `total`, the second thread calls `IncrementTotal()`. Thread 2 now enters `IncrementTotal()` and acquires the lock. It succeeds in acquiring a different lock, because `total` gets put into a different box. Thread 1 has a lock on one box containing the value of `total`. Thread 2 has a lock on another box containing the value of `total`. You've got extra code in place, and no synchronization.

Then you get bitten by the second bug: When either thread tries to release the lock on `total`, the `Monitor.Exit()` method throws a `SynchronizationLockException`. That's because `total` goes into yet another box to coerce it into the method signature for `Monitor.Exit`, which also expects a `System.Object` type. When you release the lock on this box, you unlock a resource that is different from the resource that was used for the lock. `Monitor.Exit()` fails and throws an exception.

Of course, some bright soul might try this:

```
public void IncrementTotal()
{
    // doesn't work either:
    object lockHandle = total;
    Monitor.Enter(lockHandle);
    try
    {
        total++;
    }
    finally
    {
        Monitor.Exit(lockHandle);
    }
}
```

This version doesn't throw any exceptions, but neither does it provide any synchronization protection. Each call to `IncrementTotal()` creates a new box and acquires a lock on that object. Every thread succeeds in immediately acquiring the lock, but it's not a lock on a shared resource. Every thread wins, and `total` is not consistent.

There are subtler errors that `lock` also prevents. `Enter()` and `Exit()` are two separate calls, so you can easily make the mistake of acquiring and releasing different objects. This action may cause a `Synchronization-LockException`. But if you happen to have a type that locks more than one synchronization object, it's possible to acquire two different locks in a thread and release the wrong one at the end of a critical section.

The `lock` statement automatically generates exception-safe code, something many of us humans forget to do. Also, it generates more-efficient code than `Monitor.Enter()` and `Monitor.Exit()`, because it needs to evaluate the target object only once. So, by default, you should use the `lock` statement to handle the synchronization needs in your C# programs.

However, there is one limitation to the fact that `lock` generates the same MSIL as `Monitor.Enter()`. The problem is that `Monitor.Enter()` waits forever to acquire the lock. You have introduced a possible deadlock condition. In large enterprise systems, you may need to be more defensive in how you attempt to access critical resources. `Monitor.TryEnter()` lets you specify a time-out for an operation and attempt a workaround when you can't access a critical resource.

```
public void IncrementTotal()
{
    if (!Monitor.TryEnter(syncHandle, 1000)) // wait 1 second
        throw new PreciousResourceException
            ("Could not enter critical section");
    try
    {
        total++;
    }
    finally
    {
        Monitor.Exit(syncHandle);
    }
}
```

You can wrap this technique in a handy little generic class:

```
public sealed class LockHolder<T> : IDisposable
    where T : class
{
    private T handle;
    private bool holdsLock;

    public LockHolder(T handle, int milliSecondTimeout)
    {
        this.handle = handle;
        holdsLock = System.Threading.Monitor.TryEnter(
            handle, milliSecondTimeout);
    }

    public bool LockSuccessful
    {
        get { return holdsLock; }
    }

    #region IDisposable Members
    public void Dispose()
    {
        if (holdsLock)
            System.Threading.Monitor.Exit(handle);
        // Don't unlock twice
        holdsLock = false;
    }
    #endregion
}
```

You would use this class in the following manner:

```
object lockHandle = new object();

using (LockHolder<object> lockObj = new LockHolder<object>
    (lockHandle, 1000))
{
    if (lockObj.LockSuccessful)
    {
        // work elided
    }
}
// Dispose called here.
```

The C# team added implicit language support for `Monitor.Enter()` and `Monitor.Exit()` pairs in the form of the `lock` statement because it is the most common synchronization technique that you will use. The extra checks that the compiler can make on your behalf make it easier to create synchronization code in your application. Therefore, `lock()` is the best choice for most synchronization between threads in your C# applications.

However, `lock` is not the only choice for synchronization. In fact, when you are synchronizing access to numeric types or are replacing a reference, the `System.Threading.Interlocked` class supports synchronizing single operations on objects. `System.Threading.Interlocked` has a number of methods that you can use to access shared data so that a given operation completes before any other thread can access that location. It also gives you a healthy respect for the kinds of synchronization issues that arise when you work with shared data.

Consider this method:

```
public void IncrementTotal()
{
    total++;
}
```

As written, interleaved access could lead to an inconsistent representation of the data. An increment operation is not a single machine instruction. The value of `total` must be fetched from main memory and stored in a register. Then the value of the register must be incremented, and the new value from the register must be stored back into the proper location in main memory. If another thread reads the value after the first thread, the second thread grabs the value from main memory but before storing the new value, thereby causing data inconsistency.

Suppose two threads interleave calls to `IncrementTotal`. Thread A reads the value of 5 from `total`. At that moment, the active thread switches to thread B. Thread B reads the value of 5 from `total`, increments it, and stores 6 in the value of `total`. At this moment, the active thread switches back to thread A. Thread A now increments the register value to 6 and stores that value in `total`. As a result, `IncrementTotal()` has been called twice—once by thread A, and once by thread B—but because of untimely interleaved access, the end effect is that only one update has occurred. These errors are hard to find, because they result from interleaved access at exactly the wrong moment.

You could use `lock()` to synchronize this operation, but there is a better way. The `Interlocked` class has a simple method that fixes the problem: `InterlockedIncrement`. If you rewrite `IncrementTotal` as follows, the increment operation cannot be interrupted and both increment operations will always be recorded:

```
public void IncrementTotal()
{
    System.Threading.Interlocked.Increment(ref total);
}
```

The `Interlocked` class contains other methods to work with built-in data types. `Interlocked.Decrement()` decrements a value. `Interlocked.Exchange()` switches a value with a new value and returns the current value. You'd use `Interlocked.Exchange()` to set new state and return the preceding state. For example, suppose you want to store the user ID of the last user to access a resource. You can call `Interlocked.Exchange()` to store the current user ID while at the same time retrieving the previous user ID.

Finally, there is the `CompareExchange()` method, which reads the value of a piece of shared data and, if the value matches a sought value, updates it. Otherwise, nothing happens. In either case, `CompareExchange` returns the preceding value stored at that location. In the next section, Item 14 shows how to use `CompareExchange` to create a private lock object inside a class.

The `Interlocked` class and `lock()` are not the only synchronization primitives available. The `Monitor` class also includes the `Pulse` and `Wait` methods, which you can use to implement a consumer/producer design. You can also use the `ReaderWriterLockSlim` class for those designs in which many threads are accessing a value that few threads are modifying. `ReaderWriterLockSlim` contains several improvements over the earlier version of `ReaderWriterLock`. You should use `ReaderWriterLockSlim` for all new development.

For most common synchronization problems, examine the `Interlocked` class to see whether you can use it to provide the capabilities you need. With many single operations, you can. Otherwise, your first choice is the `lock()` statement. Look beyond those only when you need special-purpose locking capability.

Item 14: Use the Smallest Possible Scope for Lock Handles

When you write concurrent programs, you want to localize the synchronization primitives to the best of your ability. The more places there are in an application where you can use a synchronization primitive, the more difficult it will be to avoid deadlocks, missing locks, or other concurrent programming issues. It's a matter of scale: The more places you have to look, the harder it will be to find a particular issue.

In object-oriented programming, you use private member variables to minimize (not remove, but minimize) the number of locations you need to search for state changes. In concurrent programs, you want to do the same thing by localizing the object that you use to provide synchronization.

Two of the most widely used locking techniques are just plain wrong when seen from that viewpoint. lock(this) and lock(TypeOf(MyType)) have the nasty effect of creating your lock object based on a publicly accessible instance.

Suppose you write code like this:

```
public class LockingExample
{
    public void MyMethod()
    {
        lock (this)
        {
            // elided
        }
    }
    // elided
}
```

Now suppose that one of your clients—let's call him Alexander—figures he needs to lock something. Alexander writes this:

```
LockingExample x = new LockingExample();
lock (x)
    x.MyMethod();
```

That type of locking strategy can easily cause deadlock. Client code has acquired a lock on the LockingExample object. Inside MyMethod, your code acquires another lock on the same object. That's all fine and good, but one day soon, different threads will lock the `LockingExample` object from somewhere in the program. Deadlock issues happen, and there's no good way to find where the lock was acquired. It could be anywhere.

You need to change your locking strategy. There are three strategies to avoid this problem.

First, if you are protecting an entire method, you can use `MethodImpl-Attribute` to specify that a method is synchronized:

```
[MethodImpl(MethodImplOptions.Synchronized)]
public void IncrementTotal()
{
    total++;
}
```

Of course, that's not the most common practice.

Second, you can mandate that a developer can create a lock only on the current type or the current object. Namely, you recommend that everyone use `lock(this)` or `lock(MyType)`. That would work—if everyone followed your recommendation. It relies on all clients in the entire world knowing that they can never lock on anything except the current object or the current type. It will fail, because it can't be enforced.

The best answer is the third choice. In general cases, you can create a handle that can be used to protect access to the shared resources of an object. That handle is a private member variable and therefore cannot be accessed outside the type being used. You can ensure that the object used to synchronize access is private and is not accessible by any nonprivate properties. That policy ensures that any lock primitives on a given object are local to a given location.

In practice, you create a variable of `System.Object` to use as a synch handle. Then you lock that handle when you need to protect access to any of the members of the class. But you need to be a bit careful when you create the synch handle. You want to make sure that you do not end up with extra copies of the synch handle because you've had threads interleave memory access at the wrong time. The `Interlocked` class's `CompareExchange` method tests a value and replaces it if necessary. You can use that method to ensure that you allocate exactly one synch handle object in your type.

Here's the simplest code:

```
private object syncHandle = new object();

public void IncrementTotal()
{
    lock (syncHandle)
    {
        // code elided
    }
}
```

You may find that you don't often need the lock and you want to create the synch object only when you need it. In those cases, you can get a little fancier with the synch handle creation:

```
private object syncHandle;

private object GetSyncHandle()
{
    System.Threading.Interlocked.CompareExchange(
        ref syncHandle, new object(), null);
    return syncHandle;
}

public void AnotherMethod()
{
    lock (GetSyncHandle())
    {
        // ... code elided
    }
}
```

The syncHandle object is used to control access to any of the shared resources in your class. The private method GetSyncHandle() returns the single object that acts as the synch target. The CompareExchange call, which can't be interrupted, ensures that you create only one copy of the synch handle. It compares the value of syncHandle with null, and, if syncHandle is null, then CompareExchange creates a new object and assigns that object to syncHandle.

That handles any locking that you might do for instance methods, but what about static methods? The same technique works, but you create a static synch handle so that there is one synch handle that is shared by all instances of the class.

Of course, you can lock sections of code that are smaller than a single method. You can create synchronization blocks around any section of code inside a method (or, for that matter, a property accessor or indexer). However, whatever the scope is, you need to do what you can to minimize the scope of locked code.

```
public void YetAnotherMethod()
{
    DoStuffThatIsNotSynchronized();
    int val = RetrieveValue();
    lock (GetSyncHandle())
    {
        // ... code elided
    }
    DoSomeFinalStuff();
}
```

If you create or use a lock inside a lambda expression, however, you must be careful. The C# compiler creates a closure around lambda expressions. This, combined with the deferred execution model supported by C# 3.0 constructs, means that it will be difficult for developers to determine when the lexical scope of the lock ends. That makes this approach more prone to deadlock issues, because developers may not be able to determine whether code is inside a locked scope.

I close with a couple of other recommendations on locking. If you find that you want to create different locking handles for different values in your class, that is a strong indication that you should break the current class into multiple classes. The class is trying to do too many things. If you need to protect access to some variables and use other locks to protect other variables in the class, that's a strong indication that you should split the class into different types having different responsibilities. It will be much easier to control the synchronization if you view each type as a single unit. Each class that holds shared data—data that must be accessed or updated by different threads—should use a single synchronization handle to protect access to those shared resources.

When you decide what to lock, pick a private field that's not visible to any callers. Do not lock a publicly visible object. Locking publicly visible objects requires that all developers always and forever follow the same practice, and it enables client code to easily introduce deadlock issues.

Item 15: Avoid Calling Unknown Code in Locked Sections

At one end of the scale are problems that are caused by not locking enough. Then when you begin creating locks, the next most likely problem is that you may create deadlocks. Deadlocks occur when a thread blocks on a resource already held by another. In the .NET Framework, you can have a special case in which cross-thread calls are marshaled in such a way that they emulate synchronous calls. It's possible to have two threads deadlocked when only one resource is locked. (Item 16, in the next section, demonstrates one such situation.)

You've already learned one of the simplest ways to avoid this problem: Item 13 discusses how using a private nonvisible data member as the target of the lock localizes the locking code in your application. But there are other ways to introduce a deadlock. If you invoke unknown code from inside a synchronized region of code, you introduce the possibility that another thread will deadlock your application.

For example, suppose you write code like this to handle a background operation:

```csharp
public class WorkerClass
{
    public event EventHandler<EventArgs> RaiseProgress;
    private object syncHandle = new object();

    public void DoWork()
    {
        for(int count = 0; count < 100; count++)
        {
            lock (syncHandle)
            {
                System.Threading.Thread.Sleep(100);
                progressCounter++;
                if (RaiseProgress != null)
                    RaiseProgress(this, EventArgs.Empty);
            }
        }
    }
```

```
private int progressCounter = 0;
public int Progress


{
    get
    {
        lock (syncHandle)
            return progressCounter;
    }
}
}
```

The `raiseProgress()` method notifies all listeners of updated progress. Note that any listeners can be registered to handle that event. In a multi-threaded program a typical event handler might look like this:

```
static void engine_RaiseProgress(object sender, EventArgs e)
{
    WorkerClass engine = sender as WorkerClass;
    if (engine != null)
        Console.WriteLine(engine.Progress);
}
```

Everything runs fine, but only because you got lucky. It works because the event handler runs in the context of the background thread.

However, suppose this application were a Windows Forms application, and you needed to marshal the event handler back to your UI thread (see Item 16). `Control.Invoke` marshals the call to the UI thread, if necessary. Furthermore, `Control.Invoke` blocks the original thread until the target delegate has completed. That sounds innocent enough. You're operating on a different thread now, but that should be just fine.

The second important action causes the whole process to deadlock. Your event handler makes a callback into the engine object in order to get the status details. The `Progress` accessor, now running on a different thread, can't acquire the same lock.

The `Progress` accessor locks the synchronization handle. That looks correct from the local context of this object, but it's not. The UI thread is trying to lock the same handle already locked in the background thread. But the background thread is suspended waiting for the event handler to return, and the background thread already has the synch handle locked. You're deadlocked.

Table 2.1 shows the call stack. The table shows why it's difficult to debug these problems. This scenario has eight methods on the call stack between the first lock and the second attempted lock. Worse, the thread interleaving happens inside the framework code. You may not even see it.

The root problem is that you've tried to reacquire a lock. Because you cannot know what actions may be taken by code outside your control, you should try to avoid invoking the callback from inside the locked region. In this example, this means that you must raise the progress-reporting event from outside the locked section:

```
public void DoWork()
{
    for(int count = 0; count < 100; count++)
    {
        lock (syncHandle)
        {
            System.Threading.Thread.Sleep(100);
            progressCounter++;
        }
        if (RaiseProgress != null)
            RaiseProgress(this, EventArgs.Empty);
    }
}
```

Now that you've seen the problem, it's time to make sure you understand the various ways that calls to unknown code might creep into your applications. Obviously, raising any publicly accessible event is a callback. Invoking a delegate that was passed as a parameter, or set through a public API, is a callback. Invoking a lambda expression that's passed in as a parameter might also be calling unknown code (see Item 40, Chapter 5).

Table 2.1 Call Stack for Code That Marshals Execution Between a Background Thread and a Foreground Thread That Updates a Window Display

Method	Thread
DoWork	BackgroundThread
raiseProgress	BackgroundThread
OnUpdateProgress	BackgroundThread
engine_OnUpdateProgress	BackgroundThread
Control.Invoke	BackgroundThread
UpdateUI	UIThread
Progress (property access)	UIThread (deadlock)

Those sources of unknown code are rather easy to spot. But there is another possible location lurking in most classes: virtual methods. Any virtual method you invoke can be overridden by a derived class. That derived class, in turn, can invoke any method (public or protected) in your class. Any of those invocations can try to lock a shared resource again.

No matter how it happens, the pattern is similar. Your class acquires a lock. Then, while still in the synchronized section, it invokes a method that calls code beyond your control. That client code is an open-ended set of code that may eventually trace back into your class, even on another thread. You can't do anything to prevent that open-ended set of code from doing something that might be evil. So instead, you must prevent the situation: Don't call unknown code from inside locked sections of your code.

Item 16: Understand Cross-Thread Calls in Windows Forms and WPF

If you've done any Windows Forms programming, you've seen that occasionally an event handler throws an `InvalidOperationException` with the cryptic message, "Cross-thread operation not valid: Control accessed from a thread other than the thread it was created on." One of the most annoying behaviors associated with cross-thread calls in Windows Forms is that sometimes they work, and sometimes they don't. That behavior has been changed in Windows Presentation Foundation (WPF). In WPF, cross-thread invocations always fail. At least that makes it easier to find and fix them before you ship an application.

In Windows Forms, the fix is to check the `Control.InvokeRequired` property and then use `ControlInvoke()` if `InvokeRequired` is true. In WPF, you use the `System.Windows.Threading.Dispatcher` methods `Invoke()` and `BeginInvoke()`. In both cases, there is a lot happening in those two steps, and you have other options. Those two API methods do more work than you might think. And, under some conditions, they do not work correctly. Because these methods exist to handle cross-thread calls, you can introduce subtle race conditions if you use them incorrectly—or even correctly if you don't understand how they work.

The underlying reason for this code is the same in both Windows Forms and WPF: Windows controls use the Component Object Model (COM) single-threaded apartment (STA) model because those underlying controls are apartment-threaded. Furthermore, many of the controls use the

message pump for many operations. This model says that all function calls to each control must be on the same thread that created the control. Invoke (and BeginInvoke and EndInvoke) marshals method calls to the proper thread. The underlying code for both models is similar, so I focus the discussion on the Windows Forms API. When there are differences in the calling conventions, I give both versions. There's quite a bit of complicated code doing this, but we'll get to the bottom of it.

First, let's look at a simple bit of generic code that will make your life much easier when you run into this situation. **Anonymous delegates** provide a shortcut for wrapping small methods that are used only in one context. Unfortunately, anonymous delegates don't work with methods—such as Control.Invoke—that use the abstract System.Delegate type. This means that you need to define a nonabstract delegate type and assign it when you use Control.Invoke.

```
private void OnTick(object sender, EventArgs e)
{
    Action action = () =>
        toolStripStatusLabel1.Text =
            DateTime.Now.ToLongTimeString();
    if (this.InvokeRequired)
        this.Invoke(action);
    else
        action();
}
```

C# 3.0 has tightened this code quite a bit. The System.Core.Action delegate defines a concrete delegate type for a method that takes no parameters and has a void return. The lambda syntax supports a concise definition of the body. If you still need to support C# 2.0, you need to create this extra code:

```
delegate void Invoker();
private void OnTick20(object sender, EventArgs e)
{
    Action action = delegate()
    {
        toolStripStatusLabel1.Text =
            DateTime.Now.ToLongTimeString();
    };
    if (this.InvokeRequired)
        this.Invoke(action);
```

```
    else
        action();
}
```

In WPF, you use the `System.Threading.Dispatcher` object attached to the control to perform the marshaling:

```
private void UpdateTime()
{
    Action action = () => textBlock1.Text =
        DateTime.Now.ToString();
    if (System.Threading.Thread.CurrentThread !=
        textBlock1.Dispatcher.Thread)
    {
        textBlock1.Dispatcher.Invoke
            (System.Windows.Threading.DispatcherPriority.Normal,
            action);
    }
    else
    {
        action();
    }
}
```

That idiom further obscures the actual logic of the event handler, making the code less readable and harder to maintain. It also introduces a delegate definition whose only purpose is to provide a method signature for the abstract delegate.

A small bit of generic coding can make that much easier. The following `ControlExtensions` static class contains generic methods for any invoke delegate having up to two parameters. You can add more overloads by adding more parameters. Further, it contains methods that use those delegate definitions to call the target, either directly or through the marshaling provided by `Control.Invoke`.

```
public static class ControlExtensions
{
    public static void InvokeIfNeeded(this Control ctl,
        Action doit)
    {
        if (ctl.InvokeRequired)
            ctl.Invoke(doit);
```

```
        else
            doit();
    }

    public static void InvokeIfNeeded<T>(this Control ctl,
        Action<T> doit, T args)
    {
        if (ctl.InvokeRequired)
            ctl.Invoke(doit, args);
        else
            doit(args);
    }
}
```

Using `InvokeIfNeeded` greatly simplifies the code that handles events in a (possibly) multithreaded environment:

```
private void OnTick(object sender, EventArgs e)
{
    this.InvokeIfNeeded(() => toolStripStatusLabel1.Text =
        DateTime.Now.ToLongTimeString());
}
```

You can create a similar set of extensions for WPF controls:

```
public static class WPFControlExtensions
{
    public static void InvokeIfNeeded(
        this System.Windows.Threading.DispatcherObject ctl,
        Action doit,
        System.Windows.Threading.DispatcherPriority priority)
    {
        if (System.Threading.Thread.CurrentThread !=
            ctl.Dispatcher.Thread)
        {
            ctl.Dispatcher.Invoke(priority,
                doit);
        }
        else
        {
            doit();
        }
    }
}
```

```
public static void InvokeIfNeeded<T>(
    this System.Windows.Threading.DispatcherObject ctl,
    Action<T> doit,
    T args,
    System.Windows.Threading.DispatcherPriority priority)
{
    if (System.Threading.Thread.CurrentThread !=
        ctl.Dispatcher.Thread)
    {
        ctl.Dispatcher.Invoke(priority,
            doit, args);
    }
    else
    {
        doit(args);
    }
}
}
```

The WPF version does not have an InvokeRequired() method call. Instead, you examine the identity of the current thread and compare it to the thread on which all control interaction should take place. DispatcherObject is the base class for many of the WPF controls. It handles the dispatch operations between threads for WPF controls. Also, notice that in WPF, you can specify the priority for the event handler action. That's because WPF applications use two UI threads. One thread handles the UI rendering pipeline so that the UI can always continue to render any animations or other actions. You can specify the priority to control which actions are more important for your users: either the rendering or the handling of a particular background event.

This code has several advantages. The body of the event handler logic is read inside the event handler, even though it is using an anonymous delegate definition. It's much more readable and easier to maintain than using Control.IsInvokeRequired and ControlInvoke in your application code. Inside the ControlExtensions class, the generic method handles the check for InvokeRequired, or comparing thread identities, meaning that you don't need to remember it each time. I don't use these methods if I know I'm writing code for a single-threaded application, but if I think my code might end up in a multithreaded environment, I use this version for generality.

To support C# 2.0, you have extra work to do. You can't use the extension method syntax nor the lambda expression syntax. Thus, the code becomes this slightly more verbose version:

```
// Define your own versions of Action:
public delegate void Action;
public delegate void Action<T>(T arg);
// versions with 3, 4 parameters elided.

public static class ControlExtensions
{
    public static void InvokeIfNeeded(Control ctl, Action doit)
    {
        if (ctl.InvokeRequired)
            ctl.Invoke(doit);
        else
            doit();
    }

    public static void InvokeIfNeeded<T>( Control ctl,
        Action<T> doit, T args)
    {
        if (ctl.InvokeRequired)
            ctl.Invoke(doit, args);
        else
            doit(args);
    }
}

// Elsewhere:

private void OnTick20(object sender, EventArgs e)
{
    ControlExtensions.InvokeIfNeeded(this, delegate()
    {
        toolStripStatusLabel1.Text =
            DateTime.Now.ToLongTimeString();
    });
}
```

Before you use this idiom in all your event handlers, let's look closely at the work done by `InvokeRequired` and `Control.Invoke`. These aren't free calls, and it's not advisable to simply apply this idiom everywhere. `Control.InvokeRequired` determines whether the current code, on the one hand, is executing on the thread that created the control or, on the other hand, is executing on another thread and therefore needs to be marshaled. In most cases, this property contains a reasonably simple implementation. It checks the current thread ID and compares it to the thread ID for the control in question. If they match, `Invoke` is not required. If they don't match, `Invoke` is required. That comparison doesn't take much time. You'll notice that the WPF version of the extension methods do exactly the same check.

But there are some interesting edge cases. Suppose the control in question has not yet been created. That can happen when a parent control has been created and the current control is in the process of being instantiated. The C# object exists, but the underlying window handle is still `null`. In that case, there's nothing to compare. The framework wants to help you out, and that takes time. The framework walks the tree of parent controls to see whether any of them has been created. If the framework finds a window that has been created, that window is used as the marshaling window. That's a reasonably safe conclusion, because parent controls are responsible for creating child controls. This approach guarantees that the child controls will be created on the same thread as the parent control found by the framework. After finding a suitable parent control, the framework performs the same check mentioned earlier, checking the current thread ID against the control thread ID.

But, of course, if the framework can't find any parent window that's been created, the framework needs to find some kind of window. If none of the windows in the hierarchy exists, the framework looks for the **parking window,** a special window that's used to hide from you some of the strange behavior of the Win32 API. In short, there are some changes to windows that require destroying and re-creating the Win32 windows. (Modifying certain styles requires a window be destroyed and re-created.) The parking window is used to hold child windows whenever a parent window must be destroyed and re-created. During that time, there is a period when the UI thread can be found only from the parking window.

In WPF, some of this has been simplified through the use of the `Dispatcher` class. Each thread has a dispatcher. The first time you ask a control for its dispatcher, the library looks to see whether that thread already has a dispatcher. If it does, the library returns that dispatcher. If not, a new `Dispatcher` object is created and associated with the control and its thread.

But there are still holes and possible failures. It's possible that none of the windows is yet created, even the parking window. In that case, Invoke-Required always returns false, indicating that you don't need to marshal the call to another thread. This situation is somewhat dangerous, because it has a chance of being wrong, but it's the best that the framework can do. Any method call you make that requires the window handle to exist will fail. There's no window, so trying to use it will fail. On the other hand, marshaling will certainly fail. If the framework can't find any marshaling control, then there's no way for the framework to marshal the current call to the UI thread. The framework chooses a possible later failure instead of a certain immediate failure. Luckily, this situation is rather rare in practice. In WPF, the Dispatcher contains extra code to protect against this situation.

Let's summarize what you've learned about InvokeRequired. Once your controls are created, InvokeRequired is reasonably fast and always safe. However, if the target control has not been created, InvokeRequired can take much longer, and if none of the controls has been created, Invoke-Required takes a long time to give you an answer that's probably not even correct. Even though Control.InvokeRequired can be a bit expensive, it's still quite a bit cheaper than a call to Control.Invoke when it's not necessary. In WPF, some of the edge cases have been optimized and work better than they do in the Windows Forms implementation.

Now let's look at Control.Invoke and what it does. (Control.Invoke can do quite a bit of work, so this discussion is greatly simplified.) First, there's the special case when you've called Invoke even though you're running on the same thread as the control. It's a short-circuit path, and the framework simply calls your delegate. Calling Control.Invoke() when InvokeRequired() returns false means that your code does a bit of extra work, but it is safe.

The interesting case happens when you actually need to call Invoke. ControlInvoke handles the cross-thread calls by posting a message to the target control's message queue. Control.Invoke creates a private structure that contains everything needed to call the delegate. That includes all parameters, a copy of the call stack, and the delegate target. The parameters are copied to avoid any modification of the value of the parameters before the target delegate is called (remember that this is a multithreaded world.)

After this structure is created and added to a queue, a message is posted to the target control. Control.Invoke then does a combination of spin-wait and sleep while it waits for the UI thread to process the message and invoke the delegate. This part of the process contains an important timing issue. When the target control processes the `Invoke` message, it doesn't simply process one delegate. It processes all `Invoke` delegates in the queue. If you always use the synchronous version of `Control.Invoke`, you won't see any effects. However, if you mix `Control.Invoke` and `Control.Begin-Invoke()`, you'll see different behavior. I return to this toward the end of this item, but for now, understand that the control's `WndProc` processes every waiting `Invoke` message whenever it processes any `Invoke` messages. You have a little more control in WPF, because you can control the priority of the asynchronous operation. You can instruct the dispatcher to queue the message for processing (1) based on system or application conditions, (2) in the normal order, or (3) as a high-priority message.

Of course, these delegates can throw exceptions, and exceptions can't cross thread boundaries. The control wraps the call to your delegate in a `try` / `catch` block and catches all exceptions. Any exceptions are copied into a structure that is examined in the worker thread after the UI thread has finished its processing.

After the UI thread process finishes, `Control.Invoke` looks for any exceptions that were thrown from the delegate on the UI thread. If there are any exceptions, `Invoke` rethrows them on the background thread. If there aren't any exceptions, normal processing continues. As you can see, that's quite a bit of processing to call a method.

`Control.Invoke` blocks the background thread while the marshaled call is being processed. It gives the impression of synchronous behavior even though multiple threads are involved.

But that may not be what you need for your application. Many times, a progress event is raised by a worker thread and you want the worker thread to continue processing rather than wait for a synchronous update to the UI. That's when you use `BeginInvoke`. This method does much of the same processing as `Control.Invoke`. However, after posting the messages to the target control, `BeginInvoke` returns immediately rather than wait for the target delegate to finish. `BeginInvoke` allows you to post a message for future processing and immediately unblock the calling thread. You can add corresponding generic asynchronous methods to the `ControlExtensions` class to make it easier to process cross-thread UI calls asynchronously. You gain less benefit from these methods than the earlier ones, but for consistency, let's add them to the `ControlExtensions` class:

```
public static void QueueInvoke(this Control ctl, Action doit)
{
    ctl.BeginInvoke(doit);
}

public static void QueueInvoke<T>(this Control ctl,
    Action<T> doit, T args)
{
    ctl.BeginInvoke(doit, args);
}
```

The QueueInvoke method does not test InvokeRequired first. That's because you may want to invoke a method asynchronously even if you are currently executing on the UI thread. BeginInvoke() does that for you. Control.Invoke posts the message to the control and returns. The target control processes that message when it next checks its message queue. It's not really asynchronous if BeginInvoke is called on the UI thread. Rather, the processing is still synchronous; you just perform the action some time after the current operation.

I'm ignoring the Asynch result returned from BeginInvoke. In practice, UI updates rarely have return values. That makes it much easier to process those messages asynchronously. Simply call BeginInvoke and expect the delegate methods to be invoked at some later time. You need to code these delegate methods defensively, because any exceptions are swallowed in the cross-thread marshaling.

Before we finish this item, let's clean up a loose end inside the control's WndProc. Recall that when WndProc receives the Invoke message WndProc processes every delegate on InvokeQueue. You can run into timing problems if you expect events to be processed in a certain order and you are using a mixture of Invoke and BeginInvoke. You can guarantee that the delegates called by Control.BeginInvoke (or Control.Invoke) are processed in the order they are received. BeginInvoke adds a delegate to the queue. Any later calls to Control.Invoke process all messages on the queue, including those previously added with a call to BeginInvoke(). Processing a delegate "some time later" means that you can't control when "some time later" actually happens. Processing a delegate "now" means that the application processes all waiting asynchronous delegates and then processes this one. It is possible that one of the waiting delegate targets for BeginInvoke will change program state before your Invoke delegate is called. You need to code defensively and ensure that you recheck program state inside the delegate rather than rely on the state passed from some time in the past when `Control.Invoke` was called.

Very simply, this version of the original handler rarely displays the extra text:

```
private void OnTick(object sender, EventArgs e)
{
    this.InvokeAsynch(() => toolStripStatusLabel1.Text =
        DateTime.Now.ToLongTimeString());
    toolStripStatusLabel1.Text += "  And set more stuff";
}
```

That's because the code invokes the first change by queuing up the message, and the change is made when the next messages are handled. That's after the next statement adding more text to the label.

`Invoke` and `InvokeRequired` do quite a bit of work on your behalf. All this work is required because Windows Forms controls are built on the single-threaded apartment model. That legacy behavior continues under the new WPF libraries. Underneath all the new .NET Framework code, the Win32 API and window messages are still lurking. That message passing and thread marshaling can lead to unexpected behavior. You need to understand what those methods do and work with their behavior.

3 | C# Design Practices

Software design is usually independent of the programming language you use. Still, to produce any running software you must express those designs in a programming language. There are many ways to express the same concept in any language, including C#. To produce the best possible software, you must express your designs in the clearest possible code. That clarity enables other developers to immediately understand your design intent, making it easier to maintain and extend their applications in the future. This chapter discusses how you can best express common designs in the C# language.

Item 17: Create Composable APIs for Sequences

You've probably written code that contains loops. In most programs, you tend to write algorithms that operate more often on a sequence of items than on a single item. It's common to use keywords such as `foreach`, `for` loops, `while`, and so on. As a result, you create methods that take a collection as input, examine or modify it or its items, and return a different collection as output.

The problem is that the strategy of operating on entire collections introduces a lot of inefficiencies. That's because it's rare that you have only one operation to perform. More likely, you'll perform several transformations between the source collection and the ultimate result. Along the way, you create collections (perhaps large ones) to store the interim results. You don't begin the next step, even on the first item, until the preceding step has completely finished. Furthermore, this strategy means iterating the collection once for every transformation. That increases the execution time for algorithms that contain many transformations of the elements.

Another alternative is to create one method that processes every transformation in one loop, producing the final collection in one iteration. That approach improves your application's performance by iterating the collection only once. It also lowers the application's memory footprint because it doesn't create collections of *N* elements for every step. However, this strategy sacrifices reusability. You're far more likely to reuse the algorithm for each individual transformation than you would for a multistep operation.

C# **iterators** enable you to create methods that operate on a sequence but process and return each element as it is requested. C# 2.0 adds the `yield return` statement, which lets you create methods that return sequences. These iterator methods have a sequence as one input (expressed as `IEnumerable<T>`) and produce a sequence as output (another `IEnumerable<T>`). By leveraging the `yield return` statement, these iterator methods do not need to allocate storage for the entire sequence of elements. Instead, these methods ask for the next element on the input sequence only when needed, and they produce the next value on the output sequence only when the calling code asks for it.

It's a shift from your usual way of thinking to create input and output parameters from `IEnumerable<T>` or from a specific instance of `IEnumerable<T>`. That's why many developers don't do it. But making that shift provides many benefits. For example, you naturally create building blocks that can be combined in many ways, promoting reuse. Moreover, you can apply multiple operations while iterating a sequence only once, increasing runtime efficiency. Each iterator method executes the code to produce the *N*th element when that element is requested and not before. This **deferred execution model** (see Item 37, Chapter 5) means that your algorithms use less storage space and compose better (see Item 40, Chapter 5) than traditional imperative methods. And, as libraries evolve, you'll be able to assign different operations to different CPU cores, promoting even better performance. Further, the bodies of these methods often do not make any assumptions about the types that they operate on. This means that you can turn these methods into generic methods to gain more reuse.

To see the benefits of writing iterator methods, let's take a simple example and examine the translation. The following method takes as its input an array of integers and writes all the unique values to the output console:

```csharp
public static void Unique(IEnumerable<int> nums)
{
    Dictionary<int, int> uniqueVals =
        new Dictionary<int, int>();

    foreach (int num in nums)
    {
        if (!uniqueVals.ContainsKey(num))
```

```
        {
            uniqueVals.Add(num, num);
            Console.WriteLine(num);
        }
    }
}
```

It's a simple method, but you can't reuse any of the interesting parts. But chances are, this search for unique numbers would be useful in other places in your program.

Suppose that instead you wrote the routine this way:

```
public static IEnumerable<int> Unique(IEnumerable<int> nums)
{
    Dictionary<int, int> uniqueVals = new
        Dictionary<int, int>();
    foreach (int num in nums)
    {
        if (!uniqueVals.ContainsKey(num))
        {
            uniqueVals.Add(num, num);
            yield return num;
        }
    }
}
```

Unique returns a sequence that contains the unique numbers. Here's how you use it:

```
foreach (int num in Unique(nums))
    Console.WriteLine(num);
```

It may look as if we haven't gained anything—or even as if the second version is much less efficient—but that's not the case. I added several tracing statements to the Unique method that will help you see how methods like Unique do their magic.

This is the updated Unique:

```
public static IEnumerable<int> Unique(IEnumerable<int> nums)
{
    Dictionary<int, int> uniqueVals =
        new Dictionary<int, int>();
    Console.WriteLine("\tEntering Unique");
```

```
foreach (int num in nums)
{
    Console.WriteLine("\tevaluating {0}", num);
    if (!uniqueVals.ContainsKey(num))
    {
        Console.WriteLine("\tAdding {0}", num);
        uniqueVals.Add(num, num);
        yield return num;
        Console.WriteLine
            ("\tReentering after yield return");
    }
}
Console.WriteLine("\tExiting Unique ");
}
```

When you run this version, here's the output:

```
Entering Unique
evaluating 0
Adding 0
```
0
```
Reentering after yield return
evaluating 3
Adding 3
```
3
```
Reentering after yield return
evaluating 4
Adding 4
```
4
```
Reentering after yield return
evaluating 5
Adding 5
```
5
```
Reentering after yield return
evaluating 7
Adding 7
```
7
```
Reentering after yield return
evaluating 3
evaluating 2
Adding 2
```
2

```
Reentering after yield return
evaluating 7
evaluating 8
Adding 8
8

Reentering after yield return
evaluating 0
evaluating 3
evaluating 1
Adding 1
1

Reentering after yield return
Exiting Unique
```

The `yield return` statement plays an interesting trick: It returns a value and retains information about its current location and the current state of its internal iteration. You've got a method that operates on an entire sequence: Both the input and the output are iterators. Internally, the iteration continues to return the next item in the output sequence while it keeps track of its current location in the input sequence. That's a continuation method. **Continuation methods** keep track of their state and resume execution at their current location when code enters them again.

The fact that `Unique()` is a continuation method provides two important benefits. First, that's what enables the deferred evaluation of each element. Second, and more important, the deferred execution provides a composability that would be difficult to achieve if each method had its `foreach` loop.

Notice that `Unique()` does not exploit the fact that the input sequence contains integers. It is an excellent candidate to be converted to a generic method:

```
public static IEnumerable<T> UniqueV3<T>
    (IEnumerable<T> sequence)
{
    Dictionary<T, T> uniqueVals = new Dictionary<T, T>();
    foreach (T item in sequence)
    {
        if (!uniqueVals.ContainsKey(item))
        {
            uniqueVals.Add(item, item);
```

```
            yield return item;
        }
    }
}
```

The true power of an iterator method like this comes when you compose it into a many-step process. Suppose you want the final output to be a sequence containing the square of each of the unique numbers. Square as an iterator method is a simple set of code:

```
public static IEnumerable<int> Square(IEnumerable<int> nums)
{
    foreach (int num in nums)
        yield return num * num;
}
```

The call location is a simple nested call:

```
foreach (int num in Square(Unique(nums)))
    Console.WriteLine("Number returned from Unique: {0}", num);
```

No matter how many different iterator methods you call, the iteration happens only once. In pseudocode, the algorithm proceeds as though it were written as shown in Figure 3.1.

The code in Figure 3.1 illustrates the composability of multiple iterator methods. These multiple iterator methods do their work in one enumeration of the entire sequence. In contrast, traditional implementation idioms would have a new iteration of the entire sequence for each action.

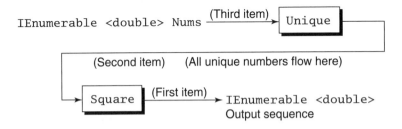

Figure 3.1 Items are pulled through a series of iterator methods. When each iterator method is ready for the next item, that item is pulled from the iterator method it uses for a source sequence. Only one element is at a given stage of the process at a given time.

When you build iterator methods that take one sequence as input and one sequence as output, other ideas emerge. For example, you can combine two sequences to form a single sequence:

```
public static IEnumerable<string> Join(
    IEnumerable<string> first,
    IEnumerable<string> second)
{
    using (IEnumerator<string> firstSequence =
        first.GetEnumerator())
    {
        using (IEnumerator<string> secondSequence =
            second.GetEnumerator())
        {
            while (firstSequence.MoveNext() &&
                secondSequence.MoveNext())
            {
                yield return string.Format("{0} {1}",
                    firstSequence.Current,
                    secondSequence.Current);
            }
        }
    }
}
```

As shown in Figure 3.2, Join forms a single sequence that concatenates each pair of items in two different string sequences, returning a sequence

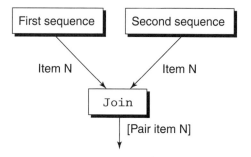

Figure 3.2 Join pulls individual items from two different source sequences. As each new output is requested, one element is pulled from each of the source sequences. Those two elements are combined into one output value, and that value is passed in the output sequence.

of those concatenations. And yes, `Join` is another possible generic method, although it's a bit more complicated than `Unique`. That's the subject of Item 6, Chapter 1.

The `Square()` iterator method shows that iterator methods can modify the source elements, modifying the contents of the sequences as part of its processing. The `Unique()` iterator method shows how an iterator method can modify the sequence itself as part of its processing: Only the first copy of each value is returned by the `Unique()` iterator method. However, iterator methods do not mutate the source sequence. Instead, they produce a new sequence as output. If the sequence contains reference types, however, the items may be modified.

These iterator methods fit together like a child's marble chute toy—you know, the kind where you drop in marbles one at a time, and they proceed to roll through tubes and past obstacles, tripping various action features along the way. The marbles don't group at each obstacle; the first marbles may be several obstacles ahead of the last ones. Each iterator method performs one action on each element of the input sequence, adding the new object to the output sequence. Individually, iterator methods do very little. But because these methods are based on a single input and output stream, it's easy to combine them. If you create these small iterator methods, it is much simpler to create complicated algorithms that are a single pipeline of many small transformations.

Item 18: Decouple Iterations from Actions, Predicates, and Functions

I've just discussed using `yield return` to create methods that operate on sequences rather than individual data types. As you gain experience with these methods, you'll often find code that has two portions: a portion that modifies the iteration of a sequence, and a portion that performs an action on each element in the sequence. For example, you might want to iterate only those items in a list that match certain criteria, or you might want to sample every Nth element or skip groups of elements.

These latter enumerations are distinct from the actions you might perform on every element that matches the criteria. Maybe you're writing different reports with the data, or summing certain values, or even modifying the properties of the items in the collection. No matter what you are doing, the enumeration pattern is not related to the action performed, and the two things should be handled separately. Putting them together means tighter coupling and probably duplicated code.

The reason many developers combine various operations into one method is that the portion to be customized falls between the standard opening and closing parts. The only way to customize the inner portion of such an algorithm is to pass a method call or function object to the enclosing method. In C#, the way to do that is to use delegates to define the inner operation. With the advent of generics and anonymous delegates in C# 2.0, it is relatively easy to create these operations so that they can be customized easily for various uses. In the following samples, I show both the anonymous delegate syntax (C# 2.0) and the even more concise lambda expression syntax added in C# 3.0.

There are two main idioms that you use with anonymous delegates: functions and actions. You'll also find references to a special case of function: a predicate. A **predicate** is a Boolean method that determines whether an element in a sequence matches some condition. An **action delegate** performs some action on an element in the collection. These method signatures are so common that the .NET library contains definitions for `Action<T>`, `Func<T, TResult>`, and `Predicate<T>`.

```
namespace System
{
    public delegate bool Predicate<T>( T obj);
    public delegate void Action<T>( T obj);
    public delegate TResult Func<T, TResult>(T arg);
}
```

For example, the `List<T>.RemoveAll()` method is a method with a predicate. The following invocation removes all instances of 5 from a list of integers:

```
// RemoveAll using anonymous delegate syntax
myInts.RemoveAll(
    delegate(int collectionMember)
    {
        return collectionMember == 5;
    });


// RemoveAll using lambda syntax
myInts.RemoveAll((collectionMember) => collectionMember == 5);
```

Internally, `List<T>.RemoveAll()` calls your delegate method (defined earlier anonymously) successively for every item in the list. Whenever the delegate returns true, that element is removed from the list. (It's a bit more complicated, because `RemoveAll()` actually creates new internal storage so that the original list isn't modified during the enumeration, but that's an implementation-specific detail.)

Action methods are called successively for every item in the collection. The `List<T>.ForEach()` method contains an example. The following invocation prints to the console every integer in the collection.

```
// ForEach using an anonymous delegate
myInts.ForEach(delegate(int collectionMember)
{
    Console.WriteLine(collectionMember);
});

// ForEach using a lambda
myInts.ForEach((collectionMember) =>
    Console.WriteLine(collectionMember));
```

Sure, that's boring, but the concept can be extended to any action you might need performed. The anonymous delegate performs the action, and the `ForEach` method calls the anonymous method on each element in the collection.

With these two methods, you can see different ways to expand the techniques to execute complex operations on collections. Let's look again at other examples of operations wherein you can save code by using predicates and actions.

Filter methods use `Predicate` to perform their tests. `Predicate` defines which objects should be passed or blocked by the filter. Following the advice in Item 17 (earlier in this chapter), you can build a generic filter that returns a sequence of all items that meet some criterion.

```
public static IEnumerable<T> Filter<T>
    (IEnumerable<T> sequence,
    Predicate<T> filterFunc)
{
    if (filterFunc == null)
        throw new ArgumentNullException
            ("Predicate must not be null");
    foreach (T item in sequence)
```

```
        if (filterFunc(item))
            yield return item;
}
```

Each element in the input sequence is evaluated using the `Predicate` method. If the `Predicate` returns `true`, that element is returned as part of the output sequence. Any developer can write a method on a type that tests a condition, and the method will be compatible with this filter method.

You can also sample a sequence and return every *N*th element:

```
public static IEnumerable<T> EveryNthItem<T>(
    IEnumerable<T> sequence, int period)
{
    int count = 0;
    foreach (T item in sequence)
        if (++count % period == 0)
            yield return item;
}
```

You can apply that filter to any sequence you want, sampling only selected items.

An `Action` delegate can be used in combination with any enumeration pattern. Here, we create a transform method that builds a new sequence from an existing sequence by calling a method:

```
public delegate T Transformer<T>(T element);
public static IEnumerable<T> Transform<T>(
    IEnumerable<T> sequence, Transformer<T> method)
{
    foreach( T element in sequence)
        yield return method(element);
}
```

Here's how you would call `Transform` to convert a sequence of integers into a sequence containing the squares of those integers:

```
// transform as anonymous delegate
foreach (int i in Transform(myInts, delegate(int value)
    {
        return value * value;
    }))
    Console.WriteLine(i);
```

```
// Transform as lambda
foreach (int i in Transform(myInts, (value)=> value * value))
    Console.WriteLine(i);
```

The `Transform` method need not return the same type of element. You can modify the `Transform` method to support changes from one type to another:

```
public delegate Tout Transformer<Tin,Tout>(Tin element);
public static IEnumerable<Tout> Transform<Tin,Tout>(
    IEnumerable<Tin> sequence, Transformer<Tin,Tout> method)
{
    foreach (Tin element in sequence)
        yield return method(element);
}
```

And you call this version as follows:

```
// Anonymous Delegate
foreach (string s in Transform(myInts, delegate(int value)
{
    return value.ToString();
}))
    Console.WriteLine(s);


// Lambda:
foreach (string s in Transform(myInts, (value)
    => value.ToString()))
    Console.WriteLine(s);
```

As you saw in Item 17, it isn't difficult to write or use any of these methods. The key is that you've separated two distinct operations: (1) iterating a sequence and (2) operating on the individual elements in the sequence. You've applied anonymous delegates or lambda expressions to create building blocks that you can use in various ways with various techniques. Any of these routines can be used as larger building blocks in your applications. You can implement many modifications to a sequence as a function (including the special case of predicates), and you can use an action delegate (or similar definition) to manipulate the items in a collection while enumerating a subset of the elements.

Item 19: Generate Sequence Items as Requested

Iterator methods do not necessarily need to take a sequence as an input parameter. An iterator method that uses the `yield return` approach can create a new sequence, essentially becoming a factory for a sequence of elements. Instead of creating the entire collection before proceeding with any operations, you create the values only as requested. This means that you avoid creating elements that aren't used by the consumers of the sequence.

Let's look at a simple example that generates a sequence of integral numbers. You might write it like this:

```
static IList<int> CreateSequence(int numberOfElements,
    int startAt, int stepBy)
{
    List<int> collection =
        new List<int>(numberOfElements);
    for (int i = 0; i < numberOfElements; i++)
        collection.Add(startAt + i * stepBy);

    return collection;
}
```

It works, but it has many deficiencies compared with using `yield return` to create the sequence. First, this technique assumes that you're putting the results into a `List<double>`. If clients want to store the results in some other structure, such as `BindingList<double>`, they must convert it:

```
BindingList<int> data = new
    BindingList<int>(CreateSequence(100, 0, 5));
```

There may be a subtle bug lurking in that construct. The `BindingList<T>` constructor does not copy the elements of the list but instead uses the same storage location as the list given in the constructor. If the storage location used to initialize the `BindingList<T>` is reachable by other code, you could introduce data integrity errors. Multiple references are synonyms for the same storage location.

Moreover, creating the entire list doesn't give client code a chance to stop the generation function based on a specified condition. The `Create-Sequence` method always generates a requested number of elements. As written, it can't be stopped if the user wants to stop the process—for paging or for any other reason.

Also, this method could be the first stage of several transformations on a sequence of data (see Item 17 earlier in this chapter). In that case, this method would be a bottleneck in the pipeline: Every element would have to be created and added to the internal collection before the next step could continue.

You can remove all those limitations by making the generation function an iterator method:

```
static IEnumerable<int> CreateSequence(int numberOfElements,
    int startAt, int stepBy)
{
    for (int i = 0; i < numberOfElements; i++)
        yield return startAt + i * stepBy;
}
```

The core logic is still the same: It generates a sequence of numbers.

It is important to note that there is a change in the way this version executes. Each time code enumerates the sequence, it regenerates the sequence of numbers. Because the code always generates the same sequence of numbers, this change does not affect the behavior. This version does not make any assumptions about what the client code will do with that storage location. If the client code wants values as a List<double>, there's a constructor that takes an IEnumerable<double> as the initial collection:

```
List<int> listStorage = new List<int>(
    CreateSequence(100, 0, 5));
```

That's necessary to ensure that only one sequence of numbers is generated. You would create a BindingList<double> collection this way:

```
BindingList<int> data = new
    BindingList<int>(CreateSequence(100,0,5).ToList());
```

This code might look a bit inefficient. The BindingList<T> class does not support a constructor that takes an IEnumerable<T>. It really isn't inefficient, though, because BindingList holds the reference to the existing list; it doesn't create another copy. ToList() creates one list object that contains all the elements in the sequence generated by CreateSequence. That List object is also held by BindingList<int>.

It's easy to stop the enumeration if you use the following method. You simply don't ask for the next element. The code works with both versions of CreateSequence(). However, if you use the first implementation of CreateSequence(), all 1,000 elements are generated, no matter where in the collection the caller wishes to stop enumerating the list. Using the enumerator version, the generation short-circuits as soon as the first non-conforming value is found. That can result in a significant performance improvement.

```
// Using an anonymous delegate
IEnumerable<int> sequence = CreateSequence(10000, 0, 7).
    TakeWhile(delegate(int num) { return num < 1000; });

// using lambda notation
IEnumerable<int> sequence = CreateSequence(10000, 0, 7).
    TakeWhile((num) => num < 1000);
```

Of course, any condition can be used to determine when the enumeration should stop. You can check to see whether the user wishes to continue, poll another thread for input, or do anything else needed by your application. The enumerator method provides a simple means of interrupting the enumeration anywhere in the sequence. This deferred execution means that only the elements requested are generated. Essentially, client code requests that an algorithm create a new element only when that element is actually used in the algorithm.

However, you should use this idiom only when your algorithm actually creates the sequence. It does not serve any purpose to use an iterator method to return a collection that already exists:

```
// Values added elsewhere
private List<string> labels = new List<string>();

// No value: creating a second compiler-generated
// Enumerator class
public IEnumerable<string> LabelsBad()
{
    foreach (string label in labels)
        yield return label;
}

// List<string> already supports an enumerator
public IEnumerable<string> LabelsBetter()
{
    return labels;
}
```

Any collection already contained in your type will support IEnumerable<T> for whatever type it stores. There's no need to add code to support the concept.

It's best to generate sequence items only when each item is requested by the consumer of the sequence. You'll avoid doing extra work when the consumer needs only a portion of the algorithm to perform its work. It may be a small savings, or the savings may be much greater if the cost of creating elements is large. In any case, the code that creates the sequence will be clearer when you generate the sequence items only as needed.

Item 20: Loosen Coupling by Using Function Parameters

Developers often reach for the most familiar language features to describe contracts between components. For most developers, that means defining a base class or an interface to declare the methods needed by a new class and then coding against those defined interfaces. Often that is the correct answer, but using function parameters can make it easier for other developers to create code that can work with your components and libraries. Using **function parameters** means that your component is not responsible for creating the concrete type of the classes it needs. Rather, your component uses any dependencies through an abstract definition.

You should be familiar with the separation of interfaces and classes. But sometimes even defining and implementing an interface are too cumbersome for a particular usage. Probably you'll most often use traditional object-oriented techniques, but these other techniques can make for a simpler API. You can create contracts by using delegates to minimize the requirements on client code.

The challenge for you is to isolate your work from these dependencies and from assumptions you implicitly make about the client developers who use your code. There are various reasons for this difficulty from both sides of your code. The more your code relies on other pieces, the harder it is to unit-test or use your code in other environments. From the other side, the more closely you rely on a particular implementation pattern from those developers who use your code, the more constraints you place on them.

You can use function parameters to decouple your components from the code that uses those components. However, each of those possible techniques comes with a cost. There is more work for you, and a little less clarity for your users, if you adopt techniques that loosen the coupling between code that must work together. You need to balance the potential needs of client developers against the lack of understanding that decoupled techniques can provide. In addition, implementing looser coupling—by using delegates or other communication mechanisms—also means that you need to work around some of the checking that the compiler provides for you.

At one end of the spectrum, you have likely specified a base class for your client classes. Doing so is the simplest way for clients to develop code that works with your component. The contract is clear: Derive from this specified base class, implement these known abstract (or other virtual) methods, and it just works. In addition, you can implement any common functionality in the abstract base class. Users of your component do not need to reimplement any of that code.

From your component's perspective, this approach is also a little less work. You can assume that certain behavior has been implemented. The compiler won't allow someone to build a derived class without providing an implementation for all the abstract methods. Nothing can force a correct implementation, but you know that a proper method exists.

However, forcing client code to derive from a base class you define is the most restrictive way to demand certain behaviors from client code. For example, all .NET languages mandate single inheritance for classes. Creating a component that demands a base class can be very limiting to all your users. You're mandating a certain class hierarchy. There's no other way to use it.

Creating interfaces and coding against them results in looser coupling than does relying on base classes. You've likely created an interface and forced client coders to implement that interface. This practice creates a relationship that's similar to the relationship you establish by using a base class. There are only two important differences: First, using an interface does not enforce any class hierarchy on your users. But, second, you can't easily provide a default implementation for any of the behavior necessary for client code.

Often, either of those mechanisms will be too much work for your purpose. Do you really need to define an interface? Or will a more loosely coupled approach, such as defining a delegate signature, be better?

You have already seen an example of this in Item 17 earlier in this chapter. The `List.RemoveAll()` method signature takes a delegate of type `Predicate<T>`:

```
void List<T>.RemoveAll (Predicate<T> match);
```

The .NET Framework designers could have implemented this method by defining an interface:

```
// Improper extra coupling.
public interface IPredicate<T>
{
    bool Match(T soughtObject);
}
public class List<T>
{
    public void RemoveAll(IPredicate<T> match)
    {
        // elided
    }
    // Other APIs elided
}
//The usage for this second version is quite a bit more work:
public class MyPredicate : IPredicate<int>
{
    public bool Match(int target)
    {
        return target < 100;
    }
}
```

Look back at Item 17 to see how much easier it is to use the version that is defined for `List<T>`. Often, it is much easier on all the developers who use your class when you define your interfaces using delegates or other loose-coupling mechanisms.

The reason for using delegates instead of an interface is that the delegate is not a fundamental attribute of the type. It's not the number of methods. Several interfaces in the .NET Framework contain only one method. `ICom-parable<T>` and `IEquatable<T>` are perfectly good interface definitions. Implementing those interfaces says something about your type: that it supports comparisons or equality. Implementing this hypothetical `IPredi-cate<T>` doesn't say anything interesting about a particular type. You really need only one method definition for one single API.

You often can use function parameters in conjunction with generic methods when you may have considered defining interfaces or creating base classes. Item 17 contains this version of a `Join` method that merges two sequences:

```
public static IEnumerable<string> Join(
    IEnumerable<string> first,
    IEnumerable<string> second)
{
    using (IEnumerator<string> firstSequence =
        first.GetEnumerator())
    {
        using (IEnumerator<string> secondSequence =
            second.GetEnumerator())
        {
            while (firstSequence.MoveNext() &&
                secondSequence.MoveNext())
            {
                yield return string.Format("{0} {1}",
                    firstSequence.Current,
                    secondSequence.Current);
            }
        }
    }
}
```

You can make a generic method and use function parameters to build the output sequence:

```
public static IEnumerable<TResult> Join<T1, T2,
TResult>(IEnumerable<T1> first,
    IEnumerable<T2> second, Func<T1, T2, TResult> joinFunc)
{
    using (IEnumerator<T1> firstSequence =
        first.GetEnumerator())
    {
        using (IEnumerator<T2> secondSequence =
            second.GetEnumerator())
        {
            while (firstSequence.MoveNext() &&
                secondSequence.MoveNext())
            {
                yield return joinFunc(firstSequence.Current,
                    secondSequence.Current);
            }
        }
    }
}
```

The caller must now define the body of the `joinFunc`:

```
IEnumerable<string> result = Join(first, second, (one, two) =>
    string.Format("{0} {1}", one, two));
```

Or, if the callers are not using C# 3.0, the lambda expression could be replaced with an anonymous delegate:

```
IEnumerable<string> result = Join(first, second,
    delegate(string one, string two)
    {
        return string.Format("{0} {1}", one, two);
    });
```

That creates much looser coupling between the `Join` method and its callers.

The `CreateSequence` method from Item 19 (earlier in this chapter) would benefit from the same kinds of changes. The version in Item 19 creates a sequence of integers. You can make that a generic method and use a function parameter to specify how that sequence should be generated:

```
public static IEnumerable<T> CreateSequence<T>
    (int numberOfElements, Func<T> generator)
{
    for (int i = 0; i < numberOfElements; i++)
        yield return generator();
}
```

A caller defines the original behavior this way:

```
int startAt = 0;
int nextValue = 5;
IEnumerable<int> sequence = CreateSequence(1000,
    () => startAt += nextValue);
```

Or, using anonymous delegate syntax, one defines it this way:

```
IEnumerable<int> sequence = CreateSequence(1000,
    delegate()
    {
        return startAt += nextValue;
    });
```

At other times, you'll want to perform an algorithm on all the items in a sequence, returning a single scalar value. For example, this method creates the sum of a sequence of integers:

```
public static int Sum(IEnumerable<int> nums)
{
    int total = 0;
    foreach (int num in nums)
    {
        total += num;
    }
    return total;
}
```

You can make this method a general-purpose accumulator by factoring out the Sum algorithm and replacing it with a delegate definition:

```
public static T Sum<T>(IEnumerable<T> sequence, T total,
    Func<T,T, T> accumulator)
{
    foreach (T item in sequence)
    {
        total = accumulator(total, item);
    }
    return total;
}
```

You would call it this way:

```
int total = 0;
total = Sum(sequence, total, (sum, num) => sum + num);
```

Using an anonymous delegate, you call it as follows:

```
total = Sum(sequence, total, delegate(int sum, int num)
{
    return sum + num;
});
```

The Sum method is still too limiting. As written, it must use the same type for the sequence, the return value, and the initial value. You'd like to use it with different types:

```
List<Employee> peeps = new List<Employee>();
// All employees added elsewhere.
// Calculate the total salary:
decimal totalSalary = Sum(peeps, 0M, (person, sum) =>
    sum + person.Salary);
```

All you need is a bit of modification to the Sum method definition, allowing different parameter types for the sequence element and the accumulated sum:

```
public static TResult Sum<T, TResult>(IEnumerable<T>
sequence,
    TResult total,
    Func<T,TResult, TResult> accumulator)
{

    foreach (T item in sequence)
    {
        total = accumulator(item, total);
    }
    return total;
}
```

Using functions as parameters does a great deal to separate algorithms from the specific data types on which they operate. However, as you loosen the coupling, you increase the amount of work you might need to do to ensure proper error handling when these decoupled components communicate. For example, suppose you've created code that defines events. You know that you must check that event member against null whenever you intend to raise that event. Client code may not have created the event handlers. You'll have the same work when you create interfaces using delegates. What is the correct behavior when your client passes a null delegate? Is it an exception, or is there a correct default behavior? What happens if client code delegates throw exceptions? Can you recover? If so, how?

Finally, when you switch from using inheritance to using delegates to define your expectations, you must understand that you have the same runtime coupling you would have by holding a reference to an object or an interface. If your object stores a copy of the delegate that it can call later, your object now controls the lifetime of the object to which that delegate refers. You may be extending the lifetime of those objects. This is no different from having your object hold a reference to an object (by storing a reference to an interface or a base class) that your object will invoke later. It's a little harder to see by reading the code, though.

The default choice is still to create interface contracts that mandate how your component will communicate with client code. Abstract base classes give you the extra ability to provide a default implementation of some of the work that otherwise would be done by client code. Defining delegates for the methods you expect gives you the most flexibility, but it also means you have less support from tools. You buy more work but gain greater flexibility.

Item 21: Create Method Groups That Are Clear, Minimal, and Complete

The more possible overloads you create for a method, the more often you'll run into ambiguity. It's also more likely that the compiler won't find the one best function method. Worse, when you make what seem to be innocent changes to your code, you can cause different methods to be called and therefore unexpected results to be generated.

In many cases, it's easier to work with fewer overloaded methods than with more overloads. Your goal should be to create precisely the right number of overloads: enough of them that your type is easy for client developers to use but not so many that you complicate the API and make it harder for the compiler to create exactly the one best method.

The greater the ambiguity you create, the more difficult it is for other developers to create code that uses new C# features such as type inference. The more ambiguous methods you have in place, the more likely it is that the compiler cannot conclude that exactly one method is best.

The C# language specification describes all the rules that determine which method will be interpreted as the best match. As a C# developer, you should have some understanding of the rules. More importantly, as an API writer, you should have a solid understanding of the rules. It is your responsibility to create an API that minimizes the chances for compilation errors caused by the compiler's attempt to resolve ambiguity. It's even more important that you don't lead your users down the path of misunderstanding which of your methods the compiler chooses in reasonable situations.

The C# compiler can follow quite a lengthy path as it determines whether there is one best method to call and, if there is, what that one best method is. When a class has only nongeneric methods, it's reasonably easy to follow and to know which methods will be called. The more possible variations you add, the worse the situation gets, and the more likely it is that you can create ambiguity.

Several conditions change the way the compiler resolves these methods. The process is affected by the number and the type of parameters, whether generic methods are potential candidates, whether any interface methods are possible, and whether any extension methods are candidates and are imported into the current context.

The compiler can look in numerous locations for candidate methods. Then, after it finds all candidate methods, it must try to pick the one best method. If there are no candidate methods or if there are multiple candidate methods, you get a compiler error. But those are the easy cases. You can't ship code that has compiler errors. The hard problems occur when you and the compiler disagree about which method is best. In those cases, the compiler always wins, and you may get undesired behavior.

I begin by noting that any methods having the same name should perform essentially the same function. For example, two methods in the same class named Add() should do the same thing. If the methods do semantically different things, then they should have different names. For example, you should never write code like this:

```csharp
public class Vector
{
    private List<double> values = new List<double>();

    // Add a value to the internal list.
    public void Add(double number)
    {
        values.Add(number);
    }

    // Add values to each item in the sequence.
    public void Add(IEnumerable<double> sequence)
    {
        int index = 0;
        foreach (double number in sequence)
        {
            if (index == values.Count)
                return;
            values[index++] += number;
        }
    }
}
```

Either of the two Add() methods is reasonable, but there is no way both should be part of the same class. Different overloaded methods should provide different parameter lists, never different actions.

That rule alone limits the possible errors caused when the compiler calls a different method from the one you expect. If both methods perform the same action, it really shouldn't matter which one gets called, right?

Of course, different methods with different parameter lists often have different performance metrics. Even when multiple methods perform the same task, you should get the method you expect. You as the class author can make that happen by minimizing the chances for ambiguity.

Ambiguity problems arise when methods have similar arguments and the compiler must make a choice. In the simplest case, there is only one parameter for any of the possible overloads:

```
public void Scale(short scaleFactor)
{
    for (int index = 0; index < values.Count; index++)
        values[index] *= scaleFactor;
}


public void Scale(int scaleFactor)
{
    for (int index = 0; index < values.Count; index++)
        values[index] *= scaleFactor;
}


public void Scale(float scaleFactor)
{
    for (int index = 0; index < values.Count; index++)
        values[index] *= scaleFactor;
}


public void Scale(double scaleFactor)
{
    for (int index = 0; index < values.Count; index++)
        values[index] *= scaleFactor;
}
```

By creating all these overloads, you have avoided introducing any ambiguity. Every numeric type except decimal is listed, and therefore the compiler always calls the version that is a correct match. (Decimal has been omitted because a conversion from decimal to double requires an explicit conversion.) If you have a C++ background, you probably wonder why I haven't recommended replacing all those overloads with a single generic method. That's because C# generics don't support that practice in the way C++ templates do. With C# generics, you can't assume that arbitrary methods or operators are present in the type parameters. You must specify your expectations using constraints (see Item 2, Chapter 1). Of course, you might think about using delegates to define a method constraint (see Item 6, Chapter 1). But in this case, that technique only moves the problem to another location in the code where both the type parameter and the delegate are specified. You're stuck with some version of this code.

However, suppose you left out some of the overloads:

```csharp
public void Scale(float scaleFactor)
{
    for (int index = 0; index < values.Count; index++)
        values[index] *= scaleFactor;
}


public void Scale(double scaleFactor)
{
    for (int index = 0; index < values.Count; index++)
        values[index] *= scaleFactor;
}
```

Now it's a bit trickier for users of the class to determine which method will be called for the short and the double cases. There are implicit conversions from short to float, and from short to double. Which one will the compiler pick? And if it can't pick one method, you've forced coders to specify an explicit cast to get their code to compile. Here, the compiler decides that float is a better match than double. However, most of your users may not come to the same conclusion. Here's how to avoid this problem: When you create multiple overloads for a method, make sure that most developers would immediately recognize which method the compiler will pick as a best match. That's best achieved by providing a complete set of method overloads.

Single-parameter methods are rather simple, but it can be difficult to understand methods that have multiple parameters. Here are two methods with two sets of parameters:

```
public class Point
{
    public double X
    {
        get;
        set;
    }
    public double Y
    {
        get;
        set;
    }

    public void Scale(int xScale, int yScale)
    {
        X *= xScale;
        Y *= yScale;
    }

    public void Scale(double xScale, double yScale)
    {
        X *= xScale;
        Y *= yScale;
    }
}
```

Now, what happens if you call with `int`, `float`? Or with `int`, `long`?

```
Point p = new Point { X = 5, Y = 7 };
// Note that second parameter is a long:
p.Scale(5, 7L); // calls Scale(double,double)
```

In both cases, only one of the parameters is an exact match to one of the overloaded method parameters. That method does not contain an implicit conversion for the other parameter, so it's not even a candidate method. Some developers would probably guess wrong in trying to determine which method gets called.

But wait—method lookup can get a lot more complicated. Let's throw a new wrench into the works and see what happens. What if there is a better method available in a base class than exists in a derived class?

```csharp
public class Point
{
    // earlier code elided
    public void Scale(int scale)
    {
        X *= scale;
        Y *= scale;
    }
}
public class Point3D : Point
{
    public double Z
    {
        get;
        set;
    }

    // Not override, not new. Different parameter type.
    public void Scale(double scale)
    {
        X *= scale;
        Y *= scale;
        Z *= scale;
    }
}
Point3D p2 = new Point3D { X = 1, Y = 2, Z = 3 };
p2.Scale(3);
```

There are quite a few mistakes here. `Point` should declare `Scale()` as a virtual method if the class author intends for `Scale` to be overridden. But the author of the overriding method—let's call her Kaitlyn—made a different mistake: By creating a new method (rather than hiding the original), Kaitlyn has ensured that the user of her type will generate code that calls the wrong method. The compiler finds both methods in scope and determines (based on the type of the parameters) that `Point.Scale(int)` is a better match. By creating a set of method signatures that conflict, Kaitlyn has created this ambiguity.

Adding a generic method to catch all the missing cases, using a default implementation, creates an even more sinister situation:

```
public static class Utilities
{
    // Prefer Math.Max for double:
    public static double Max(double left, double right)
    {
        return Math.Max(left, right);
    }

    // Note that float, int, etc. are handled here:
    public static T Max<T>(T left, T right)
        where T : IComparable<T>
    {
        return (left.CompareTo(right) > 0 ? left : right);
    }
}
double a1 = Utilities.Max(1,3 );
double a2 = Utilities.Max(5.3, 12.7f);
double a3 = Utilities.Max(5, 12.7f);
```

The first call instantiates a generic method for Max<int>. The second call goes to Max(double, double). The third call goes to a generic method for Max<float>. That's because for generic methods, one of the types can always be a perfect match, and no conversion is required. A generic method becomes the best method if the compiler can perform the correct type substitution for all type parameters. Yes, even if there are obvious candidate methods that require implicit conversions, the generic method is considered a better method match whenever it is accessible.

But I'm not finished throwing complications at you. Extension methods can also be considered in the mix. What happens if an extension method appears to be a better match than does an accessible member function? Well, a better match means a method that has a better-matching parameter list. If the extension method is a better match—meaning that none of the parameters needs any conversions—then the compiler prefers the extension method to an accessible member function that requires conversions. Given that generic methods always create a better match, you can see why extension methods can wreak havoc with method lookup.

As you can see, the compiler examines quite a few places to find candidate methods. As you put more methods in more places, you expand that list. The larger the list, the more likely it is that the potential methods will present an ambiguity. Even if the compiler is certain which method is the one best method, you've introduced potential ambiguity for your users. If only one in twenty developers can correctly identify which method overload gets called when he invokes one of a series of overloaded methods, you've clearly made your API too complex. Users should be able to know immediately which of the possible set of accessible overloads the compiler has chosen as the best. Anything less is obfuscating your library.

To provide a complete set of functionality for your users, create the minimum set of overloads. Then stop. Adding methods will only increase your library's complexity without enhancing its usefulness.

Item 22: Prefer Defining Methods to Overloading Operators

Every object-oriented language has taken its own stance on the practice of overloading operators. Some languages support overloading almost any operator for your type. Other languages disallow overloading operators altogether. C# takes a middle approach: Some, but not all, operators can be overloaded. The C# language designers took a liberal approach; you may never have a good reason to overload some of the operators that you can overload.

Because languages treat operator overloading differently, the Common Language Specification (CLS) takes an interesting approach. Overloaded operators are not CLS compliant, but each operator maps to a special method name. This practice allows languages that do not support overloaded operators to invoke overloaded operators defined in languages that allow them.

The names of those overloaded operators are not necessarily friendly API names. Developers using other languages would need to call a method named `op_Equality` to invoke the == operator you created in C#. Some languages may not even allow code to invoke the methods that underlie overloaded operators. For example, C# does not call a user-defined `op_Assign` method, even if you have defined one using another language that supports such a method. Instead, the C# compiler always performs a simple bitwise copy for assignment.

This kind of mismatch between languages means that you should never create a public interface that relies on operators alone. .NET developers using your type may not be able to access those methods at all. If they do, they may need to explicitly use the `op_` version of the method. You should always define your public interface in terms of CLS-compliant members, and then add overloaded operators only as a convenience for those languages that support them. For the remainder of this item, I discuss the common operators you can overload and explain the conditions that apply to the operation.

The simplest decision is whether to overload `operator ==`. If your type overrides `System.Object.Equals` or implements `IEquatable<T>` for your type, you should overload `operator ==`. The C# language specification mandates that if you overload `operator ==`, then you must also overload `operator !=` and override `System.Object.GetHashCode()`. All three of those methods must follow the same semantics for equality, although the language cannot enforce that. To enforce it, you must implement those methods correctly. It follows that if you overload `operator ==`, then you must implement `IEquatable<T>` and override `System.Object.Equals()`.

The next most common set of overloaded operators is the comparison operators. If you implement `IComparable<T>` for your type, you should also overload `operator <` and `operator >`. If your type also implements `IEquatable<T>`, you should also overload `operator <=` and `operator >=`. As with `operator ==`, the C# specification mandates that you must override those operators in pairs. Overloading `operator <` means that you must override `operator >`, and overloading `operator <=` means that you must overload `operator >=`.

Notice that in both of those descriptions, the directive is to overload operators when your type defines methods that implement the same functionality using standard .NET BCL interfaces. That's the most important point in this item: Whenever you define overloaded operators, you must provide an alternative public API that implements the same behavior. If you fail to do this, it means that your type will be much less friendly to developers who are using languages that don't support operator overloading.

Once you move beyond the equality and ordering relations, it's much less likely that you'll overload operators. It's also much less clear-cut when you should overload operators.

You should consider overloading the mathematical operators if your type models numeric data. More importantly, remember that you must provide an alternative for languages that don't support operator overloading. Defining `operator +` means that you should create an `Add()` method. (`System.String` has a `Concat()` method, which is consistent with the semantics of + for strings.)

You'll find that it's much easier to define the set of operators you want to overload by first defining the set of methods you want to support and then deriving the operators you want to support based on the methods your type supports. For example, if you create `Add()` and `Subtract()`, you should define `operator +` and `operator -` but probably not any other mathematical operators. If you define multiple `Add()` methods with dissimilar parameters, you should define multiple `operator +` overloads. Furthermore, because addition is commutative, you should define `operator +` methods with both parameter orderings. If A + B is valid, then B + A is also valid, and it must produce the same result even if A and B are different types (except for `System.String`).

Define the methods first, and then you can more easily decide whether certain operator expressions are valid based on your type. Should your type support the unary as well as the binary operators? For example, is A + (- B) supported? For that construct to work, you must support the unary `operator -`. If it is supported, every developer using your class will expect it to produce the same result as A - B. This means that you should define a `Negate()` method, or something similar, to provide a method call that provides the same functionality as the overloaded unary `operator -`. Would you have defined a `Negate()` method if you'd started by defining the methods for your interface? If not, that's an indication that you don't need to add those overloaded operators.

Overloading mathematical operators in C# is a little easier because of restrictions defined by the language. You cannot overload the mathematical assignment operators (+=, -=, etc.), but they are evaluated using the corresponding mathematical operator, so your user-defined behavior still provides the result.

You will rarely, if ever, overload the remaining operators. Those include the logical operators, operator `true`, and operator `false`.

Overloaded operators can provide intuitive syntax in those languages that support them. However, not every .NET language supports operator overloading. You should start your design by defining your type's public interface using CLS-compliant members. Once you have done that, consider implementing overloaded operators for those languages that support types. The most common operators you will overload are `operator ==` and `operator !=`. You must overload those when your type implements `IEquatable<T>`. Many C# developers use the operators and expect them to behave consistently with the `IEquatable<T>.Equals()` method. You'll also override the comparison operators: <, >, <=, and >=. You should implement those when your type implements IComparable<T>.

If your type models a numeric type, consider overloading mathematical operators. Start with the methods you intend to support, and then add overloaded operators to match for developers using languages that support overloaded operators (such as C#). In all cases, though, ensure that your type is useful even if you do not implement any overloaded operators. Developers using languages that don't support overloaded operators cannot access that portion of your type's public interface. Prefer methods to overloaded operators.

Item 23: Understand How Events Increase Runtime Coupling Among Objects

Events seem to provide a way to completely decouple your class from those types it needs to notify. Thus, you'll often provide outgoing event definitions. Let subscribers, whatever type they might be, subscribe to those events. Inside your class, you raise the events. Your class knows nothing about the subscribers, and it places no restrictions on the classes that can implement those interfaces. Any code can be extended to subscribe to those events and create whatever behavior they need when those events are raised.

And yet, it's not that simple. There are coupling issues related to event-based APIs. To begin with, some event argument types contain status flags that direct your class to perform certain operations.

```
public class WorkerEngine
{
    public event EventHandler<WorkerEventArgs> OnProgress;
    public void DoLotsOfStuff()
    {
        for (int i = 0; i < 100; i++)
        {
            SomeWork();
            WorkerEventArgs args = new WorkerEventArgs();
            args.Percent = i;
            EventHandler<WorkerEventArgs> progHandler =
                OnProgress;
            if (progHandler != null)
            {
```

```
                    progHandler(this, args);
            }
            if (args.Cancel)
                return;
        }
    }
    private void SomeWork()
    {
        // elided
    }
}
```

Now, every subscriber to that event is coupled. Suppose you have multiple subscribers on a single event. One subscriber might request a cancel, and the second might reverse that request. The foregoing definition does not guarantee that this behavior can't happen. Having multiple subscribers and a mutable event argument means that the last subscriber in the chain can override every other subscriber. There's no way to enforce having only one subscriber, and there is no way to guarantee that you're the last subscriber. You could modify the event arguments to ensure that once the cancel flag is set, no subscriber can turn it off:

```
public class WorkerEventArgs : EventArgs
{
    public int Percent
    {
        get;
        set;
    }
    public bool Cancel
    {
        get;
        private set;
    }
    public void RequestCancel()
    {
        Cancel = true;
    }
}
```

Changing the public interface works here, but it might not work in some cases. If you need to ensure that there is exactly one subscriber, you must choose another way of communicating with any interested code. For example, you can define an interface and call that one method. Or you can ask for a delegate that defines the outgoing method. Then your single subscriber can decide whether it wants to support multiple subscribers and how to orchestrate the semantics of cancel requests.

At runtime, there's another form of coupling between event sources and event subscribers. Your event source holds a reference to the delegate that represents the event subscriber. The event subscriber's object lifetime now will match the event source's object lifetime. The event source is now a root for the event subscriber. As long as the event source holds the reference and is reachable, the event subscriber is also reachable and therefore is not eligible for garbage collection. Even if the event subscriber would otherwise be eligible for destruction, the delegate handle in the event source keeps a live root, and keeps it alive.

As a result, event subscribers need to modify their implementation of the dispose pattern to unhook event handlers as part of the `Dispose()` method. Otherwise, subscriber objects continue to live on because reachable delegates exist in the event source object. It's another case where runtime coupling can cost you. Even though it appears that there is looser coupling because the compile-time dependencies are minimized, runtime coupling does have costs.

Event-based communication loosens the static coupling between types, but it comes at the cost of tighter runtime coupling between the event generator and the event subscribers. The multicast nature of events means that all subscribers must agree on a protocol for responding to the event source. The event model, in which the event source holds a reference to all subscribers, means that all subscribers must either (1) remove event handlers when the subscriber wants to be disposed of or (2) simply cease to exist. Also, the event source must unhook all event handlers when the source should cease to exist. You must factor those issues into your design decision to use events.

Item 24: Declare Only Nonvirtual Events

Like many other class members in C#, events can be declared as virtual. It would be nice to think that it's as easy as declaring any other C# language element as virtual. Unfortunately, because you can declare events using field-like syntax as well as `add` and `remove` syntax, it's not that simple. It's remarkably simple to create event handlers across base and derived classes that don't work the way you expect. Even worse, you can create hard-to-diagnose crash bugs.

Let's modify the worker engine from the preceding item to provide a base class that defines the basic event mechanism:

```
public abstract class WorkerEngineBase
{
    public virtual event EventHandler<WorkerEventArgs>
        OnProgress;

    public void DoLotsOfStuff()
    {
        for (int i = 0; i < 100; i++)
        {
            SomeWork();
            WorkerEventArgs args = new WorkerEventArgs();
            args.Percent = i;
            EventHandler<WorkerEventArgs> progHandler =
                OnProgress;
            if (progHandler != null)
            {
                progHandler(this, args);
            }
            if (args.Cancel)
                return;
        }
    }

    protected abstract void SomeWork();
}
```

The compiler creates a private backing field, along with public add and remove methods. The generated code is similar to the following code. Notice the Synchronized attribute on the event handler (see Item 13, Chapter 2).

```
private EventHandler<WorkerEventArgs> progressEvent;

public virtual event EventHandler<WorkerEventArgs> OnProgress
{
    [MethodImpl(MethodImplOptions.Synchronized)]
```

```
    add
    {
        progressEvent += value;
    }
    [MethodImpl(MethodImplOptions.Synchronized)]
    remove
    {
        progressEvent -= value;
    }
}
```

Because that private backing field is compiler generated, you can't write code to access it directly. You can invoke it only through the publicly accessible event declaration. That restriction, obviously, also applies to derived events. You can't manually write code that accesses the private backing field of the base class. However, the compiler can access its own generated fields, so the compiler can create the proper code to override the events in the correct manner. In effect, creating a derived event hides the event declaration in the base class. This derived class does exactly the same work as in the original example:

```
public class WorkerEngineDerived : WorkerEngineBase
{
    protected override void SomeWork()
    {
        // elided
    }
}
```

The addition of an `override` event breaks the code:

```
public class WorkerEngineDerived : WorkerEngineBase
{
    protected override void SomeWork()
    {
        Thread.Sleep(50);
    }
    // Broken. This hides the private event field in
    // the base class
    public override event
        EventHandler<WorkerEventArgs> OnProgress;
}
```

The declaration of the overridden event means that the hidden backing field in the base class is not assigned when user code subscribes to the event. The user code subscribes to the derived event, and there is no code in the derived class to raise the event.

Therefore, when the base class uses a field-like event, overriding that event definition hides the event field defined in the base class. Code in the base class that raises the event doesn't do anything. All subscribers have attached to the derived class. It doesn't matter whether the derived class uses a field-like event definition or a property-like event definition. The derived class version hides the base class event. No events raised in the base class code actually call a subscriber's code.

Derived classes work only if they use the `add` and `remove` accessors:

```
public class WorkerEngineDerived : WorkerEngineBase
{
    protected override void SomeWork()
    {
        Thread.Sleep(50);
    }
    public override event
        EventHandler<WorkerEventArgs> OnProgress
    {
        add
        {
            base.OnProgress += value;
        }
        remove
        {
            base.OnProgress -= value;
        }
    }
    // Important: Only the base class can raise the event.
    // Derived cannot raise the events directly.
    // If derived classes should raise events, the base
    // class must provide a protected method to
    // raise the events.
}
```

You can also make this idiom work if the base class declares a property-like event.

The base class needs to be modified to contain a protected event field, and the derived class property can then modify the base class variable:

```
public abstract class WorkerEngineBase
{
    protected EventHandler<WorkerEventArgs> progressEvent;

    public virtual event
        EventHandler<WorkerEventArgs> OnProgress
    {
        [MethodImpl(MethodImplOptions.Synchronized)]
        add
        {
            progressEvent += value;
        }
        [MethodImpl(MethodImplOptions.Synchronized)]
        remove
        {
            progressEvent -= value;
        }
    }

    public void DoLotsOfStuff()
    {
        for (int i = 0; i < 100; i++)
        {
            SomeWork();
            WorkerEventArgs args = new WorkerEventArgs();
            args.Percent = i;
            EventHandler<WorkerEventArgs> progHandler =
                progressEvent;
            if (progHandler != null)
            {
                progHandler(this, args);
            }
            if (args.Cancel)
                return;
        }
    }

    protected abstract void SomeWork();
}
```

```
public class WorkerEngineDerived : WorkerEngineBase
{
    protected override void SomeWork()
    {
        //elided
    }
    // Works. Access base class event field.
    public override event
        EventHandler<WorkerEventArgs> OnProgress
    {
        [MethodImpl(MethodImplOptions.Synchronized)]
        add
        {
            progressEvent += value;
        }
        [MethodImpl(MethodImplOptions.Synchronized)]
        remove
        {
            progressEvent -= value;
        }
    }
}
```

However, this code still constrains your derived class's implementations. The derived class cannot use the field-like event syntax:

```
public class WorkerEngineDerived : WorkerEngineBase
{
    protected override void SomeWork()
    {
        //elided
    }
    // Broken. Private field hides the base class
    public override event
        EventHandler<WorkerEventArgs> OnProgress;
}
```

You are left with two options here to fix the problem. First, whenever you create a virtual event, never use field-like syntax. You can't use field-like syntax in the base class nor in any derived classes. The other solution is to create a virtual method that raises the event whenever you create a virtual event definition. Any derived class must override the raise event method as well as override the virtual event definition.

```
public abstract class WorkerEngineBase
{
    public virtual event
        EventHandler<WorkerEventArgs> OnProgress;

    protected virtual WorkerEventArgs
        RaiseEvent(WorkerEventArgs args)
    {
        EventHandler<WorkerEventArgs> progHandler =
            OnProgress;
        if (progHandler != null)
        {
            progHandler(this, args);
        }
        return args;
    }

    public void DoLotsOfStuff()
    {
        for (int i = 0; i < 100; i++)
        {
            SomeWork();
            WorkerEventArgs args = new WorkerEventArgs();
            args.Percent = i;
            RaiseEvent(args);
            if (args.Cancel)
                return;
        }
    }

    protected abstract void SomeWork();
}

public class WorkerEngineDerived : WorkerEngineBase
{
    protected override void SomeWork()
    {
        Thread.Sleep(50);
    }
```

```
public override event
    EventHandler<WorkerEventArgs> OnProgress;

protected override WorkerEventArgs
    RaiseEvent(WorkerEventArgs args)
{
    EventHandler<WorkerEventArgs> progHandler =
        OnProgress;
    if (progHandler != null)
    {
        progHandler(this, args);
    }
    return args;
}
}
```

Of course, when you look at this code, you'll see that you really don't gain anything by declaring the event as virtual. The existence of the virtual method to raise the event is all you need to customize the event-raising behavior in the derived class. There really isn't anything you can do by overriding the event itself that you can't do by overriding the method that raises the event: You can iterate all the delegates by hand, and you can provide different semantics for handling how event args are changed by each subscriber. You can even suppress events by not raising anything.

At first glance, events seem to provide a loose-coupling interface between your class and those other pieces of code that are interested in communicating with your class. If you've created virtual events, there is both compile-time and runtime coupling between your event sources and those classes that subscribe to your events. The fixes you need to add to your code to make virtual events work usually mean you don't need a virtual event anyway.

Item 25: Use Exceptions to Report Method Contract Failures

Any method that cannot perform its stated actions should report that failure by throwing an exception. Error codes can be ignored and can pollute the normal flow of execution with constant error checks. But exceptions should not be used as a general flow-control mechanism. This means that you must provide other public methods that enable your library's users to minimize the chances that exceptions will be thrown under an application's normal operating conditions. Exceptions are costly at runtime, and writing exception-proof code is difficult. If you don't provide APIs for developers to test conditions without writing many `try/catch` blocks, you aren't providing a robust library.

Exceptions are the preferred failure-reporting mechanism because they have many advantages over return codes as an error-reporting mechanism. Return codes are part of a method's signature, and they often convey information other than error reporting. Whereas return codes are often the result of a computation, exceptions have one purpose only: to report failures. Because exceptions are class types and you can derive your own exception types, you can use exceptions to convey rich information about the failure.

Error return codes must be processed by the method caller. In contrast, thrown exceptions propagate up the call stack until a suitable `catch` clause is found. That gives developers the freedom to isolate error handling from error generation by many levels in the call stack. No error information is lost in this separation because of the richness of your exception classes.

Finally, exceptions cannot be ignored. If a program does not contain a suitable `catch` clause, then a thrown exception terminates the application. You can't continue running after an unnoticed failure, something that would cause data corruption.

Using exceptions to report contract failures does not mean that any method that cannot do what you want must exit by throwing an exception. This doesn't mean that every failure is an exception. `File.Exists()` returns `true` if a file exists, and `false` if it doesn't. `File.Open()` throws an exception if the file does not exist. The difference is simple: `File.Exists()` satisfies its contract by telling whether or not a file exists. The method succeeds even when the file does not exist. In contrast, `File.Open()` succeeds only when the file exists, the current user can read the file, and the current process can open the file for read access. In the first case, the method succeeds even when it tells you an answer you don't desire. In the second case, the method fails, and your program can't continue. An undesired answer from a method is different from a failure. The method succeeds; it gives you the information you requested.

This is a distinction that has an important influence on how you name your methods. Methods that perform actions should be named to clearly state the action that must be performed. In contrast, methods that test particular actions should be named to indicate the test action. What's more, you should provide test methods to minimize the need to use the exceptions as a flow-control mechanism. Writing exception-safe code is difficult. Also, exceptions take more time than do normal method calls. You should strive to create methods in your classes that enable users to test possible failure conditions before performing work. This practice lets them program more defensively, and you can still throw exceptions if developers choose not to test conditions before calling methods.

Whenever you write methods that may throw exceptions, you should also provide methods that test for the conditions that would cause those exceptions. Internally, you can use those test methods to check for any prerequisites before you continue, throwing the exception in those cases when it fails.

Suppose you have a worker class that fails when certain widgets aren't in place. If your API includes only the worker methods but does not provide an alternative path through the code, you'll encourage developers to write code like this:

```
// Don't promote this:
DoesWorkThatMightFail worker = new DoesWorkThatMightFail();
try
{
    worker.DoWork();
}
catch (WorkerException e)
{
    ReportErrorToUser(
        "Test Conditions Failed. Please check widgets");
}
```

Instead, you should add public methods that enable developers to explicitly check conditions before doing the work:

```
public class DoesWorkThatMightFail
{
    public bool TryDoWork()
    {
        if (!TestConditions())
            return false;
        Work(); // may throw on failures, but unlikely
        return true;
    }
```

```csharp
public void DoWork()
{
    Work(); // will throw on failures.
}

private bool TestConditions()
{
    // body elided
    // Test conditions here
    return true;
}

private void Work()
{
    // elided
    // Do the work here
}
}
```

This pattern requires you to write four methods: two public methods, and two private methods. The TryDoWork() method validates all input parameters and any internal object state necessary to perform the work. Then it calls the Work() method to perform the task. DoWork() simply calls the Work() method and lets any failures generate exceptions. This idiom is used in .NET because there are performance implications involved in throwing exceptions, and developers may wish to avoid those costs by testing conditions before allowing methods to fail.

Now, after adding the foregoing extra code, developers who wish to test conditions before performing the work can do so in a much cleaner way:

```csharp
if (!worker.TryDoWork())
{
    ReportErrorToUser
        ("Test Conditions Failed. Please check widgets");
}
```

In practice, testing the preconditions enables more checking, such as parameter checking and internal state. You use this idiom most often when your worker class processes some form of untrusted input, such as user input, file input, or parameters from unknown code. Those failures have application-defined recovery scenarios and are rather common occurrences.

You need to support them by using a control mechanism that does not involve exceptions. Notice that I have not made any claims that `Work()` won't throw any exceptions. Other, more unexpected failures may occur even after normal parameter checking. Those failures would be reported using exceptions, even if the user calls `TryDoWork()`.

It is your responsibility to throw an exception whenever your method cannot complete its contract. Contract failures are always reported by throwing exceptions. Because exceptions should not be used as a general flow-control mechanism, you should also provide an alternative set of methods that enables developers to test for possible invalid conditions before calling methods that might throw exceptions.

Item 26: Ensure That Properties Behave Like Data

Properties lead dual lives. From the outside, they appear to be passive data elements. However, on the inside they are implemented as methods. This dual life can lead you to create properties that don't live up to your users' expectations. Developers using your types will assume that accessing a property behaves the same as accessing a data member. If you create properties that don't live up to those assumptions, your users will misuse your types. Property access gives the impression that calling those particular methods will have the same characteristics as accessing a data member directly.

When properties correctly model data members, they live up to client developers' expectations. First, client developers will believe that subsequent calls to a `get` accessor without any intervening statements will produce the same answer:

```
int someValue = someObject.ImportantProperty;
Debug.Assert(someValue == someObject.ImportantProperty);
```

Of course, multiple threads could violate this assumption, whether you're using properties or fields. But otherwise, repeated calls to the same property should return the same value.

Finally, developers using your type will not expect property accessors to do much work. A property getter should never be an expensive operation. Similarly, property `set` accessors will likely do some validation, but it should not be expensive to call them.

Why do developers using your types have these expectations? It's because they view properties as data. They access properties in tight loops. You've done the same thing with .NET collection classes. Whenever you enumerate an array with a `for` loop, you retrieve the value of the array's `Length` property repeatedly:

```
for (int index = 0; index < myArray.Length; index++)
```

The longer the array, the more times you access the `Length` property. If you had to count all elements every time you accessed the array's `Length` property, every loop would have quadratic performance. No one would use loops.

Living up to your client developers' expectations is not hard. First, use implicit properties. **Implicit properties** are a thin wrapper around a compiler-generated backing store. Their characteristics closely match those of data access. In fact, because the property accessors are simple implementations, they are often inlined. Whenever you can implement properties in your design using implicit properties, you will live up to client expectations.

However, if your properties contain behavior that isn't implemented in implicit properties, that's not always a concern. You'll likely add validation in your property setters, and that will satisfy users' expectations. Earlier I showed you this implementation of a property setter for a `LastName`:

```
public string LastName
{
    // getter elided
    set
    {
        if (string.IsNullOrEmpty(value))
            throw new ArgumentException(
            "last name can't be null or blank");
        lastName = value;
    }
}
```

That validation code doesn't break any of the fundamental assumptions about properties. It executes quickly, and it protects the validity of the object.

Also, property `get` accessors often perform some computation before returning the value. Suppose you have a `Point` class that includes a property for its distance from the origin:

```
public class Point
{
    public int X
    {
        get;
        set;
    }
    public int Y
    {
        get;
        set;
    }
    public double Distance
    {
        get { return Math.Sqrt(X * X + Y * Y); }
    }
}
```

Computing the distance is quick, and your users won't see performance problems if you have implemented `Distance` in this way. However, if `Distance` did turn out to be a bottleneck, you could cache the distance the first time you compute it. Of course, this also means that you need to invalidate the cached value whenever one of the component values changes. (Or you could make `Point` an immutable type.)

```
public class Point
{
    private int xValue;
    public int X
    {
        get { return xValue; }
        set
        {
            xValue = value;
            distance = default(double?);
        }
    }
    private int yValue;
    public int Y
    {
        get { return yValue; }
```

```
        set
        {
            yValue = value;
            distance = default(double?);
        }
    }
    private double? distance;
    public double Distance
    {
        get
        {
            if (!distance.HasValue)
                distance = Math.Sqrt(X * X + Y * Y);
            return distance.Value;
        }
    }
}
```

If computing the value returned by a property getter is much more expensive, you should rethink your public interface.

```
// Bad Property Design. Lengthy operation required for getter
public class MyType
{
    // lots elided
    public string ObjectName
    {
        get { return RetrieveNameFromRemoteDatabase(); }
    }
}
```

Users don't expect that accessing a property will require round trips to remote storage. You need to change the public API to meet users' expectations. Every type is different, so your implementation must depend on the usage pattern for the type. You may find that caching the value is the right answer:

```
// One possible path: evaluate once and cache the answer
public class MyType
{
    // lots elided
    private string objectName;
```

```
public string ObjectName
{
    get
    {
        if (objectName == null)
            objectName = RetrieveNameFromRemoteDatabase();
        return objectName;
    }
}
}
```

This technique works well when the ObjectName property is needed only occasionally. You save the work of retrieving the value when it's not needed. In return, the first caller to ask for the property pays an extra penalty. If this type almost always uses the ObjectName property and it's valid to cache the name, you could load the value in the constructor and use the cached value as the property return value. The preceding code also assumes that ObjectName can be safely cached. If other portions of the program or other processes in the system change the remote storage for the object name, then this design fails.

The operations of pulling data from a remote database and later saving changes back to the remote database are common enough, and certainly valid. You can live up to your users' expectations by performing those operations in methods, giving those methods names that match the operations. Here's a different version of MyType that lives up to expectations:

```
//Better solution: Use methods to manage cached values
public class MyType
{
    public void LoadFromDatabase()
    {
        objectName = RetrieveNameFromRemoteDatabase();
        // other fields elided.
    }
    public void SaveToDatabase()
    {
        SaveNameToRemoteDatabase(objectName);
        // other fields elided.
    }
```

```
    // lots elided
    private string objectName;
    public string ObjectName
    {
        get { return objectName; }
        set { objectName = value; }
    }
}
```

Of course, once you've made that change, you can see that ObjectName could be replaced with an implicit property:

```
//Replace properties with implicit properties
public class MyType
{
    public void LoadFromDatabase()
    {
        ObjectName = RetrieveNameFromRemoteDatabase();
        // other fields elided.
    }

    public void SaveToDatabase()
    {
        SaveNameToRemoteDatabase(ObjectName);
        // other fields elided.
    }

    // lots elided

    public string ObjectName
    {
        get;
        set;
    }
}
```

It's not only get accessors that can break client developer assumptions. You can create code that breaks your users' assumptions in the property setter as well. Suppose that ObjectName is a read-write property. If the setter wrote the value to the remote database it would break your users' assumptions:

```
// Poor property design: setter is too expensive
public class MyType
{
    // lots elided
    private string objectName;
    public string ObjectName
    {
        get
        {
            if (objectName == null)
                objectName = RetrieveNameFromRemoteDatabase();
            return objectName;
        }
        set
        {
            objectName = value;
            SaveNameToRemoteDatabase(objectName);
        }
    }
}
```

This extra work in the setter breaks several assumptions made by your users. Client code developers won't expect that a setter is making a remote call to a database. It will take longer than they expect. It also has the chance of failing in many ways they don't expect.

Properties set different expectations for client developers than do methods. Client developers expect properties to execute quickly and to provide a view into object state. They expect properties to be like data fields, both in behavior and in their performance characteristics. When you create properties that violate those assumptions, you should modify the public interface to create methods that represent the operations that don't live up to users' expectations for properties. That practice lets you return the properties to their purpose of providing a window into object state.

Item 27: Distinguish Between Inheritance and Composition

One of the most powerful constructs available in any object-oriented language is inheritance. Maybe that's why developers seem to reach for inheritance to the exclusion of any other programming idiom. That's unfortunate, because inheritance is not always the best representation of your design. Inheritance creates the tightest coupling between two classes. The derived class contains all the members of the base class. And because the derived class is an instance of the base class, an object of the derived class type can be substituted for an object of the base class at any time.

That's a strong statement about a strong relationship between two types. If that's not true for your design, you should use another idiom, such as composition. **Composition** allows the outer object to expose selected methods from the inner object, without such tight coupling of the public and protected interfaces.

Both class inheritance and composition provide ways to reuse implementation from another class. Inheritance is often the first choice of developers. When you derive your class from another type, your class automatically includes all the public members of the base class.

```
public class MyDerived : MyBase
{
    // Every public method of MyBase is part of the public API
    // for MyDerived.
}
```

If you use composition, you must reimplement every method in the base class's public interface. You can delegate the implementation to the base class explicitly:

```
public class MyOuterClass
{
    private MyInnerClass implementation =
        new MyInnerClass();

    public void SampleImplMethod()
    {
        implementation.SampleImplMethod();
    }
    // repeat for every public method in MyInnerClass
}
```

Explicitly delegating method implementation to the inner class gives you control over exposing methods defined in the inner class. Inheritance always exposes every public member in the base class. In contrast, composition allows you to selectively choose which, if any, of the public methods available in the inner class are exposed as part of the outer class's interface. They aren't part of your type's public interface unless you explicitly add them.

Your class's interface is also insulated against future updates of the inner class. Using inheritance, upgrades to base types are automatically part of your class's interface. Using composition, you must explicitly modify your outer class in order to expose any new methods in the inner class. This constraint may be important if the inner class was created by a third party. Your user community can get newer versions of those components without getting an upgrade of your system.

Of course, you've probably noticed that the version using composition has lost polymorphism. You can't substitute `MyOuterClass` when `MyInnerClass` is expected. But if you apply one more bit of indirection, you can get closer to that behavior. You need to create an interface that supports the interface contract you need. Then you can make your outer class implement that interface:

```
internal interface IContract
{
    void SampleImplMethod();
    // other methods elided
}


internal class MyInnerClass : IContract
{
    public void SampleImplMethod()
    {
        // elided
    }
}


public class MyOuterClass : IContract
{
    private MyInnerClass impl = new MyInnerClass();
    // remainder elided

    public void SampleImplMethod()
    {
        impl.SampleImplMethod();
    }
}
```

Callers now work with `MyOuterClass` through its `IContract` interface. This separation between interfaces and classes provides granularity and loose coupling in your public interfaces. You can define the interface to contain the minimum members needed by callers. The implementation class, and the outer classes, can have more methods available as public members, but callers depend only on the interface contract. It's not the same as inheritance: `MyOuterClass` cannot be used by a method that declares parameters of type `MyInnerClass`.

Composition makes it easier to create outer classes that aggregate more than one inner type. You can contain multiple implementation classes that represent different pieces of functionality that make up this class:

```
internal class InnerClassOne
{
    internal void SampleImplMethodOne();
}


internal class InnerClassTwo
{
    internal void SampleImplMethodTwo();
}


public class MyOuterClass
{
    private InnerClassOne implOne = new InnerClassOne();
    private InnerClassTwo implTwo = new InnerClassTwo();

    public void SampleImplMethodOne()
    {
        implOne.SampleImplMethodOne();
    }
    public void SampleImplMethodTwo()
    {
        implTwo.SampleImplMethodTwo();
    }
}
```

Of course, it would make sense to extract interfaces from those implementations so that the outer class can be used wherever code expects a type that implements the particular contract:

```csharp
public interface IContractOne
{
    void SampleImplMethodOne();
    // other methods elided
}

public interface IContractTwo
{
    void SampleImplMethodTwo();
    // other methods elided.
}

public class MyOuterClass : IContractOne, IContractTwo
{
    // remainder elided
}
```

Finally, containment lets you change the inner class at runtime. You can examine various runtime conditions and create various inner classes. That requires you to have defined interfaces that your inner classes implement. It allows you to treat different inner classes polymorphically:

```csharp
public interface IContract
{
    void SomeMethod();
}

internal class InnerTypeOne : IContract
{
    public void SomeMethod()
    {
        // elided
    }
}

internal class InnerTypeTwo : IContract
{
    public void SomeMethod()
    {
        // elided
    }
}
```

```
public class MyOuterClass : IContract
{
    private readonly IContract impl;
    public MyOuterClass(bool flag)
    {
        if (flag)
            impl = new InnerTypeOne();
        else
            impl = new InnerTypeTwo();
    }

    public void SomeMethod()
    {
        impl.SomeMethod();
    }
}
```

This concept can be as complex as needed to satisfy your requirements. You can switch between more than two inner classes. You can also modify the behavior by creating new inner objects if the situation changes over time. It's not much extra work, because you reuse the same interface contract that you've created for your external clients. Now you're overloading that same concept internally to perform your own method call dispatch between multiple inner classes.

The examples I've described so far look at the differences between these two design strategies at one point in time. Over time, composition gains advantages because of its reduced interface coupling in your derived class. That's because your derived class automatically includes every public member of the base class. If the base class developer adds any new methods, your type automatically includes those types. Whether or not those methods belong in your type, you've got them. Using composition, you must decide for yourself whether or not to include those methods. Although you must write code to export these new methods, they don't automatically leak into your public interface.

Before I conclude, don't misinterpret this advice as a complete recommendation against inheritance. When the object model correctly models an Is A relationship, inheritance provides more reuse with less work. Furthermore, when it models everything correctly, it's clearer to developers who later examine your code. The .NET BCL uses inheritance throughout the Windows Forms library and the Web Forms library. Inheritance models work very well for UI controls. Throughout other parts of the .Net BCL, the inheritance libraries are not nearly as deep. In other areas, the developers choose composition more often.

You should expand your set of design choices and use both composition and inheritance. When you create types that reuse implementation from other types, you should use composition. If your types model an Is A relationship in every way, inheritance is the better choice. Composition requires more work to expose the implementation from the inner objects, but the payoff is more control over the coupling between your type and the type whose implementation you wish to reuse. Using inheritance means that your derived type is a special case of the base class in every way.

4 | C# 3.0 Language Enhancements

The C# 3.0 release has added several new and interesting features to the C# language. Many of these features were added to support Language-Integrated Query (LINQ). However, the C# language features can be used for many things other than LINQ queries. In this chapter, I discuss the new language features, explain how they provide new techniques you can use to solve your current development problems, and describe some practices to avoid when you use these new features.

Item 28: Augment Minimal Interface Contracts with Extension Methods

Extension methods provide a mechanism for C# developers to define behavior in interfaces. You can define an interface with minimal capabilities and then create a set of extension methods defined on that interface to extend its capabilities. In particular, you can add behavior instead of just defining an API.

The `System.Linq.Enumerable` class provides a great example of this technique. `System.Enumerable` contains more than 50 extension methods defined on `IEnumerable<T>`. Those methods range from `Where` to `OrderBy` to `ThenBy` to `GroupInto`. Defining these as extension methods to `IEnumerable<T>` provides great advantages. First, none of these capabilities requires modifications to any class that already implements `IEnumerable<T>`. No new responsibilities have been added for classes that implement `IEnumerable<T>`. Implementers still need define only `GetEnumerator()`, and `IEnumerator<T>` still need define only `Current`, `MoveNext()`, and `Reset()`. Yet by creating extension methods, the C# compiler ensures that all collections now support query operations.

You can follow the same pattern yourself. `IComparable<T>` follows a pattern from the days of C. If `left < right`, then `left.CompareTo(right)` returns a value less than 0. If `left > right`, then `left.CompareTo(right)` returns a value greater than 0. When `left` and `right` are equivalent, `left.CompareTo(right)` returns 0. This pattern has been used so often that many of us have it memorized, but that doesn't make it very approachable. It would be much more readable to write something like `left.LessThan(right)` or `left.GreaterThanEqual(right)`. That's easy to do with extension methods. Here's an implementation:

```
public static class Comparable
{
    public static bool LessThan<T>(this T left, T right)
        where T : IComparable<T>
    {
        return left.CompareTo(right) < 0;
    }

    public static bool GreaterThan<T>(this T left, T right)
        where T : IComparable<T>
    {
        return left.CompareTo(right) < 0;
    }

    public static bool LessThanEqual<T>(this T left, T right)
        where T : IComparable<T>
    {
        return left.CompareTo(right) <= 0;
    }

    public static bool GreaterThanEqual<T>(this T left, T right)
        where T : IComparable<T>
    {
        return left.CompareTo(right) <= 0;
    }
}
```

Every class that implements `IComparable<T>` now appears to include these additional methods if the proper `using` declaration is in scope. Implementers still need only create one method (`CompareTo`), and the client code can use other, easier-to-read signatures.

You should also follow the same pattern with interfaces you've created in your applications. Rather than define rich interfaces, use the interface to define the minimal functionality necessary to satisfy the requirements. Any convenience methods that can be built on that minimal interface should be created using extension methods. Compared with richer interface contracts, using extension methods enables implementers to write fewer methods and still provide a richer interface to client code.

By using interfaces and extension methods in this way, you can provide a default implementation for methods that are part of an interface. This practice provides a way for classes to reuse implementations based on an interface definition. Whenever you define an interface, consider methods that could be implemented using existing interface members. Those methods are candidates to be defined as extension methods that can be reused by all interface implementers.

Be aware that you could cause strange behavior by defining extension methods on an interface when some classes may want to define their own implementation of that extension method. Although the rules of method resolution mean that the class method will be called in favor of an extension method, that is a compile-time resolution. Any code that is typed to use the interface will call the extension method rather than the method defined on its type.

Let's look at a small, rather contrived example. Here's a simple interface that keeps a marker on an object:

```
public interface IFoo
{
    int Marker
    {
        get;
        set;
    }
}
```

You could write an extension method to increment the marker:

```
public static class FooExtensions
{
    public static void NextMarker(this IFoo thing)
    {
        thing.Marker += 1;
    }
}
```

Throughout your code, you use this extension method:

```
private static void UpdateMarker(IFoo item)
{
    item.NextMarker();
}


public class MyType : IFoo
{
    #region IFoo Members
    public int Marker
    {
        get;
        set;
    }
    #endregion

    // Elided
}


// elsewhere
MyType t = new MyType();
UpdateMarker(t); // t.Marker == 1
```

Time passes, and one of your developers creates a new version of a type and introduces that type's own (semantically different) version of NextMarker. It's important to note that MyType has a different implementation of NextMarker:

```
// MyType version 2
public class MyType : IFoo
[
    public int Marker
    {
        get;
        set;
    }

    public void NextMarker()
    {
        Marker += 5;
    }
}
```

That introduces a breaking change in the application. This code snippet sets the value of `Marker` to 5:

```
MyType t = new MyType();
t.NextMarker(); // t.Marker == 5
```

You can't avoid this problem entirely, but you can minimize its effects. This sample was contrived to exhibit bad behavior. In production code, the behavior of the extension method should be semantically the same as that of the class method having the same signature. If you can create a better, more efficient algorithm in a class, you should do that. However, you must ensure that the behavior is the same. If you do that, then this behavior won't affect program correctness.

When you find that your design calls for making an interface definition that many classes will be forced to implement, consider creating the smallest possible set of members defined in the interface. Then provide an implementation of convenience methods in the form of extension methods. In that way, class designers who implement your interface will have the least amount of work to do, and developers using your interface can get the greatest possible benefit.

Item 29: Enhance Constructed Types with Extension Methods

You'll probably use a number of constructed generic types in your application. You'll create specific collection types: `List<int>`, `Dictionary<EmployeeID, Employee>`, and many other collections. The purpose of creating these collections is that your application has a specific need for a collection of a certain type and you want to have specific behavior defined for those specific constructed types. To implement that functionality in a low-impact way, you can create a set of extension methods on specific constructed types.

You can see this pattern in the `System.Linq.Enumerable` class. Item 28 (in this chapter) discusses the extension pattern used by `Enumerable<T>` to implement many common methods on sequences as extension methods on `IEnumerable<T>`. In addition, `Enumerable` contains a number of methods that are implemented specifically for particular constructed types that implement `IEnumerable<T>`. For example, several numeric methods are implemented on numeric sequences (`IEnumerable<int>`, `IEnumerable<double>`, `IEnumerable<long>`, and `IEnumerable<float>`). Here

are a few of the extension methods implemented specifically for
IEnumerable<int>:

```
public class Enumerable
{
    public static int Average(this IEnumerable<int>
        sequence);
    public static int Max(this IEnumerable<int> sequence);
    public static int Min(this IEnumerable<int> sequence);
    public static int Sum(this IEnumerable<int> sequence);


    // other methods elided
}
```

Once you recognize the pattern, you can see many ways you could implement the same kind of extensions for the constructed types in your own
domain. If you were writing an e-commerce application and you wanted
to send e-mail coupons to a set of customers, the method signature might
look something like this:

```
public static void SendEmailCoupons(this
    IEnumerable<Customer>
    customers, Coupon specialOffer);
```

Similarly, you could find all customers with no orders in the past month:

```
public static IEnumerable<Customer> LostProspects(
    this IEnumerable<Customer> targetList);
```

If you didn't have extension methods, you could achieve a similar effect by
deriving a new type from the constructed generic type you used. For example, the Customer methods just shown could be implemented like this:

```
public class CustomerList : List<Customer>
{
    public void SendEmailCoupons(Coupon specialOffer);
    public static IEnumerable<Customer> LostProspects();


}
```

It works, but it is actually much more limiting than extension methods on
IEnumerable<Customer> to the users of this list of customers. The difference in the method signatures provides part of the reason. The extension methods use IEnumerable<Customer> as the parameter, but the
methods added to the derived class are based on List<Customer>. They

mandate a particular storage model. For that reason, they can't be composed as a set of iterator methods (see Item 17, Chapter 3). You've placed unnecessary design constraints on the users of these methods. That's a misuse of inheritance.

Another reason to prefer the extension methods as a way to implement this functionality has to do with the way queries are composed. The `Lost-Prospects()` method probably would be implemented something like this:

```
public static IEnumerable<Customer> LostProspects(
    IEnumerable<Customer> targetList)
{
    IEnumerable<Customer> answer =
        from c in targetList
        where DateTime.Now - c.LastOrderDate >
            TimeSpan.FromDays(30)
        select c;
    return answer;
}
```

Item 34 (later in this chapter) discusses why lambda expressions are preferred over methods in queries. Implementing these features as extension methods means that they provide a reusable query expressed as a lambda expression. You can reuse the entire query rather than try to reuse the predicate of the `where` clause.

If you examine the object model for any application or library you are writing, you'll likely find many constructed types used for the storage model. You should look at these constructed types and decide what methods logically would be added to each of them. It's best to create the implementation for those methods as extension methods by using either the constructed type or a constructed interface implemented by the type. You'll turn a simple generic instantiation into a class having all the behavior you need. Furthermore, you'll create that implementation in a manner that decouples the storage model from the implementation to the greatest extent possible.

Item 30: Prefer Implicitly Typed Local Variables

Implicitly typed local variables were added to the C# language to support anonymous types. A second reason for using implicitly typed locals is that some queries create results that are an `IQueryable<T>`, whereas others return `IEnumerable<T>`. If you coerce an `IQueryable<T>` collection into an `IEnumerable<T>` collection, you miss out on any enhancements provided by the `IQueryProvider` (see Item 42, Chapter 5). Using `var` also improves a developer's comprehension of the code. `Dictionary<int, Queue<string>>` doesn't add much comprehension, but the variable name `JobsQueuedByRegion` does.

I prefer `var` and use it to declare many local variables, because I find that it focuses the developer's attention on the important part (the semantic meaning) and not on the particulars of a variable's type. The compiler still warns me if I have created any construct that doesn't type-check. Variable type safety is not the same as developers typing more keystrokes. In many cases, the differences between `IQueryable` and `IEnumerable` do not add any information to you as a developer. However, if you try to tell the compiler which type it is, you'll find that you can change the behavior by getting it wrong (see Item 42, Chapter 5). There are times when it's better to use implicitly typed variables, because the compiler will pick a better type than you will. At other times, however, overusing `var` only decreases the readability of your code. Even worse, using implicitly typed variables can lead to subtle conversion bugs.

Let's begin with the problems of readability. Many times, the type of a local variable is clear from its initialization statement:

```
var foo = new MyType();
```

Any competent developer can tell the type of `foo` from the declaration. Similarly, most factory methods are clear:

```
var foo = AnotherType.CreateObject();
```

However, in some cases, the return type might not always be clear from the method name:

```
var foo = someObject.DoSomeWork(anotherParameter);
```

Of course, that's a contrived example, and I hope that most of the methods in your codebase have names that give a better indication of what's returned. Even in this contrived example, a better variable name would give most developers a better indication of the meaning:

```
var HighestSellingProduct =
    someObject.DoSomeWork(anotherParameter);
```

Even without any type information, most developers would correctly assume the type of `Product`.

Depending on the actual signature of `DoSomeWork`, of course, `Highest-SellingProduct` might not actually be a `Product`. It might be any class derived from `Product` or even any interface implemented by `Product`. The compiler believes that `HighestSellingProduct` is whatever type it has been told by the method signature for `DoSomeWork`. It doesn't matter that the runtime type is actually `Product`. When the compile-time type is different from the runtime type, the compiler always wins. You don't get a say unless you use some kind of cast.

So we've started to enter the realm where `var` introduces questions of readability. Introducing `var` for a variable returned from some method is one of the ways that the use of `var` can confuse developers reading your code. A human reading the code will assume one type. At runtime, the human may be correct. But the compiler does not have the luxury of examining the runtime type of the object. The compiler examines the compile-time type and infers the type of the local variable based on those declarations. What's changed is that now the compiler determines the declared type of the variable. When you declare the type yourself, other developers can see the declared type. In contrast, when you use `var`, the compiler determines the type, but developers may not see the type written. Because of the way you've written your code, the human reader and the compiler come to different conclusions about the types involved. That will lead to maintenance errors and avoidable bugs.

Let's continue looking at problems caused by implicitly typed locals when you declare variables of built-in numeric types. There are numerous conversions between the built-in numeric types: Widening conversions, such as from `float` to `double`, are always safe. There are also narrowing conversions, such as from `long` to `int`, that involve a loss of precision. By explicitly declaring the types of all numeric variables, you retain some control over the types used, and you help the compiler warn you about possible dangerous conversions.

Examine this small bit of code:

```
static void Main(string[] args)
{
    var f = GetMagicNumber();
    var total = 100 * f / 6;
    Console.WriteLine("Type: {0}, Value: {1}",
```

```
        total.GetType().Name, total);
}
```

What is `total`? It depends on the type returned from `GetMagicNumber`. Here are five outputs, all from different declarations of `GetMagicNumber`:

```
Declared Type: Double, Value: 166.666666666667
Declared Type: Single, Value: 166.6667
Declared Type: Decimal, Value: 166.6666666666666666666666667
Declared Type: Int32, Value: 166
Declared Type: Int64, Value: 166
```

The differences in the type are caused by the way the compiler infers the type of `f`, which modifies the inferred type of `total`. The compiler gives `f` the same type that it gives the declared return type of `GetMagicNumber()`. Because the constants used in the calculation of `total` are literals, the compiler converts those literals to the type of `f`, and the calculation is done using the rules appropriate for that type. The different rules of the different types create the different answers.

This isn't a problem with the language. The C# compiler is doing exactly what you requested. By using local type inference, you told the compiler that it knew more about your types than you did. It made the best decision it could based on the right side of the assignment. When you work with built-in numeric types, you need to be very careful. That's because many implicit conversions are available on numeric types. Furthermore, because the various numeric types have different degrees of precision, it's not only readability that suffers but also accuracy.

Of course, it's not the use of `var` that causes the problem. The cause is that it's not clear from reading the code which type is returned by `GetMagic-Number()` and which built-in conversions may be in play. The same problems occur when the variable declaration `f` is removed from the method:

```
static void Main(string[] args)
{
    var total = 100 * GetMagicNumber() / 6;
    Console.WriteLine("Type: {0}, Value: {1}",
        total.GetType().Name, total);
}
```

The problem is that developers can't see the actual type of the return value from `GetMagicNumber()` and can't easily determine which numeric conversions have been performed.

Contrast that with the results of the same routine if you explicitly declare the expected return type of GetMagicNumber(). Now the compiler tells you whether your assumptions are wrong. If there is an implicit conversion from the return type of GetMagicNumber to the declared type of f, it just works. That would be the case if f were declared as a decimal and GetMagicNumber() returned an int. However, if there is not an implicit conversion, you'll receive a compiler error. You must change your assumptions. That will give you the chance to look at the code and understand the conversions that should be in place.

That one example shows the scenarios when local variable type inference can make it harder for developers who are maintaining code. The compiler works in the same way, and it is the tool that performs the type checking. However, developers can't easily see which rules and conversions apply. In these situations, local type inference can hamper the view of the types involved.

Local type inference doesn't have any real effect on the static typing used in C#. Why is that? First, you need to understand that local type inference is not the same thing as dynamic typing. Variables declared with var are not dynamic but instead are implicitly declared with the type of the right side of the assignment. You are not telling the compiler which type you're creating; the compiler declares the type for you. When the type you want is not the same as the type the compiler would pick, you introduce problems in your code.

Sometimes, though, the compiler may be smarter than you are. Examine this simple routine, which retrieves customer names starting with *A* from a database.

```csharp
public IEnumerable<string> FindCustomersStartingWith
    (string start)
{
    IEnumerable<string> q =
        from c in db.Customers
        select c.ContactName;

    var q2 = q.Where(s => s.StartsWith(start));
    return q2;
}
```

This code has a serious performance problem. The original query, which defines the entire list of customer contact names, has been declared by the developer as `IEnumerable<string>`. Because the query is running against a database, it's actually in `IQueryable<string>`. However, by strongly declaring the return value, you've lost that information. `IQueryable<T>` derives from `IEnumerable<T>`, so the compiler does not even warn you about this assignment. Yet when the second portion of the query is compiled, `Enumerable.Where` will be used, rather than `Queryable.Where`. In this case, the compiler would have correctly determined a better type (`IQueryable<string>`) than the one you forced on it (`IEnumerable<string>`). If you were wrong in such a way that there was no implicit conversion from `IQueryable<string>`, then the compiler would give you an error. However, because `IQueryable<T>` derives from `IEnumerable<T>`, the compiler allows the conversion, letting you hurt yourself.

The second query does not call `Queryable.Where`; instead, it calls `Enumerable.Where`. That has a large negative implication for performance. In Item 38 (Chapter 5), you will learn that `IQueryable` composes multiple query expression trees into a single operation that can be executed at once, often at the remote server where the data is located. In this instance, the second portion of the query (the `where` clause) sees the source as an `IEnumerable<string>`. That change is significant, because only the first part of the query is built on the remote machine. The entire list of customer names will be returned from the source. The second statement (the `where` clause) locally examines the entire list of customer contact names and returns only those matching the search string.

Contrast that with this version:

```
public IEnumerable<string> FindCustomersStartingWith
    (string start)
{
    var q =
        from c in db.Customers
        select c.ContactName;

    var q2 = q.Where(s => s.StartsWith(start));
    return q2;
}
```

Now `q` is an `IQueryable<string>`. The compiler infers the return type because of the source of the query. The second statement composes the query, adding the `Where` clause to the query, and holds a new, more complete expression tree. The actual data is retrieved only when the caller examines the query. The expression to filter the query gets passed to the data source, and the result sequence contains only those contact names that match the filter. Any network traffic is reduced, and the query is more efficient.

This miraculous change is that q is now declared (by the compiler) as `IQueryable<string>` instead of `IEnumerable<string>`. Extension methods cannot be virtual, and the dispatch does not depend on the runtime type of the object. Instead, extension methods are static methods, and the compiler decides which method is the best match based on the compile-time type and not the runtime type. There's no late binding mechanism going on here. Even if the runtime type contains instance members that would match the call, they're not visible to the compiler and therefore are not candidates.

It's important to note that any extension method can be written to examine the runtime type of its parameters. Extension methods could create a different implementation based on the runtime type. In fact, `Enumerable.Reverse()` does just that to get increased performance when the parameter implements either `IList<T>` or `ICollection<T>` (see Item 3, Chapter 1).

You, the developer, must decide whether letting the compiler silently declare the compile-time type of the variable harms readability. If not being able to immediately see the exact type of a local variable creates ambiguity when someone reads the code, it's best to declare that type explicitly. However, in many cases, the code clearly conveys the semantic information about the variable. In the examples you've seen, you know that q is a sequence of contact names (which happen to be strings). The semantic information is clear from the initialization statement. That is often the case when a variable is initialized from a query expression. Whenever the semantic information of the variable is clear, you can use var. Going back to my first point, you should avoid var when the initialization expression does not clearly show developers the semantic information about the variable but an explicit type declaration does convey that information.

In short, it's best to declare local variables using var unless developers (including you, in the future) need to see the declared type to understand the code. The title of this item says "prefer," not "always." I recommend explicitly declaring all numeric types (int, float, double, and others) rather than use a var declaration. In addition, use the type parameter in generics (for example T, TResult) rather than var. For everything else, just use var. Merely typing more keystrokes—to explicitly declare the type—doesn't promote type safety or improve readability. You may also introduce inefficiencies that the compiler will avoid if you pick the wrong declared type.

Item 31: Limit Type Scope by Using Anonymous Types

You should use anonymous types whenever you need simple data containers that store interim results. Anonymous types save you quite a bit of work and help you gain features because the compiler can generate some code you can't. Furthermore, these types don't cause the code bloat many people think they do. When you combine all these features, anonymous types should be in your arsenal more often than they likely are. You should create concrete types only when you need to add behavior or need to assign a name to a type so that you can use it as a parameter to a method or as a member of a class.

Let's start with saving work. Suppose you write this assignment:

```
var aPoint = new { X = 5, Y = 67 };
```

You've told the compiler several things. You've indicated that you need a new internal sealed class. You've told the compiler that this new type is an immutable type and that it has two public read-only properties surrounding two backing fields (X, Y).

You've told the compiler to write something like this for you:

```
internal sealed class AnonymousMumbleMumble
{
    private readonly int x;

    public int X
    {
        get { return X; }
    }

    private readonly int y;
    public int Y
    {
        get { return y; }
    }
}
```

```
public AnonymousMumbleMumble(int xParm, int yParm)
{
    x = xParm;
    y = yParm;
}
}
```

The complier defines the actual type by deriving from a generic `Tuple` (see Item 9, Chapter 1), giving the properties the names you specify.

Instead of writing this by hand, I'd rather let the compiler write it for me. There are a great many advantages. Most simply, the compiler is faster. I can't type the full class definition nearly as fast as I can type the new expression. Second, the compiler generates the same definition for these repetitive tasks. As developers, we occasionally miss something. This is pretty simple code, so the chances of error aren't very great, but they're not zero. The compiler does not make those human mistakes. Third, letting the compiler generate the code minimizes the amount of code to maintain. No other developer needs to read this code, figure out why you wrote it, figure out what it does, and find where it is used. Because the compiler generates the code, there is less to figure out and less to look at.

The obvious drawback of using anonymous types is that you don't know the name of the type. Because you don't name the type, you can't use an anonymous type as a parameter to a method or as its return value. Still, there are ways to work with single objects or sequences of anonymous types. You can write methods or expressions that work with anonymous types inside a method. You must define them as lambda expressions or anonymous delegates so that you can define them inside the body of the method where the anonymous type was created. If you mix in generic methods that contain function parameters, you can create methods that work with anonymous methods. For example, you can double both the x and Y values for a `Point` by creating a transform method:

```
static T Transform<T>(T element, Func<T, T> transformFunc)
{
    return transformFunc(element);
}
```

You can pass an anonymous type to the `Transform` method:

```
var aPoint = new { X = 5, Y = 67 };
var anotherPoint = Transform(aPoint, (p) =>
    new { X = p.X * 2, Y = p.Y * 2});
```

Of course, complicated algorithms will require complicated lambda expressions, and probably multiple calls to various generic methods. But it's only more of the simple example I've shown. That is what makes anonymous types great vehicles for storing interim results. The scope of an anonymous type is limited to the method where it is defined. The anonymous type can store results from the first phase of an algorithm and pass those interim results into the second phase. Using generic methods and lambdas means that you can define any necessary transformations on those anonymous types within the scope of the method where the anonymous type is defined.

What's more, because the interim results are stored in anonymous types, those types do not pollute the application's namespace. You can have the compiler create these simple types and shield developers from needing to understand them to understand the application. Anonymous types are scoped inside the method where they are declared. Using an anonymous type clearly shows other developers that a particular type is scoped inside that single method.

You may have noticed that I use some weasel words earlier when I describe how the compiler defines an anonymous type. The compiler generates "something like" what I wrote when you tell it you need an anonymous type. The compiler adds some features that you can't write yourself. Anonymous types are immutable types that support object initializer syntax. If you create your own immutable type, you must hand-code your constructors so that client code can initialize every field or property in that type. Hand-coded immutable types would not support object initializer syntax, because there are no accessible property setters. Still, you can and must use object initializer syntax when you construct an instance of an anonymous type. The compiler creates a public constructor that sets each of the properties, and it substitutes a constructor call for the property setters at the call point.

For example, suppose you have this call:

```
var aPoint = new { X = 5, Y = 67 };
```

It is translated by the compiler into this:

```
AnonymousMumbleMumble aPoint = new AnonymousMumbleMumble
    (5, 67);
```

The only way you can create an immutable type that supports object initializer syntax is to use an anonymous type. Hand-coded types do not get the same compiler magic.

Finally, I've said that there is less runtime cost for anonymous types than you might have thought. You might naively think that each time you new up any anonymous type, the compiler blindly defines a new anonymous type. Well, the compiler is a little smarter than that. Whenever you create the same anonymous type, the compiler reuses the same anonymous type as before.

I need to be a little more precise about what the compiler views as the same anonymous types if they're used in different locations. First, obviously that happens only if the multiple copies of the anonymous type are declared in the same assembly.

Second, for two anonymous types to be considered the same, the property names and types must match, and the properties must be in the same order. The following two declarations produce two different anonymous types:

```
var aPoint = new { X = 5, Y = 67 };
var anotherPoint = new { Y = 12, X = 16 };
```

By putting the properties in different orders, you have created two different anonymous types. You would get the same anonymous type only by ensuring that all properties are declared in the same order every time you declare an object that is meant to represent the same concept.

Before we leave anonymous types, a special case deserves mention. Because anonymous types follow value semantics for equality, they can be used as composite keys. For example, suppose you need to group customers by salesperson and ZIP code. You could run this query:

```
var query = from c in customers
            group c by new { c.SalesRepresentative,
                c.ZipCode };
```

This query produces a dictionary in which the keys are a pair of `SalesRepresentative` and `ZipCode`. The values are lists of `Customers`.

Anonymous types aren't as exotic as they seem, and they don't harm readability when they are used correctly. If you have interim results that you need to keep track of and if they're modeled well with an immutable type, then you should use anonymous types. When you need to define behaviors on those types, that's when you need to create concrete types to represent those concepts. In the meantime, the compiler can generate all the boilerplate code you need. You clearly communicate to other developers that the type is used only within the context of that method and those generic methods it calls.

Item 32: Create Composable APIs for External Components

You can use extension methods to increase the composability of method signatures that originate in other libraries. **Composable methods** are member methods of one of the input parameters, and they return a result that is composed from the transformation involved in the method. Composable methods are recombinant methods that can be reassembled in different orders to satisfy different requirements.

Unfortunately, many of the .NET Framework APIs are not constructed in this way. One of the best examples of this problem is the `TryParse` method, which returns a Boolean and returns the parsed value as its result. `TryParse` returns two different pieces of information: the success value and the parsed number. Because it must examine the success value before continuing, `TryParse` can't be composed with other methods.

Here's a routine that reads a comma-separated value (CSV) file of numeric data and returns a list of arrays, where each array contains the values in one line:

```
private static IEnumerable<int[]>
    ParseNumbersInCsv(TextReader src)
{
    List<int[]> values = new List<int[]>();
    string line = src.ReadLine();
    while (line != null)
    {
        List<int> lineOfValues = new List<int>();
        string[] fields = line.Split(',');
        foreach (var s in fields)
        {
            int dataValue = 0;
            bool success = int.TryParse(s, out dataValue);
            // Because success isn't checked, add 0 on failure
            lineOfValues.Add(dataValue);
        }
        values.Add(lineOfValues.ToArray());
        line = src.ReadLine();
    }
```

```
        return values;
}
```

It works, but this implementation is imperative, and it doesn't support composition very well. Furthermore, because it's an imperative implementation you lose some other benefits. Suppose the files were very large and contained marker values that would indicate when you could stop reading the file. To modify this method for new requirements, you'd need to add parameters, add logic to support changes, and increase the overall complexity of the method. Because you've chosen an imperative model, whenever any changes are needed you must change the description of how the method works.

What's needed is to modify the API signatures to provide composability of the actions, something that will allow callers to modify the behavior by using different expressions. Let's start this conversion in the inside with the conversion of a string to a nullable integer:

```
public static int? DefaultParse(this string input)
{
    int answer;
    return (int.TryParse(input, out answer))
        ? answer : default(int?);
}
```

You may also want to build a variation that returns a default value for any invalid inputs:

```
public static int DefaultParse(this string input,
    int defaultValue)
{
    int answer;
    return (int.TryParse(input, out answer))
        ? answer : defaultValue;
}
```

Next, you put `DefaultParse` to work on a single input line:

```
public static IEnumerable<int> ParseLine(this string line,
    int defaultValue)
{
    string[] fields = line.Split(',');
    foreach (string s in fields)
        yield return (s.DefaultParse(defaultValue));
}
```

You can also build a second `ParseLine` that returns an `IEnumerable<int?>`:

```
public static IEnumerable<int?> ParseLine(this string line)
{
    string[] fields = line.Split(',');
    foreach (string s in fields)
        yield return (s.DefaultParse());
}
```

You can also build an extension method that returns each line in succession:

```
public static IEnumerable<string> EatLines
    (this TextReader reader)
{
    string line = reader.ReadLine();
    while (null != line)
    {
        yield return line;
        line = reader.ReadLine();
    }
}
```

After those API signatures are converted, a single query generates the sequence of lines, each containing a sequence of values:

```
var values = from l in src.EatLines()
             select l.ParseLine(0);
```

Or, if you use nullable `int`s, as in the following, the first query returns an `IEnumerable<IEnumerable<int>>`, and the second returns an `IEnumerable<IEnumerable<int?>>`.

```
var values = from l in src.EatLines()
             select l.ParseLine();
```

These methods can be extended quickly for other purposes. Let's suppose that a string value indicates the end of the input. You can modify the query as follows to read only until the query detects the first invalid input:

```
var values = (from l in src.EatLines()
              select l.ParseLine()).TakeWhile(
              (lineOfValues) =>
              !lineOfValues.Contains(default(int?)));
```

All this is possible because we've used extension methods to modify the API signature into a composable form. You can use the same kind of composability throughout your code. Note that even though the method signatures have changed, the underlying semantics have not. That's an important consideration when you create extension methods. Be sure not to change the caller's assumption about the behavior of the objects involved in the extension method.

There are a number of problems with creating extension methods that change the semantics of an API. First, it changes the semantics of a method signature. Instance methods cannot be called using a null reference, because the .NET runtime will throw a null reference exception instead of calling your routine. You can't intercept that condition or take any corrective action. That matters even when you're adding an extension method for the first time. Extension methods are the lowest-priority match when the compiler performs its method resolution. Therefore, if someone later adds a specific method that replaces your extension method, existing code will throw exceptions in locations that previously worked.

The most common way to abuse this technique is to write extension methods designed to work with null objects:

```
// Bad idea. Don't change the semantics of a null this pointer
public static int StorageLength(this string target)
{
    if (target == null)
        return 0;
    else
        return target.Length;
}
```

Anyone using this method will be confused by its behavior. The .NET runtime checks for null object pointers and generates a null reference exception before any instance methods can be called. Extension methods specifically designed to work with null violate that principle and lead to code that will be hard to maintain or extend over time.

You should also avoid creating extension methods that have a high likelihood of failure. Unfortunately, this often occurs when you extend the .NET collection interfaces. Examine this method, which extends ICollection<T> by providing support for AddRange():

```
public static void AddRange<T>(this ICollection<T> coll,
    IEnumerable<T> range)
{
    foreach (T item in range)
        coll.Add(item);
}
```

It works fine—if the type that implements ICollection happens to be a type that supports Add. However, if you use an array to call that routine, the compiler throws an exception:

```
string[] sample = { "one", "two", "three", "four", "five", };
// Throws a NotSupportedException:
sample.AddRange(range);
```

Most types that implement ICollection<T> and support Add already have their own version of AddRange included. You've added no capabilities but have increased the likelihood that someone calling your new extension method will get frustrated by exceptions. It doesn't make sense to create extension methods that are likely to fail.

You can prompt similar user dissatisfaction when you create extension methods that have significantly worse performance than users expect. The following extension method, which reverses a collection based on the IList<T> interface, is a useful little extension.

```
// Good use: no impact on performance
public static IEnumerable<T> Reverse<T>(this IList<T> sequence)
{
    for (int index = sequence.Count-1; index >= 0; index--)
        yield return sequence[index];
}
```

The same extension method on IEnumerable<T> takes on totally different performance metrics:

```
// Bad idea. Creates copy, slower performance
public static IEnumerable<T> Reverse<T>
    (this IEnumerable<T> sequence)
{
    IList<T> temp = new List<T>(sequence);
    return temp.Reverse();
}
```

The IEnumerable<T> method consumes memory equal to the size of the original collection, and it takes longer to execute. Most users will assume (incorrectly) that the performance of Reverse is linear. That's true if you write the method against IList<T>. However, if you write it against a general interface that forces you to create a slower, more complicated algorithm, you mislead users, who will think that you've created a better alternative.

Worse, because a type that implements IList<T> or ICollection<T> also implements IEnumerable<T>, you may find yourself using an inferior algorithm because of the way the compiler resolves method calls. The compiler calls the IList<T> version of Reverse() only if the compile-time type implements IList<T>. Even if the runtime type implements IList<T>, if the compile-time type declares only IEnumerable<T> support, you're stuck with the inferior method.

The System.Linq.Enumerable class does contain a Reverse method, using IEnumerable<T> as a parameter. The .NET Framework team gets around these issues by examining the runtime type of the sequence. If the sequence implements IList<T> or ICollection<T>, the compiler uses the algorithm that is faster and less memory intensive.

Extension methods are a great way to massage the signature of an API so that it can be composed into complicated expressions. However, when you create extension methods to change the composability of an API, you need to ensure that the API doesn't hide errors nor change the performance metrics of an implied API.

Item 33: Avoid Modifying Bound Variables

The following small code snippet illustrates what can happen when you capture variables in a closure and then modify those variables.

```
int index = 0;
Func<IEnumerable<int>> sequence =
    () => Utilities.Generate(30, () => index++);

index = 20;
foreach (int n in sequence())
    Console.WriteLine(n);
Console.WriteLine("Done");
```

```
index = 100;
foreach (int n in sequence())
    Console.WriteLine(n);
```

This snippet prints the numbers from 20 through 50, followed by the numbers 100 through 130. That result may surprise you. During the rest of this item, I discuss the code the compiler produces that creates this result. The behavior makes sense, and you'll learn to use it to your advantage.

The C# compiler does quite a bit of work in translating your query expressions into executable code. Even though there are a great many new features in the C# language, all those new constructs compile down to IL that is compatible with the 2.0 version of the .NET CLR. Query syntax depends on new assemblies but not on any new CLR features. The C# compiler converts your queries and lambda expressions into static delegates, instance delegates, or closures. It chooses which one to create based on the code inside the lambda. Which path the compiler takes depends on the body of the lambda. That may sound like so much language trivia, but it has important implications for your code. Which construct the compiler uses does change some subtle behaviors of your code.

Not all lambda expressions create the same code. The simplest work for the compiler is to generate the delegate for this style of code:

```
int[] someNumbers = { 0, 1, 2, 3, 4, 5, 6, 7, 8, 9, 10 };
IEnumerable<int> answers = from n in someNumbers
                           select n * n;
```

The compiler implements the lambda expression `select n * n` using a static delegate definition. The compiler writes code as though you had written it:

```
private static int HiddenFunc(int n)
{
    return (n * n);
}
private static Func<int, int> HiddenDelegateDefinition;

// usage:
int[] someNumbers = new int[] { 0, 1, 2, 3, 4, 5,
    6, 7, 8, 9, 10 };
if (HiddenDelegateDefinition == null)
{
```

```
        HiddenDelegateDefinition  = new
            Func<int, int>(HiddenFunc);
}
IEnumerable<int> answers =
    someNumbers.Select<int, int>( HiddenDelegateDefinition);
```

The body of the lambda expression does not access any instance variables nor local variables. The lambda expression accesses only its parameters. Therefore, the C# compiler creates a static method for the target of the delegate. That's the simplest path the compiler can take. The compiler generates a private static method and corresponding delegate definition whenever the expression to be enclosed can be implemented in a private static method. That includes simple expressions such as the example here or a method that accesses any static class variables.

The sample lambda expression is only concise syntax for a method call wrapped in a delegate. Simple as can be. The next simplest version is a lambda expression that requires access to instance variables but not to any local variables:

```
public class ModFilter
{
    private readonly int modulus;

    public ModFilter(int mod)
    {
        modulus = mod;
    }

    public IEnumerable<int> FindValues(
        IEnumerable<int> sequence)
    {
        return from n in sequence
                where n % modulus == 0 // New expression
                select n * n; // previous example
    }
}
```

Here the compiler creates an instance method to wrap the delegate for the new expression. It's the same basic concept as before but now uses an instance method so that the delegate can read and modify the object's state. As with the static delegate sample, here the compiler converts the lambda expression to code that you are already familiar with. It's a combination of delegate definitions and method calls:

```csharp
// Equivalent pre-LINQ version
public class ModFilter
{
    private readonly int modulus;

    // New method
    private bool WhereClause(int n)
    {
        return ((n % this.modulus) == 0);
    }

    // original method
    private static int SelectClause(int n)
    {
        return (n * n);
    }

    // original delegate
    private static Func<int, int> SelectDelegate;

    public IEnumerable<int> FindValues(
        IEnumerable<int> sequence)
    {
        if (SelectDelegate == null)
        {
            SelectDelegate = new Func<int, int>(SelectClause);
        }
        return sequence.Where<int>(
            new Func<int, bool>(this.WhereClause)).
            Select<int, int>(SelectClause);
    }
    // Other methods elided.
}
```

Whenever the code inside your lambda expression accesses member variables for your object instances, the compiler generates an instance method representing the code in your lambda expression. There's nothing magical going on here. The compiler saves you some typing, but that's all you gain. It's just plain old method calls.

However, the compiler does quite a bit more work if any of the code in your lambda expressions accesses local variables or accesses parameters to methods. Here, you need a closure. The compiler generates a private nested class to implement the closure for your local variables. The local variable must be passed to the delegate that implements the body of the lambda expression. In addition, any changes to that local variable performed by the lambda expression must be visible in the outer scope. *The C# Programming Language,* Third Edition, by Anders Hejlsberg, Mads Torgersen, Scott Wiltamuth, and Peter Golde (Microsoft Corporation, 2009), §7.14.4.1, describes this behavior. Of course, you may have more than one variable in both the inner and outer scopes. You also may have more than one query expression.

Let's make a small change to the sample method so that it accesses a local variable:

```
public class ModFilter
{
    private readonly int modulus;

    public ModFilter(int mod)
    {
        modulus = mod;
    }

    public IEnumerable<int> FindValues(
        IEnumerable<int> sequence)
    {
        int numValues = 0;
        return from n in sequence
                where n % modulus == 0 // New expression
                // Select clause accesses local variable:
                select n * n / ++numValues;
    }
    // other methods elided
}
```

Notice that the `select` statement needs to access the local variable, `numValues`. To create the closure, the compiler creates a nested class to implement the behavior you need. Here's a version of the code that matches what the compiler generates:

```csharp
// Pre-LINQ version of a simple closure
public class ModFilter
{
    private sealed class Closure
    {
        public ModFilter outer;
        public int numValues;

        public int SelectClause(int n)
        {
            return ((n * n) / ++this.numValues);
        }
    }

    private readonly int modulus;

    public ModFilter(int mod)
    {
        this.modulus = mod;
    }

    private bool WhereClause(int n)
    {
        return ((n % this.modulus) == 0);
    }

    public IEnumerable<int> FindValues
        (IEnumerable<int> sequence)
    {
        Closure c = new Closure();
        c.outer = this;
        c.numValues = 0;
        return sequence.Where<int>
            (new Func<int, bool>(this.WhereClause))
            .Select<int, int>(
                new Func<int, int>(c.SelectClause));
    }
}
```

In this version, the compiler creates a nested class to contain all the variables that are accessed or modified inside the lambda expression. In fact, those local variables are completely replaced by fields of that nested class. Both the code inside the lambda expression and the code outside the lambda (but in the local method) access that same field. The logic inside the lambda expression has been compiled into a method in the inner class.

The compiler treats method parameters used in lambda expressions exactly the same way that it treats local variables: It copies those parameters into the nested class representing the closure.

Let's reexamine that initial example. Now it's clear why the behavior is strange. The variable `incrementBy` is modified after it has been placed in the closure but before the query has been executed. You modified the internal structure and then expected it to move back in time and use its previous version.

Modifying the bound variables between queries can introduce errors caused by the interaction of deferred execution and the way the compiler implements closures. Therefore, you should avoid modifying bound variables that have been captured by a closure.

Item 34: Define Local Functions on Anonymous Types

Many developers have a limited view of anonymous types. Sure, these types are simple to use, and they help you with short-lived variables that don't have a major role in the logic of your application. That's because anonymous types don't live beyond the scope of one method. Many developers believe that you can't develop with anonymous types because they can't be used in more than one method.

That's not true. You can write generic methods that use anonymous methods. To do so, you need to inject any specific elements or logic into your generic method.

As a simple example, this method returns a sequence of all objects in a collection that match a sought value:

```
static IEnumerable<T> FindValue<T>(IEnumerable<T> enumerable,
    T value)
{
    foreach (T element in enumerable)
    {
        if (element.Equals(value))
```

```
        {
            yield return element;
        }
    }
}
```

You can use it with anonymous types like this:

```
static void Main(string[] args)
{
    IDictionary<int, string> numberDescriptionDictionary =
        new Dictionary<int, string>()
    {
        {1,"one"},
        {2, "two"},
        {3, "three"},
        {4, "four"},
        {5, "five"},
        {6, "six"},
        {7, "seven"},
        {8, "eight"},
        {9, "nine"},
        {10, "ten"},
    };
    List<int> numbers = new List<int>()
        { 1, 2, 3, 4, 5, 6, 7, 8, 9, 10 };
    var r = from n in numbers
            where n % 2 == 0
            select new { Number = n,
                Description =
                    numberDescriptionDictionary[n] };
    r = from n in FindValue(r, new
        { Number = 2, Description = "two" })
        select n;
}
```

The `FindValue()` method knows nothing about the type; it's simply a generic type.

Of course, such simple functions can do only so much. If you want to write methods that use particular properties in your anonymous types, you need to create and use higher-order functions. A **higher-order function** is one that either takes a function as a parameter or returns a function. Higher-order functions that take functions as parameters are useful when you're working with anonymous types. You can use higher-order functions and generics to work with anonymous methods across multiple methods. Take a look at this query:

```
Random randomNumbers = new Random();
var sequence = (from x in Utilities.Generator(100,
                   () => randomNumbers.NextDouble() * 100)
            let y = randomNumbers.NextDouble() * 100
            select new { x, y }).TakeWhile(
            point => point.x < 75);
```

The query ends in the `TakeWhile()` method, which has this signature:

```
public static IEnumerable<TSource> TakeWhile<TSource>
    (this IEnumerable<TSource> source,
    Func<TSource, bool> predicate);
```

Notice that the signature of `TakeWhile` returns an `IEnumerable<TSource>` and has an `IEnumerable<TSource>` parameter. In our simple example, `TSource` stands in for an anonymous type representing an X,Y pair. `Func<TSource, bool>` represents a function that takes a `TSource` as its parameter.

This technique gives you the pathway to creating large libraries and code that works with anonymous types. The query expressions rely on generic methods that can work with anonymous types. The lambda expression, because it's declared in the same scope as the anonymous type, knows all about the anonymous type. The compiler creates the private nested class that passes around instances of the anonymous type to the other methods.

The following code creates an anonymous type and then processes that type in many generic methods:

```
var sequence = (from x in Funcs.Generator(100,
                   () => randomNumbers.NextDouble() * 100)
            let y = randomNumbers.NextDouble() * 100
            select new { x, y }).TakeWhile(
            point => point.x < 75);

var scaled = from p in sequence
            select new {x = p.x * 5, y = p.y * 5};
var translated = from p in scaled
                select new { x = p.x - 20, y = p.y - 20};
```

```
var distances = from p in translated
                let distance = Math.Sqrt(
                  p.x * p.x + p.y * p.y)
                where distance < 500.0
                select new { p.x, p.y, distance };
```

There isn't anything amazing going on here. It's simply the compiler generating delegates and calling them. Every one of those query methods results in a compiler-generated method that takes your anonymous type as a parameter. The compiler creates a delegate that is bound to each of those methods and uses that delegate as the parameter to the query method.

As this first sample continues to grow, it's easy to let algorithms get out of hand, create multiple copies of algorithms, and end up with a large investment in repeated code. So let's look at how to modify this code so that as more capabilities are needed, you can continue to keep the code simple, modular, and extensible.

One approach is to move some of the code around to create a simpler method and yet preserve the reusable blocks. You refactor some of the algorithms into generic methods that will take lambda expressions to perform the specific work needed by the algorithm.

Almost all of the following methods perform a simple mapping from one type to another. Some of them are an even simpler mapping to a different object of the same type.

```
// In another class define the Map function:
public static IEnumerable<TResult> Map<TSource, TResult>(this
IEnumerable<TSource> source,
    Func<TSource, TResult> mapFunc)
{
    foreach (TSource s in source)
        yield return mapFunc(s);
}


// Usage:
var sequence = (from x in Funcs.Generator(100,
                  () => randomNumbers.NextDouble() * 100)
                let y = randomNumbers.NextDouble() * 100
                select new { x, y }).TakeWhile(
                point => point.x < 75);
```

```
var scaled = sequence.Map(p => new {x = p.x * 5,
    y = p.y * 5});
var translated = scaled.Map(p => new { x = p.x - 20,
    y = p.y - 20});
var distances = translated.Map(p => new { p.x, p.y,
    distance = Math.Sqrt(p.x * p.x + p.y * p.y) });
var filtered = from location in distances
               where location.distance < 500.0
               select location;
```

The important technique here is to extract those algorithms that can be performed with minimal knowledge of the anonymous type. All anonymous types support IEquatable<T> and nothing else. So you can assume the existence only of the System.Object public members and the IEquatable<T> members. Nothing has changed here, but you should realize that anonymous types can be passed around to methods only if you also pass around the methods.

In the same vein, you may find that part of the original method will be used in other locations. In those cases, you should factor out those reusable nuggets of code and create a generic method that can be called from both locations.

That points to the need to be careful of taking these techniques too far. Anonymous types should not be used for types that are essential to many of your algorithms. The more often you find yourself using the same type and the more processing you're doing with that type, the more likely it is that you should convert that anonymous type into a concrete type. Any recommendation is arbitrary, but I suggest that if you're using the same anonymous type in more than three major algorithms, it would be better to convert it into a concrete type. If you find yourself creating longer and more complicated lambda expressions in order to continue to use an anonymous type, that should be a flag to create a concrete type.

Anonymous types are lightweight types that simply contain read and write properties that usually hold simple values. You will build many of your algorithms around these simple types. You can manipulate anonymous types using lambda expressions and generic methods. Just as you can create private nested classes to limit the scope of types, you can exploit the fact that the scope of an anonymous type is limited to a given method. Through generics and higher-order functions, you can create modular code using anonymous types.

Item 35: Never Overload Extension Methods

Earlier in this chapter (Items 28 and 29) I discuss three reasons to create extension methods for interfaces or types: adding default implementation to interfaces, creating behaviors on closed generic types, and creating composable interfaces. However, extension methods are not always a good way to express your designs. In all those cases, you made some enhancements to an existing type definition, but those enhancements did not fundamentally change the behavior of the type.

Item 22 explains that you can create extension methods to provide a default implementation for common actions that can be built using a minimal interface definition. You may be tempted to use the same technique to enhance class types. You may even be tempted to create multiple versions of class extensions that you can substitute by changing the namespaces you are using. Don't do that. Extension methods give you a great way to provide a default implementation for types that implement interfaces. However, there are much better alternatives to extending class types. Overusing and misapplying extension methods quickly create a morass of conflicting methods that will increase maintenance costs.

Let's begin with an example that misuses extension methods. Suppose you have a simple `Person` class that was generated by some other library:

```
public sealed class Person
{
    public string FirstName
    {
        get;
        set;
    }
    public string LastName
    {
        get;
        set;
    }
}
```

You might consider writing an extension method to create a report of people's names to the console:

```
// Bad start.
// extending classes using extension methods
```

```
namespace ConsoleExtensions
{
    public static class ConsoleReport
    {
        public static string Format(this Person target)
        {
            return string.Format("{0,20}, {1,15}",
                target.LastName, target.FirstName);
        }
    }
}
```

Generating the console report is simple:

```
static void Main(string[] args)
{
    List<Person> somePresidents =
        new List<Person>{
            new Person{
                FirstName = "George",
                LastName = "Washington" },
            new Person{
                FirstName = "Thomas",
                LastName = "Jefferson" },
            new Person{
                FirstName = "Abe",
                LastName = "Lincoln" }
        };

    foreach (Person p in somePresidents)
        Console.WriteLine(p.Format());
}
```

That might seem harmless enough. But requirements change. Later you find that you need to create a report in XML format. Someone might think of writing this method:

```
// Even worse.
// Ambiguous extension methods
// in different namespaces.
namespace XmlExtensions
{
```

```
public static class XmlReport
{
    public static string Format(this Person target)
    {
        return new XElement("Person",
            new XElement("LastName", target.LastName),
            new XElement("FirstName", target.FirstName)
            ).ToString();
    }
}
```

Switching a `using` statement in the source file changes the format of the report. This is a misuse of extension methods. It's a fragile way to extend a type. If a developer uses the wrong namespace, the program behavior changes. If she forgets to use any of the extension namespaces, the program won't compile. If she needs both of the namespaces in different methods, she must split the class definition into different files, based on which extension method she needs. Using both namespaces causes a compiler error on an ambiguous reference.

You clearly need a different way to implement this functionality. Extension methods force call dispatch based on the compile-time type of the object. Switching based on the namespace to determine which method is desired makes that strategy even more fragile.

This functionality isn't based on the type you're extending: Formatting a `Person` object for either XML or a console report is not part of the `Person` type, but instead more closely belongs to the outside environment that uses the `Person` object.

Extension methods should be used to enhance a type with functionality that naturally extends a type. You should create extension methods only to add functionality that would logically be part of that type. Items 28 and 29 explain two techniques for augmenting interfaces and closed types. If you look at the examples in those items, you can see that all those extension methods create methods that feel like part of the type from the standpoint of consumers of that type.

Contrast that with the examples here. Instead of being part of the `Person` type, the `Format` methods are methods that use the `Person` type. They don't belong in the `Person` type from the standpoint of code that uses that type.

The methods themselves are valid, but they should be regular static methods in a class that can be used with `Person` objects. In fact, if possible, they should be placed in the same class, with different method names:

```
public static class PersonReports
{
    public static string FormatAsText(Person target)
    {
        return string.Format("{0,20}, {1,15}",
            target.LastName, target.FirstName);
    }
    public static string FormatAsXML(Person target)
    {
        return new XElement("Person",
            new XElement("LastName", target.LastName),
            new XElement("FirstName", target.FirstName)
            ).ToString();
    }
}
```

This class contains both methods, as static methods, and the different names clearly reflect each method's purpose. You have provided both methods to your class's users without introducing ambiguity in the public interface, or the perceived public interface, for the class. Any developer can use either method, should he need those methods. You have not created any ambiguity by introducing the same method signature in different namespaces. That's critical, because very few developers would assume that changing the list of `using` statements would change the runtime behavior of a program. They may assume that it would cause compile-time errors but not runtime errors.

Of course, once you've changed the method names so that they do not collide, you could make these methods into extension methods again. There isn't much to gain from these methods, which don't seem to be extending the type but rather are using the type. However, because the names don't collide, you can put both methods in the same namespace and the same class. That avoids the pitfalls of the earlier example.

You should view the set of extension methods for a type as a single global set. Extension methods should never be overloaded on namespaces. If at any time you find yourself needing to create multiple extension methods having the same signature, stop. Instead, change the method signature, and consider creating plain old static methods. That practice avoids the ambiguity caused when the compiler selects the overload based on `using` statements.

5 | Working with LINQ

The driving force behind the language enhancements to C# 3.0 was LINQ. The new features and the implementation of those features were driven by the need to support deferred queries, translate queries into SQL to support LINQ to SQL, and add a unifying syntax to the various data stores. Chapter 4 shows you how the new language features can be used for many development idioms in addition to data query. This chapter concentrates on using those new features for querying data, regardless of source.

A goal of LINQ is that language elements perform the same work no matter what the data source is. However, even though the syntax works with all kinds of data sources, the query provider that connects your query to the actual data source is free to implement that behavior in a variety of ways. If you understand the various behaviors, it will make it easier to work with various data sources transparently. If you need to, you can even create your own data provider.

Item 36: Understand How Query Expressions Map to Method Calls

LINQ is built on two concepts: a query language, and a translation from that query language into a set of methods. The C# compiler converts query expressions written in that query language into method calls.

Every query expression has a mapping to a method call or calls. You should understand this mapping from two perspectives. From the perspective of a class user, you need to understand that your query expressions are nothing more than method calls. A `where` clause translates to a call to a method named `Where()`, with the proper set of parameters. As a class designer, you should evaluate the implementations of those methods provided by the base framework and determine whether you can create better implementations for your types. If not, you should simply defer to the base library versions. However, when you can create a better version, you must make sure that you fully understand the translation from query expressions into method calls. It's your responsibility to ensure that your method signatures correctly handle every translation case. For some of the query expressions, the correct path is rather obvious. However, it's a little more difficult to comprehend a couple of the more complicated expressions.

The full **query expression pattern** contains eleven methods. The following is the definition from *The C# Programming Language,* Third Edition, by Anders Hejlsberg, Mads Torgersen, Scott Wiltamuth, and Peter Golde (Microsoft Corporation, 2009), §7.15.3 (reprinted with permission from Microsoft Corporation):

```
delegate R Func<T1,R>(T1 arg1);
delegate R Func<T1,T2,R>(T1 arg1, T2 arg2);
class C
{
    public C<T> Cast<T>();
}

class C<T> : C
{
    public C<T> Where(Func<T,bool> predicate);
    public C<U> Select<U>(Func<T,U> selector);
    public C<V> SelectMany<U,V>(Func<T,C<U>> selector,
        Func<T,U,V> resultSelector);
    public C<V> Join<U,K,V>(C<U> inner,
        Func<T,K> outerKeySelector,
        Func<U,K> innerKeySelector,
        Func<T,U,V> resultSelector);
    public C<V> GroupJoin<U,K,V>(C<U> inner,
        Func<T,K> outerKeySelector,
        Func<U,K> innerKeySelector,
        Func<T,C<U>,V> resultSelector);
    public O<T> OrderBy<K>(Func<T,K> keySelector);
    public O<T> OrderByDescending<K>(Func<T,K> keySelector);
    public C<G<K,T>> GroupBy<K>(Func<T,K> keySelector);
    public C<G<K,E>> GroupBy<K,E>(Func<T,K> keySelector,
        Func<T,E> elementSelector);
}

class O<T> : C<T>
{
```

```
    public O<T> ThenBy<K>(Func<T,K> keySelector);
    public O<T> ThenByDescending<K>(Func<T,K> keySelector);
}


class G<K,T> : C<T>
{
    public K Key { get; }
}
```

The .NET base library provides two general-purpose reference implementations of this pattern. `System.Linq.Enumerable` provides extension methods on `IEnumerable<T>` that implement the query expression pattern. `System.Linq.Queryable` provides a similar set of extension methods on `IQueryable<T>` that supports a query provider's ability to translate queries into another format for execution. (For example, the LINQ to SQL implementation converts query expressions into SQL queries that are executed by the SQL database engine.) As a class user, you are probably using one of those two reference implementations for most of your queries.

Second, as a class author, you can create a data source that implements `IEnumerable<T>` or `IQueryable<T>` (or a closed generic type from `IEnumerable<T>` or `IQueryable<T>`), and in that case your type already implements the query expression pattern. Your type has that implementation because you're using the extension methods defined in the base library.

Before we go further, you should understand that the C# language does not enforce any execution semantics on the query expression pattern. You can create a method that matches the signature of one of the query methods and does anything internally. The compiler cannot verify that your `Where` method satisfies the expectations of the query expression pattern. All it can do is ensure that the syntactic contract is satisfied. This behavior isn't any different from that of any interface method. For example, you can create an interface method that does anything, whether or not it meets users' expectations.

Of course, this doesn't mean that you should ever consider such a plan. If you implement any of the query expression pattern methods, you should ensure that its behavior is consistent with the reference implementations, both syntactically and semantically. Except for performance differences, callers should not be able to determine whether your method is being used or the reference implementations are being used.

Translating from query expressions to method invocations is a complicated iterative process. The compiler repeatedly translates expressions to methods until all expressions have been translated. Furthermore, the compiler has a specified order in which it performs these translations, although I'm not explaining them in that order. The compiler order is easy for the compiler and is documented in the C# specification. I chose an order that makes it easier to explain to humans. For our purposes, I discuss some of the translations in smaller, simpler examples.

In the following query, let's examine the `where`, `select`, and `range` variables:

```
int[] numbers = { 0, 1, 2, 3, 4, 5, 6, 7, 8, 9 };
var smallNumbers = from n in numbers
                   where n < 5
                   select n;
```

The expression `from n in numbers` binds the range variable n to each value in `numbers`. The `where` clause defines a filter that will be translated into a `where` method. The expression `where n < 5` translates to the following:

```
numbers.Where((n) => n < 5);
```

`Where` is nothing more than a filter. The output of `Where` is a proper subset of the input sequence containing only those elements that satisfy the predicate. The input and output sequences must contain the same type, and a correct `Where` method must not modify the items in the input sequence. (User-defined predicates may modify items, but that's not the responsibility of the query expression pattern.)

That `where` method can be implemented either as an instance method accessible to `numbers` or as an extension method matching the type of `numbers`. In the example, `numbers` is an array of `int`. Therefore, n in the method call must be an integer.

`Where` is the simplest of the translations from query expression to method call. Before we go on, let's dig a little deeper into how this works and what that means for the translations. The compiler completes its translation from query expression to method call before any overload resolution or type binding. The compiler does not know whether there are any candidate methods when the compiler translates the query expression to a method call. It doesn't examine the type, and it doesn't look for any candidate extension methods. It simply translates the query expression into the method call. After all queries have been translated into method call syntax, the compiler performs the work of searching for candidate methods and then determining the best match.

Next, you can extend that simple example to include the `select` expression in the query. `Select` clauses are translated into `Select` methods. However, in certain special cases the `Select` method can be optimized away. The sample query is a **degenerate select**, selecting the `range` variable. Degenerate select queries can be optimized away, because the output sequence is not equal to the input sequence. The sample query has a `where` clause, which breaks that identity relationship between the input sequence and the output sequence. Therefore, the final method call version of the query is this:

```
var smallNumbers = numbers.Where(n => n < 5);
```

The `select` clause is removed because it is redundant. That's safe because the `select` operates on an immediate result from another query expression (in this example, `where`).

When the `select` does not operate on the immediate result of another expression, it cannot be optimized away. Consider this query:

```
var allNumbers = from n in numbers select n;
```

It will be translated into this method call:

```
var allNumbers = numbers.Select(n => n);
```

While we're on this subject, note that `select` is often used to transform or project one input element into a different element or into a different type. The following query modifies the value of the result:

```
int[] numbers = { 0, 1, 2, 3, 4, 5, 6, 7, 8, 9 };
var smallNumbers = from n in numbers
                   where n < 5
                   select n * n;
```

Or you could transform the input sequence into a different type as follows:

```
int [] numbers = {0,1,2,3,4,5,6,7,8,9};
var squares = from n in numbers
              select new { Number = n, Square = n * n};
```

The select clause maps to a Select method that matches the signature in the query expression pattern:

```
var squares = numbers.Select(n =>
    new { Number = n, Square = n * n});
```

Select transforms the input type into the output type. A proper select method must produce exactly one output element for each input element. Also, a proper implementation of Select must not modify the items in the input sequence.

That's the end of the simpler query expressions. Now we discuss some of the less obvious transformations.

Ordering relations map to the OrderBy and ThenBy methods, or Order-ByDescending and ThenByDescending. Consider this query:

```
var people = from e in employees
            where e.Age > 30
            orderby e.LastName, e.FirstName, e.Age
            select e;
```

It translates into this:

```
var people = employees.Where(e => e.Age > 30).
    OrderBy(e => e.LastName).
    ThenBy(e => e.FirstName).
    ThenBy(e => e.Age);
```

Notice in the definition of the query expression pattern that ThenBy operates on a sequence returned by OrderBy or ThenBy. Those sequences can contain markers that enable ThenBy to operate on the sorted subranges when the sort keys are equal.

This transformation is not the same if the orderby clauses are expressed as different clauses. The following query sorts the sequence entirely by LastName, then sorts the entire sequence again by FirstName, and then sorts again by Age:

```
// Not correct. Sorts the entire sequence three times.
var people = from e in employees
            where e.Age > 30
            orderby e.LastName
            orderby e.FirstName
            orderby e.Age
            select e;
```

As separate queries, you could specify that any of the orderby clauses use descending order:

```
var people = from e in employees
             where e.Age > 30
             orderby e.LastName descending
             thenby e.FirstName
             thenby e.Age
             select e;
```

The OrderBy method creates a different sequence type as its output so that thenby clauses can be more efficient and so that the types are correct for the overall query. OrderBy cannot operate on an unordered sequence, only on a sorted sequence (typed as O<T> in the sample). Subranges are already sorted and marked. If you create your own orderby and thenby methods for a type, you must adhere to this rule. You'll need to add an identifier to each sorted subrange so that any subsequent thenby clause can work properly. ThenBy methods need to be typed to take the output of an OrderBy or ThenBy method and then sort each subrange correctly.

Everything I've said about OrderBy and ThenBy also applies to OrderBy-Descending and ThenByDescending. In fact, if your type has a custom version of any of those methods, you should almost always implement all four of them.

The remaining expression translations involve multiple steps. Those queries involve either groupings or multiple from clauses that introduce continuations. Query expressions that contain continuations are translated into nested queries. Then those nested queries are translated into methods. Following is a simple query with a continuation:

```
var results = from e in employees
              group e by e.Department into d
              select new { Department = d.Key,
              Size = d.Count() };
```

Before any other translations are performed, the continuation is translated into a nested query:

```
var results = from d in
    from e in employees group e by e.Department
    select new { Department = d.Key, Size = d.Count()};
```

Once the nested query is created, the methods translate into the following:

```
var results = employees.GroupBy(e => e.Department).
    Select(d => new { Department = d.Key, Size = d.Count()});
```

The foregoing query shows a `GroupBy` that returns a single sequence. The other `GroupBy` method in the query expression pattern returns a sequence of groups in which each group contains a key and a list of values:

```
var results = from e in employees
              group e by e.Department into d
              select new { Department = d.Key,
              Employees = d.AsEnumerable()};
```

That query maps to the following method calls:

```
var results2 = employees.GroupBy(e => e.Department).
    Select(d => new { Department = d.Key,
        Employees = d.AsEnumerable()});
```

`GroupBy` methods produce a sequence of key/value list pairs; the keys are the group selectors, and the values are the sequence of items in the group. The query `select` clause may create new objects for the values in each group. However, the output should always be a sequence of key/value pairs in which the value contains some element created by each item in the input sequence that belongs to that particular group.

The final methods to understand are `SelectMany`, `Join`, and `GroupJoin`. These three methods are complicated, because they work with multiple input sequences. The methods that implement these translations perform the enumerations across multiple sequences and then flatten the resulting sequences into a single output sequence. `SelectMany` performs a cross join on the two source sequences. For example, consider this query:

```
int[] odds = {1,3,5,7};
int[] evens = {2,4,6,8};
var pairs = from oddNumber in odds
            from evenNumber  in evens
            select new {oddNumber, evenNumber,
            Sum=oddNumber+evenNumber};
```

It produces a sequence having 16 elements:

```
1,2, 3
1,4, 5
```

```
1,6,  7
1,8,  9
3,2,  5
3,4,  7
3,6,  9
3,8,  11
5,2,  7
5,4,  9
5,6,  11
5,8,  13
7,2,  9
7,4,  11
7,6,  13
7,8,  15
```

Query expressions that contain multiple `select` clauses are translated into a `SelectMany` method call. The sample query would be translated into the following `SelectMany` call:

```
int[] odds = { 1, 3, 5, 7 };
int[] evens = { 2, 4, 6, 8 };
var values = odds.SelectMany(oddNumber => evens,
    (oddNumber, evenNumber) =>
    new { oddNumber, evenNumber,
    Sum = oddNumber + evenNumber });
```

The first parameter to `SelectMany` is a function that maps each element in the first source sequence to the sequence of elements in the second source sequence. The second parameter (the output selector) creates the projections from the pairs of items in both sequences.

`SelectMany()` iterates the first sequence. For each value in the first sequence, it iterates the second sequence, producing the result value from the pair of input values. The output selected is called for each element in a flattened sequence of every combination of values from both sequences. One possible implementation of `SelectMany` is as follows:

```
static IEnumerable<TOutput> SelectMany<T1, T2, TOutput>(
    this IEnumerable<T1> src,
    Func<T1, IEnumerable<T2>> inputSelector,
    Func<T1, T2, TOutput> resultSelector)
{
    foreach (T1 first in src)
```

```
    {
        foreach (T2 second in inputSelector(first))
            yield return resultSelector(first, second);
    }
}
```

The first input sequence is iterated. Then the second input sequence is iterated using the current value on the input sequence. That's important, because the input selector on the second sequence may depend on the current value in the first sequence. Then, as each pair of elements is generated, the result selector is called on each pair.

If your query has more expressions and if SelectMany does not create the final result, then SelectMany creates a tuple that contains one item from each input sequence. Sequences of that tuple are the input sequence for later expressions. For example, consider this modified version of the original query:

```
int[] odds = { 1, 3, 5, 7 };
int[] evens = { 2, 4, 6, 8 };
var values = from oddNumber in odds
             from evenNumber in evens
             where oddNumber > evenNumber
             select new { oddNumber, evenNumber,
             Sum = oddNumber + evenNumber };
```

It produces this SelectMany method call:

```
odds.SelectMany(oddNumber => evens,
    (oddNumber, evenNumber) =>
    new {oddNumber, evenNumber});
```

The full query is then translated into this statement:

```
var values = odds.SelectMany(oddNumber => evens,
    (oddNumber, evenNumber) =>
    new { oddNumber, evenNumber }).
    Where(pair => pair.oddNumber > pair.evenNumber).
    Select(pair => new {
        pair.oddNumber,
        pair.evenNumber,
        Sum = pair.oddNumber + pair.evenNumber });
```

You can see another interesting property in the way `SelectMany` gets treated when the compiler translates multiple `from` clauses into `Select-Many` method calls. `SelectMany` composes well. More than two `from` clauses will produce more than one `SelectMany()` method call. The resulting pair from the first `SelectMany()` call will be fed into the second `SelectMany()`, which will produce a triple. The triple will contain all combinations of all three sequences. Consider this query:

```
var triples = from n in new int[] { 1, 2, 3 }
              from s in new string[] { "one", "two",
                  "three" }
              from r in new string[] { "I", "II", "III" }
              select new { Arabic = n, Word = s, Roman = r };
```

It will be translated into the following method calls:

```
var numbers = new int[] {1,2,3};
var words = new string[] {"one", "two", "three"};
var romanNumerals = new string[] { "I", "II", "III" };
var triples = numbers.SelectMany(n => words,
    (n, s) => new { n, s}).
    SelectMany(pair => romanNumerals,
    (pair,n) =>
        new { Arabic = pair.n, Word = pair.s, Roman = n });
```

As you can see, you can extend from three to any arbitrary number of input sequences by applying more `SelectMany()` calls. These later examples also demonstrate how `SelectMany` can introduce anonymous types into your queries. The sequence returned from `SelectMany()` is a sequence of some anonymous type.

Now let's look at the two other translations you need to understand: `Join` and `GroupJoin`. Both are applied on join expressions. `GroupJoin` is always used when the join expression contains an `into` clause. `Join` is used when the join expression does not contain an `into` clause.

A join without an `into` looks like this:

```
var numbers = new int[] { 0, 1, 2, 3, 4, 5, 6, 7, 8, 9 };
var labels = new string[] { "0", "1", "2", "3", "4", "5" };
var query = from num in numbers
            join label in labels on num.ToString() equals
                label
            select new { num, label };
```

It translates into the following:

```
var query = numbers.Join(labels, num => num.ToString(),
    label => label, (num, label) => new { num, label });
```

The `into` clause creates a list of subdivided results:

```
var groups = from p in projects
             join t in tasks on p equals t.Parent
                 into projTasks
             select new { Project = p, projTasks };
```

That translates into a `GroupJoin`:

```
var groups = projects.GroupJoin(tasks,
    p => p, t => t.Parent, (p, projTasks) =>
        new { Project = p, TaskList = projTasks });
```

The entire process of converting all expressions into method calls is complicated and often takes several steps.

The good news is that for the most part, you can happily go about your work secure in the knowledge that the compiler does the correct translation. And because your type implements `IEnumerable<T>`, users of your type are getting the correct behavior.

But you may have that nagging urge to create your own version of one or more of the methods that implement the query expression pattern. Maybe your collection type is always sorted on a certain key, and you can short-circuit the `OrderBy` method. Maybe your type exposes lists of lists, and this means that you may find that `GroupBy` and `GroupJoin` can be implemented more efficiently.

More ambitiously, maybe you intend to create your own provider and you'll implement the entire pattern. That being the case, you need to understand the behavior of each query method and know what should go into your implementation. Refer to the examples, and make sure you understand the expected behavior of each query method before you embark on creating your own implementations.

Many of the custom types you define model some kind of collection. The developers who use your types will expect to use your collections in the same way that they use every other collection type, with the built-in query syntax. As long as you support the `IEnumerable<T>` interface for any type that models a collection, you'll meet that expectation. However, your types may be able to improve on the default implementation by using the internal specifics in your type. When you choose to do that, ensure that your type matches the contract from the query pattern in all forms.

Item 37: Prefer Lazy Evaluation Queries

When you define a query, you don't actually get the data and populate a sequence. You are actually defining only the set of steps that you will execute when you choose to iterate that query. This means that each time you execute a query, you perform the entire recipe from first principles. That's usually the right behavior. Each new enumeration produces new results, in what is called **lazy evaluation.** However, often that's not what you want. When you grab a set of variables, you want to retrieve them once and retrieve them now, in what is called **eager evaluation.**

Every time you write a query that you plan to enumerate more than once, you need to consider which behavior you want. Do you want a snapshot of your data, or do you want to create a description of the code you will execute in order to create the sequence of values?

This concept is a major change in the way you are likely accustomed to working. You probably view code as something that is executed immediately. However, with LINQ queries, you're injecting code into a method. That code will be invoked at a later time. More than that, if the provider uses expression trees instead of delegates, those expression trees can be combined later by combining new expressions into the same expression tree.

Let's start with an example to explain the difference between lazy and eager evaluation. The following bit of code generates a sequence and then iterates that sequence three times, with a pause between iterations.

```
private static IEnumerable<TResult>
    Generate<TResult>(int number, Func<TResult> generator)
{
    for (int i = 0; i < number; i++)
        yield return generator();
}

private static void LazyEvaluation()
{
    Console.WriteLine("Start time for Test One: {0}",
        DateTime.Now);
    var sequence = Generate(10, () => DateTime.Now);
```

```
        Console.WriteLine("Waiting....\tPress Return");
        Console.ReadLine();

        Console.WriteLine("Iterating...");
        foreach (var value in sequence)
            Console.WriteLine(value);

        Console.WriteLine("Waiting....\tPress Return");
        Console.ReadLine();
        Console.WriteLine("Iterating...");
        foreach (var value in sequence)
            Console.WriteLine(value);
}
```

Here's one sample output:

```
Start time for Test One: 11/18/2007 6:43:23 PM
Waiting....    Press Return

Iterating...
11/18/2007 6:43:31 PM
11/18/2007 6:43:31 PM
11/18/2007 6:43:31 PM
11/18/2007 6:43:31 PM
11/18/2007 6:43:31 PM
11/18/2007 6:43:31 PM
11/18/2007 6:43:31 PM
11/18/2007 6:43:31 PM
11/18/2007 6:43:31 PM
11/18/2007 6:43:31 PM
Waiting....    Press Return

Iterating...
11/18/2007 6:43:42 PM
11/18/2007 6:43:42 PM
11/18/2007 6:43:42 PM
11/18/2007 6:43:42 PM
11/18/2007 6:43:42 PM
11/18/2007 6:43:42 PM
11/18/2007 6:43:42 PM
11/18/2007 6:43:42 PM
11/18/2007 6:43:42 PM
11/18/2007 6:43:42 PM
```

In this example of lazy evaluation, notice that the sequence is generated each time it is iterated, as evidenced by the different time stamps. The sequence variable does not hold the elements created. Rather, it holds the expression tree that can create the sequence. You should run this code yourself, stepping into each query to see exactly when the expressions are evaluated. It's the most instructive way to learn how LINQ queries are evaluated.

You can use this capability to compose queries from existing queries. Instead of retrieving the results from the first query and processing them as a separate step, you can compose queries in different steps and then execute the composed query only once. For example, suppose I modify the query to return times in universal format:

```
var sequence1 = Generate(10, () => DateTime.Now);
var sequence2 = from value in sequence1
                select value.ToUniversalTime();
```

Sequence 1 and sequence 2 share functional composition, not data. Sequence 2 is not built by enumerating the values in sequence 1 and modifying each value. Rather, it is created by executing the code that produces sequence 1, followed by the code that produces sequence 2. If you iterate the two sequences at different times, you'll see unrelated sequences. Sequence 2 will not contain the converted values from sequence 1. Instead, it will contain totally new values. It doesn't generate a sequence of dates and then convert the entire sequence into universal time. Instead, each line of code generates one set of values using universal time.

Query expressions may operate on infinite sequences. They can do so because they are lazy. If written correctly, they examine the first portion of the sequence and then terminate when an answer is found. On the other hand, some query expressions must retrieve the entire sequence before they can proceed to create their answer. Understanding when these bottlenecks might occur will help you create queries that are natural without incurring performance penalties. In addition, this understanding will help you avoid those times when the full sequence is required and will create a bottleneck.

Consider this small program:

```
static void Main(string[] args)
{
    var answers = from number in AllNumbers()
                  select number;
```

```
        var smallNumbers = answers.Take(10);
        foreach (var num in smallNumbers)
                Console.WriteLine(num);
}

static IEnumerable<int> AllNumbers()
{
    int number = 0;
    while (number < int.MaxValue)
    {
        yield return number++;
    }
}
```

This sample illustrates what I mean about a method that does not need the full sequence. The output from this method is the sequence of numbers 0,1,2,3,4,5,6,7,8,9. That's the case even though the AllNumbers() method could generate an infinite sequence. (Yes, it eventually has an overflow, but you'll lose patience long before then.)

The reason this works as quickly as it does is that the entire sequence is not needed. The Take() method returns the first *N* objects from the sequence, so nothing else matters.

However, if you rewrite this query as follows, your program will run forever:

```
class Program
{
    static void Main(string[] args)
    {
        var answers = from number in AllNumbers()
                      where number < 10
                      select number;

        foreach(var num in answers)
            Console.WriteLine(num);
    }
}
```

It runs forever because the query must examine every single number to determine which methods match. This version of the same logic requires the entire sequence.

There are a number of query operators that must have the entire sequence in order to operate correctly. `Where` uses the entire sequence. `Orderby` needs the entire sequence to be present. `Max` and `Min` need the entire sequence. There's no way to perform these operations without examining every element in the sequence. When you need these capabilities, you'll use these methods.

You need to think about the consequences of using methods that require access to the entire sequence. As you've seen, you need to avoid any methods that require the entire sequence if the sequence might be infinite. Second, even if the sequence is not infinite, any query methods that filter the sequence should be front-loaded in the query. If the first steps in your query remove some of the elements from the collection, that will have a positive effect on the performance of the rest of the query.

For example, the following two queries produce the same result. However, the second query may execute faster. Sophisticated providers will optimize the query, and both queries will have the same performance metrics. However, in the LINQ to Objects implementation (provided by `System.Linq.Enumerable`), all products are read and sorted. Then the products sequence is filtered.

```
// Order before filter.
var sortedProductsSlow =
    from p in products
    orderby p.UnitsInStock descending
    where p.UnitsInStock > 100
    select p;

// Filter before order.
var sortedProductsFast =
    from p in products
    where p.UnitsInStock > 100
    orderby p.UnitsInStock descending
    select p;
```

Notice that the first query sorts the entire series and then throws away any products whose total in stock is less than 100. The second query filters the sequence first, resulting in a sort on what may be a much smaller sequence. At times, knowing whether the full sequence is needed for a method is the difference between an algorithm that never finishes and one that finishes quickly. You need to understand which methods require the full sequence, and try to execute those last in your query expression.

So far, I've given you quite a few reasons to use lazy evaluation in your queries. In most cases, that's the best approach. At other times, though, you do want a snapshot of the values taken at a point in time. There are two methods you can use to generate the sequence immediately and store the results in a container: `ToList()` and `ToArray()`. Both methods perform the query and store the results in a `List<T>` or an `Array`, respectively.

These methods are useful for a couple of purposes. By forcing the query to execute immediately, these methods capture a snapshot of the data right now. You force the execution to happen immediately, rather than later when you decide to enumerate the sequence. Also, you can use `ToList()` or `ToArray()` to generate a snapshot of query results that is not likely to change before you need it again. You can cache the results and use the saved version later.

In almost all cases, lazy evaluation saves work and is more versatile than eager evaluation. In the rare cases when you do need eager evaluation, you can force it by running the query and storing the sequence results using `ToList()` or `ToArray()`. But unless there is a clear need to use eager evaluation, it's better to use lazy evaluation.

Item 38: Prefer Lambda Expressions to Methods

This recommendation may appear counterintuitive. Coding with lambda expressions can lead to repeated code in the body of lambdas. You often find yourself repeating small bits of logic. The following code snippet has the same logic repeated several times:

```
var allEmployees = FindAllEmployees();

// Find the first employees:
var earlyFolks = from e in allEmployees
                where e.Classification ==
                    EmployeeType.Salary
                where e.YearsOfService > 20
                where e.MonthlySalary < 4000
                select e;

// find the newest people:
var newest = from e in allEmployees
            where e.Classification == EmployeeType.Salary
            where e.YearsOfService < 2
```

```
    where e.MonthlySalary < 4000
    select e;
```

You could replace the multiple calls to `Where` with a single `Where` clause that has both conditions. There isn't any noticeable difference between the two representations. Because queries compose (see Item 17, Chapter 3) and because simple `where` predicates will likely be inlined, the performance will be the same.

You may be tempted to factor repeated lambda expressions into methods that can be reused. You'd end up with code that looks like this:

```
// factor out method:
private static bool LowPaidSalaried(Employee e)
{
    return e.MonthlySalary < 4000 &&
        e.Classification == EmployeeType.Salary;
}


// elsewhere
var allEmployees = FindAllEmployees();
var earlyFolks = from e in allEmployees
                 where LowPaidSalaried(e) &&
                 e.YearsOfService > 20
                 select e;


// find the newest people:
var newest = from e in allEmployees
             where LowPaidSalaried(e) && e.YearsOfService < 2
             select e;
```

It's a small example, so there's not much change here. But already it feels better. Now if the employee classifications change or if the low threshold changes, you're changing the logic in only one location.

Unfortunately, this method of refactoring your code makes it less reusable. The first version, as written, is actually more reusable than the second version. That's because of the way lambda expressions are evaluated, parsed, and eventually executed. If you're like most developers, you see code that has been copied as pure evil and something to be eradicated at all costs. The version with a single method is simpler. It has only one copy of the code to be modified later if needs change. It's just plain good software engineering.

Unfortunately, it's also wrong. Some code will convert the lambda expressions into a delegate to execute the code in your query expression. Other classes will create an expression tree from the lambda expression, parse that expression, and execute it in another environment. LINQ to Objects does the former, and LINQ to SQL does the latter.

LINQ to Objects performs queries on local data stores, usually stored in a generic collection. The implementation creates an anonymous delegate that contains the logic in the lambda expression and cxecutes that code. The LINQ to Objects extension methods use `IEnumerable<T>` as the input sequence.

LINQ to SQL, on the other hand, uses the expression tree contained in the query. That expression tree contains the logical representation of your query. LINQ to SQL parses the tree and uses the expression tree to create the proper T-SQL query, which can be executed directly against the database. Then, the query string (as T-SQL) is sent to the database engine and is executed there.

This processing requires that the LINQ to SQL engine parse the expression tree and replace every logical operation with equivalent SQL. All method calls are replaced with an `Expression.MethodCall` node. The LINQ to SQL engine cannot translate any arbitrary method call into a SQL expression. Instead, it throws an exception. The LINQ to SQL engine fails rather than try to execute multiple queries, bring multiple data to the client side of the application boundary, and then process it there.

If you are building any kind of reusable library for which the data source could be anything, you must anticipate this situation. You must structure the code so that it will work correctly with any data source. This means that you need to keep lambda expressions separate, and as inline code, for your library to function correctly.

Of course, this doesn't mean that you should be copying code all over the library. It means only that you need to create different building blocks for your applications when query expressions and lambdas are involved. From our simple example, you can create larger reusable blocks this way:

```
private static IQueryable<Employee> LowPaidSalariedFilter
    (this IQueryable<Employee> sequence)
{
    return from s in sequence
        where s.Classification == EmployeeType.Salary &&
```

```
                    s.MonthlySalary < 4000
                    select s;
}


// elsewhere:
var allEmployees = FindAllEmployees();

// Find the first employees:
var salaried = allEmployees.LowPaidSalariedFilter();

var earlyFolks = salaried.Where(e => e.YearsOfService > 20);

// find the newest people:
var newest = salaried.Where(e => e.YearsOfService < 2);
```

Of course, not every query is that simple to update. You need to move up the call chain a bit to find the reusable list-processing logic so that you need to express the same lambda expression only once. Recall from Item 17 (Chapter 3) that enumerator methods do not execute until you begin to traverse the items in the collection. Remembering that fact, you can create small methods that construct each portion of your query and contain commonly used lambda expressions. Each of those methods must take as input the sequence, and must return the sequence using the `yield return` keyword.

Following that same pattern, you can compose `IQueryable` enumerators by building new expression trees that can be executed remotely. Here, the expression tree for finding sets of employees can be composed as a query before it is executed. The `IQueryProvider` object (such as the LINQ to SQL data source) processes the full query rather than pull out parts that must be executed locally.

You then put together those small methods to build the larger queries you will use in your application. The advantage of this technique is that you avoid the code-copying issues that we all dislike in the first sample in this item. You also have structured the code so that it creates an expression tree for execution when you have composed your completed query and begin to execute it.

One of the most efficient ways to reuse lambda expressions in complicated queries is to create extension methods for those queries on closed generic types. You can see that the method for finding the lower-paid salaried employees is such a method. It takes a sequence of employees and returns a filtered sequence of employees. In production code, you should create a second overload that uses `IEnumerable<Employee>` as the parameter type. In that way, you support both the LINQ to SQL style implementations and the LINQ to Objects implementation.

You can build exactly the queries you need by composing the smaller building blocks from those methods that take lambda expressions and are sequence methods. You gain the advantage of creating code that works with `IEnumerable<T>` and `IQueryable<T>`. Furthermore, you haven't broken the possible evaluation of the queryable expression trees.

Item 39: Avoid Throwing Exceptions in Functions and Actions

When you create code that executes over a sequence of values and the code throws an exception somewhere in that sequence processing, you'll have problems recovering state. You don't know how many elements were processed, if any. You don't know what needs to be rolled back. You can't restore the program state at all.

Consider this snippet of code, which gives everyone a 5 percent raise:

```
var allEmployees = FindAllEmployees();
allEmployees.ForEach(e => e.MonthlySalary *= 1.05M);
```

One day, this routine runs and throws an exception. Chances are that the exception was not thrown on the first or last employee. Some employees got raises, but others didn't. It will be very difficult for your program to recover the previous state. Can you return the data to a consistent state? Once you lose knowledge of program state, you can't regain it without human examination of all the data.

This problem occurs because the code snippet modifies elements of a sequence in place. It doesn't follow the strong exception guarantee. In the face of errors, you can't know what happened and what didn't.

You fix this situation by guaranteeing that whenever the method does not complete, the observable program state does not change. You can implement this in various ways, each with its own benefits and risks.

Before talking about the risks, let's examine the reason for concern in a bit more detail. Not every method exhibits this problem. Many methods examine a sequence but do not modify it. The following method examines everyone's salary and returns the result:

```
decimal total = allEmployees.Aggregate(0M,
    (sum, emp) => sum + emp.MonthlySalary);
```

You don't need to carefully modify methods like this that do not modify any data in the sequence. In many applications, you'll find that most of your methods do not modify the sequence. Let's return again to our first method, giving every employee a 5 percent raise. What actions can you take to rework this method to ensure that the strong exception guarantee is satisfied?

The first and easiest approach is to rework the action so that you can ensure that the action method, expressed earlier in the lambda expression, never throws an exception. In many cases, it is possible to test any failure conditions before modifying each element in the sequence (see Item 25, Chapter 3). You need to define the functions and predicates so that the method's contract can be satisfied in all cases, even error conditions. This strategy works if doing nothing is the right behavior for elements that caused the exception. In the example of granting raises, imagine that all exceptions are caused by employee records that are stale and include people who no longer work for the company but are still in persistent storage. That would make it correct behavior to skip them. This modification would work:

```
allEmployees.FindAll(
    e => e.Classification == EmployeeType.Active).
    ForEach(e => e.MonthlySalary *= 1.05M);
```

Fixing the problem in this way is the simplest path to avoiding inconsistencies in your algorithms. Whenever you can write your action methods to ensure that no exceptions leave a lambda expression or action method, that's the most efficient technique to use.

However, sometimes you may not be able to guarantee that those expressions never throw an exception. Now you must take more-expensive defensive measures. You need to rework the algorithm to take into account the possibility of an exception. That means doing all the work on a copy and then replacing the original sequence with the copy only if the operation completes successfully. If you felt you could not avoid the possibility of an exception, you could rewrite our earlier algorithm:

```
var updates = (from e in allEmployees
            select new Employee
            {
                EmployeeID = e.EmployeeID,
```

```
                Classification = e.Classification,
                YearsOfService = e.YearsOfService,
                MonthlySalary = e.MonthlySalary *= 1.05M
            }).ToList();
allEmployees = updates;
```

You can see the cost of those changes here. First, there's quite a bit more code than in the earlier versions. That's more work—more code to maintain and more to understand. But you've also changed the performance metrics for the application. This newer version creates a second copy of all the employee records and then swaps the reference to the new list of employees with the reference to the old list. If the employee list is large, that could cause a big performance bottleneck. You have created duplicates of all employees in the list before swapping references. The contract for the action now might throw an exception when the `employee` object is invalid. The code outside the query now handles those conditions.

And there's still another issue with this particular fix: Whether or not it makes sense depends on how it's used. This new version limits your ability to compose operations using multiple functions. This code snippet caches the full list. This means that its modifications aren't composed along with other transformations in a single enumeration of the list. Each transformation becomes an imperative operation. In practice, you can work around this issue by creating one query statement that performs all the transformations. You cache the list and swap the entire sequence as one final step for all the transformations. Using that technique, you preserve the composability and still provide the strong exception guarantee.

In practice that means writing query expressions to return a new sequence rather than modifying each element of a sequence in place. Each composed query should be able to swap the list unless any exceptions are generated during the processing of any of the steps in the sequence.

Composing queries changes the way you write exception-safe code. If your actions or functions throw an exception, you may have no way to ensure that the data is not in an inconsistent state. You don't know how many elements were processed. You don't know what actions must be taken to restore the original state. However, returning new elements (rather than modifying the elements in place) gives you a better chance of ensuring that operations either complete or don't modify any program state.

This is the same advice for all mutable methods when exceptions may be thrown. It also applies in multithreaded environments. The problem can be harder to spot when you use lambda expressions and the code inside them may throw the exception. With the final operation, you should swap the entire sequence after you are sure that none of the operations has generated an exception.

Item 40: Distinguish Early from Deferred Execution

Declarative code is expository: It defines what gets done. **Imperative code** details step-by-step instructions that explain how something gets done. Both are valid and can be used to create working programs. However, mixing the two causes unpredictable behavior in your application.

All the imperative code you make today will calculate any needed parameters and then call the method. This line of code describes an imperative set of steps to create the answer:

```
object answer = DoStuff(Method1(),
    Method2(),
    Method3());
```

At runtime, this line of code does the following.

1. It calls `Method1` to generate the first parameter to `DoStuff()`.
2. It calls `Method2` to generate the second parameter to `DoStuff()`.
3. It calls `Method3` to generate the third parameter to `DoStuff()`.
4. It calls `DoStuff` with the three calculated parameters.

That should be a familiar style of code for you. All parameters are calculated, and the data is sent to any method. The algorithms you write are a descriptive set of steps that must be followed to produce the results.

Deferred execution, in which you use lambdas and query expressions, completely changes this process and may pull the rug out from under you. The following line of code seems to do the same thing as the foregoing example, but you'll soon see that there are important differences:

```
object answer = DoStuff(() => Method1(),
    () => Method2(),
    () => Method3());
```

At runtime, this line of code does the following.

1. It calls `DoStuff()`, passing the lambda expressions that could call `Method1`, `Method2`, and `Method3`.

2. Inside `DoStuff`, if and only if the result of `Method1` is needed, `Method1` is called.
3. Inside `DoStuff`, if and only if the result of `Method2` is needed, `Method2` is called.
4. Inside `DoStuff`, if and only if the result of `Method3` is needed, `Method3` is called.
5. `Method1`, `Method2`, and `Method3` may be called in any order, as many times (including zero) as needed.

None of those methods will be called unless the results are needed. This difference is significant, and you will cause yourself major problems if you mix the two idioms.

From the outside, any method can be replaced by its return value, and vice versa, as long as that method does not produce any side effects. In our example, the `DoStuff()` method does not see any difference between the two strategies. The same value is returned, and either strategy is correct. If the method always returns the same value for the same inputs, then the method return value can always be replaced by a call to the method, and vice versa.

However, looking at the program as a whole, there may be significant differences between the two lines of code. The imperative model always calls all three methods. Any side effects from any of those methods always occur exactly once. In contrast, the declarative model may or may not execute all or any of the methods. The declarative version may execute any of the methods more than once. This is the difference between (1) calling a method and passing the results to a method and (2) passing a delegate to the method and letting the method call the delegate. You may get different results from different runs of the application, depending on what actions take place in these methods.

The addition of lambda expressions, type inference, and enumerators makes it much easier to use functional programming concepts in your classes. You can build higher-order functions that take functions as parameters or that return functions to their callers. In one way, this is not a big change: A true function and its return value are always interchangeable. In practice, a function may have side effects, and this means that different rules apply.

If data and methods are interchangeable, which should you choose? And, more importantly, when should you choose which? The most important difference is that data must be preevaluated, whereas a method can be lazy-evaluated. When you must evaluate data early, you must preevaluate the method and use the result as the data, rather than take a functional approach and substitute the method.

The most important criterion for deciding which to use is the possibility of side effects, both in the body of the function and in the mutability of its return value. Item 37 (earlier in this chapter) shows a query whose results are based on the current time. Its return value changes depending on whether you execute it and cache the results or you use the query as a function parameter. If the function itself produces side effects, the behavior of the program depends on when you execute the function.

There are techniques you can use to minimize the contrast between early and late evaluation. Pure immutable types cannot be changed, and they don't change other program states; therefore, they are not subject to side effects. In the brief example earlier, if `Method1`, `Method2`, and `Method3` are members of an immutable type, then the observable behavior of the early and the late evaluation statements should be exactly the same.

My example does not take any parameters, but if any of those late evaluation methods took parameters, those parameters would need to be immutable to ensure that the early and late binding results were the same.

Therefore, the most important point in deciding between early and late evaluation is the semantics that you want to achieve. If (and only if) the objects and methods are immutable, then the correctness of the program is the same when you replace a value with the function that calculates it, and vice versa. ("Immutable methods" in this case means that the methods cannot modify any global state, such as performing I/O operations, updating global variables, or communicating with other processes.) If the objects and methods are not immutable, you risk changing the program's behavior by changing from early to late evaluation and vice versa. The rest of this item assumes that the observable behavior won't change between early and late evaluation. We look at other reasons to favor one or the other strategy.

One decision point is the size of the input and output space versus the cost of computing the output. For example, programs would still work if `Math.PI` calculated pi when called. The value and the computation are interchangeable from the outside. However, programs would be slower because calculating pi takes time. On the other hand, a method `CalculatePrimeFactors(int)` could be replaced with a lookup table containing all factors of all integers. In that case, the cost of the data table in memory would likely be much greater than the cost in time of calculating the values when needed.

Your real-world problems probably fall somewhere between those two extremes. The right solution won't be as obvious, nor will it be as clear-cut. In addition to analyzing the computational cost versus the storage cost, you need to consider how you will use the results of any given method. You will find that in some situations, early evaluation of certain queries will make sense. In other cases, you'll use interim results only infrequently. If you ensure that the code does not produce side effects and that either early or deferred evaluation produces the correct answer, then you can make the decision based on the measured performance metrics of both solutions. You can try both ways, measure the difference, and use the best result.

Finally, in some cases, you may find that a mixture of the two strategies will work the best. You may find that caching sometimes provides the most efficiency. In those cases, you can create a delegate that returns the cached value:

```
MyType cache = Method1();
object answer = DoStuff(() => cache,
    () => Method2(),
    () => Method3());
```

The final decision point is whether the method can execute on a remote data store. This factor has quite a bearing on how LINQ to SQL processes queries. Every LINQ to SQL query starts as a deferred query: The methods, and not the data, are used as parameters. Some of the methods may involve work that can be done inside the database engine, and some of the work represents local methods that must be processed before the partially processed query is submitted to the database engine. LINQ to SQL parses the expression tree. Before submitting the query to the database engine, it replaces any local method calls with the result from those method calls. It can do this processing only if a method call does not rely on any individual items in the input sequence being processed (see Items 37 and 38, both in this chapter).

Once LINQ to SQL has replaced any local method calls with the equivalent return values, it translates the query from expressions into SQL statements, which are sent to the database engine and executed there. The result is that by creating a query as a set of expressions, or code, the LINQ to SQL libraries can replace those methods with equivalent SQL. That provides improved performance and lower bandwidth usage. It also means that you as a C# developer can spend less time learning T-SQL. Other providers can do the same.

However, all this work is possible only because you can treat data as code, and vice versa, under the right circumstances. With LINQ to SQL, local methods can be replaced with the return values when the parameters to the method are constants that do not rely on the input sequence. Also, there is quite a bit of functionality in the LINQ to SQL libraries that translates expression trees to a logical structure that can then be translated into T-SQL.

As you create algorithms in C# now, you can determine whether using the data as a parameter or the function as a parameter causes any difference in behavior. Once you've determined that either would be correct, you must determine which would be the better strategy. When the input space is smaller, passing data might be better. However, in other cases, when the input or output space may be very large and you don't necessarily use the entire input data space, you may find that it's much wiser to use the algorithm itself as a parameter. If you're not sure, lean toward using the algorithm as a parameter, because the developer who implements the function can create that function to eagerly evaluate the output space and work with those data values instead.

Item 41: Avoid Capturing Expensive Resources

Closures create objects that contain bound variables. The length of the lives of those bound variables may surprise you, and not always in a good way. As developers we've grown accustomed to looking at the lifetimes of local variables in a very simple way: Variables come into scope when we declare them, and they are out of scope when the corresponding block closes. Local variables are eligible for garbage collection when they go out of scope. We use these assumptions to manage resource usage and object lifetimes.

Closures and captured variables change those rules. When you capture a variable in a closure, the object referenced by that variable does not go out of scope until the last delegate referencing that captured variable goes out of scope. Under some circumstances it may last even longer. After closures and captured variables escape one method, they can be accessed by closures and delegates in client code. Those delegates and closures can be accessed by other code, and so on. Eventually the code accessing your delegate becomes an open-ended set of methods with no idea when your closure and delegates are no longer reachable. The implication is that you really don't know when local variables go out of scope if you return something that is represented by a delegate using a captured variable.

The good news is that often you don't need to be concerned about this behavior. Local variables that are managed types and don't hold on to expensive resources are garbage-collected at a later point, just as regular variables are. If the only thing used by local variables is memory, there's no concern at all.

But some variables hold on to expensive resources. They represent types that implement IDisposable and need to be explicitly cleaned up. You may prematurely clean up those resources before you've actually enumerated the collection. You may find that files or connections aren't being closed quickly enough, and you're not able to access files because they are still open.

Item 33 (Chapter 4) shows you how the C# compiler produces delegates and how variables are captured inside a closure. In this item, we look at how to recognize when you have captured variables that contain other resources. We examine how to manage those resources and how to avoid pitfalls that can occur when captured variables live longer than you'd like.

Consider this construct:

```
int counter = 0;
IEnumerable<int> numbers =
    Extensions.Generate(30, () => counter++);
```

It generates code that looks something like this:

```
private class Closure
{
    public int generatedCounter;
    public int generatorFunc()
    {
        return generatedCounter ++;
    }
}

// usage
Closure c = new Closure();
c.generatedCounter = 0;
```

```
IEnumerable<int> sequence = Extensions.Generate(30, new
Func<int>(c.generatorFunc));
```

This can get very interesting. The hidden nested class members have been bound to delegates used by `Extensions.Generate`. That can affect the lifetime of the hidden object and therefore can affect when any of the members are eligible for garbage collection. Look at this example:

```
public IEnumerable<int> MakeSequence()
{
    int counter = 0;
    IEnumerable<int> numbers = Extensions.Generate(30,
        () => counter++);
    return numbers;
}
```

In this code, the returned object uses the delegate that is bound by the closure. Because the return value needs the delegate, the delegate's lifetime extends beyond the life of the method. The lifetime of the object representing the bound variables is extended. The object is reachable because the delegate instance is reachable, and the delegate is still reachable because it's part of the returned object. And all members of the object are reachable because the object is reachable.

The C# compiler generates code that looks like this:

```
public static IEnumerable<int> MakeSequence()
{
    Closure c = new Closure();
    c.generatedCounter = 0;
    IEnumerable<int> sequence = Extensions.Generate(30,
        new Func<int>(c.generatorFunc));
    return sequence;
}
```

Notice that this sequence contains a delegate reference to a method bound to c, the local object instantiating the closure. The local variable c lives beyond the end of the method.

Often, this situation does not cause much concern. But there are two cases in which it can cause confusion. The first involves `IDisposable`. Consider the following code. It reads numbers from a CSV input stream and returns the values as a sequence of sequences of numbers. Each inner sequence contains the numbers on that line. It uses some of the extension methods shown in Item 28 (Chapter 4).

```
public static IEnumerable<string> ReadLines(
    this TextReader reader)
{
    string txt = reader.ReadLine();
    while (txt != null)
    {
        yield return txt;
        txt = reader.ReadLine();
    }
}


public static int DefaultParse(this string input,
    int defaultValue)
{
    int answer;
    return (int.TryParse(input, out answer))
        ? answer : defaultValue;
}


public static IEnumerable<IEnumerable<int>>
    ReadNumbersFromStream(TextReader t)
{
    var allLines = from line in t.ReadLines()
                select line.Split(',');
    var matrixOfValues = from line in allLines
                    select from item in line
                            select item.DefaultParse(0);
    return matrixOfValues;
}
```

You would use it like this:

```
TextReader t = new StreamReader("TestFile.txt");
var rowsOfNumbers = ReadNumbersFromStream(t);
```

Remember that queries generate the next value only when that value is accessed. The `ReadNumbersFromStream()` method does not put all the data in memory, but rather it loads values from the stream as needed. The two statements that follow don't actually read the file. It's only later when you start enumerating the values in `rowsOfNumbers` that you open the file and begin reading the values.

Later, in a code review, someone—say, that pedantic Alexander—points out that you never explicitly close the test file. Maybe he found it because there was a resource leak, or he found some error because the file was open when he tried to read it again. You make a change to fix that problem. Unfortunately, it doesn't address the root concerns.

```
IEnumerable<IEnumerable<int>> rowOfNumbers;
using (TextReader t = new StreamReader("TestFile.txt"))
    rowOfNumbers = ReadNumbersFromStream(t);
```

You happily start your tests, expecting success, but your program throws an exception a couple of lines later:

```
IEnumerable<IEnumerable<int>> rowOfNumbers;
using (TextReader t = new StreamReader("TestFile.txt"))
    rowOfNumbers = ReadNumbersFromStream(t);


foreach (var line in rowOfNumbers)
{
    foreach (int num in line)
        Console.Write("{0}, ", num);
    Console.WriteLine();
}
```

What happened? You tried to read from the file after you closed it. The iteration throws an `ObjectDisposedException`. The C# compiler bound `TextReader` to the delegate that reads and parses items from the file. That set of code is represented by the variable `arrayOfNums`. Nothing has really happened yet. The stream has not been read, and nothing has been parsed. That's one of the issues that arise when you move the resource management back up to the callers. If those callers misunderstand the lifetimes of resources, they will introduce problems that range from resource leaks to broken code.

The specific fix is straightforward. You move the code around so that you use the array of numbers before you close the file:

```
using (TextReader t = new StreamReader("TestFile.txt"))
{
    var arrayOfNums = ReadNumbersFromStream(t);

    foreach (var line in arrayOfNums)
    {
```

```
        foreach (var num in line)
            Console.Write("{0}, ", num);
        Console.WriteLine();
    }
}
```

That's great, but not all your problems are that simple. This strategy will lead to lots of duplicated code, and we're always trying to avoid that. So let's look at this solution for some hints about what can lead to a more general answer. The foregoing piece of code works because it uses the array of numbers before the file is closed.

You've structured the code in such a way that it's almost impossible to find the right location to close the file. You've created an API wherein the file must be opened in one location but cannot be closed until a later point. Suppose the original usage pattern were more like this:

```
using (TextReader t = new StreamReader("TestFile.txt"))
    return ReadNumbersFromFile(t);
```

Now you're stuck with no possible way to close the file. It's opened in one routine, but somewhere up the call stack, the file needs to be closed. Where? You can't be sure, but it's not in your code. It's somewhere up the call stack, outside your control, and you're left with no idea even what the file name is and no stream handle to examine what to close.

One obvious solution is to create one method that opens the file, reads the sequence, and returns the sequence. Here's a possible implementation:

```
public static IEnumerable<string> ParseFile(string path)
{
    using (StreamReader r = new StreamReader(path))
    {
        string line = r.ReadLine();
        while (line != null)
        {
            yield return line;
            line = r.ReadLine();
        }
    }
}
```

This method uses the same deferred execution model I show you in Item 17 (Chapter 3). What's important here is that the `StreamReader` object is disposed of only after all elements have been read, whether that happens early or later. The file object will be closed, but only after the sequence has been enumerated. Here's a smaller contrived example to show what I mean.

```
class Generator : IDisposable
{
    private int count;
    public int GetNextNumber()
    {
        return count++;
    }


    #region IDisposable Members
    public void Dispose()
    {
        Console.WriteLine("Disposing now ");
    }
    #endregion
}
```

The `Generator` class implements `IDisposable`, but only to show you what happens when you capture a variable of a type that implements `IDisposable`. Here's one sample usage:

```
var query = (from n in SomeFunction()
            select n).Take(5);


foreach (var s in query)
    Console.WriteLine(s);



Console.WriteLine("Again");
foreach (var s in query)
    Console.WriteLine(s);
```

Here's the output from this code fragment:

```
0
1
2
3
4
Disposing now
```

```
Again
0
1
2
3
4
Disposing now
```

The `Generator` object is disposed of when you would hope: after you have completed the iteration for the first time. `Generator` is disposed of whether you complete the iteration sequence or you stop the iteration early, as this query does.

However, there is a problem here. Notice that "Disposing now" is printed twice. Because the code fragment iterated the sequence twice, the code fragment caused `Generator` to be disposed of twice. That's not a problem in the `Generator` class, because that's only a marker. But the file example throws an exception when you enumerate the sequence for the second time. The first enumeration finishes, and `StreamReader` gets disposed of. Then the second enumeration tries to access a stream reader that's been disposed of. It won't work.

If your application will likely perform multiple enumerations on a disposable resource, you need to find a different solution. You may find that your application reads multiple values, processing them in different ways during the course of an algorithm. It may be wiser to use delegates to pass the algorithm, or multiple algorithms, into the routine that reads and processes the records from the file.

You need a generic version of this method that will let you capture the use of those values and then use those values inside an expression before you finally dispose of the file. The same action would look like this:

```
// Usage pattern: parameters are the file
// and the action you want taken for each line in the file.
ProcessFile("testFile.txt",
    (arrayOfNums) =>
    {
        foreach (IEnumerable<int> line in arrayOfNums)
        {
            foreach (int num in line)
                Console.Write("{0}, ", num);
            Console.WriteLine();
        }
```

```
        // Make the compiler happy by returning something:
        return 0;
    }
);


// declare a delegate type
public delegate TResult ProcessElementsFromFile<TResult>(
    IEnumerable<IEnumerable<int>> values);


// Method that reads files, processing each line
// using the delegate
public static TResult ProcessFile<TResult>(string filePath,
    ProcessElementsFromFile<TResult> action)
{
    using (TextReader t = new StreamReader(filePath))
    {
        var allLines = from line in t.ReadLines()
                        select line.Split(',');

        var matrixOfValues = from line in allLines
                                select from item in line
                                    select
                                        item.DefaultParse(0);
        return action(matrixOfValues);
    }
}
```

This looks a bit complicated, but it is helpful if you find yourself using this data source in many ways. Suppose you need to find the global maximum in the file:

```
var maximum = ProcessFile("testFile.txt",
    (arrayOfNums) =>
        (from line in arrayOfNums
            select line.Max()).Max());
```

Here, the use of the file stream is completely encapsulated inside `Process-File`. The answer you seek is a value, and it gets returned from the lambda expression. By changing the code so that the expensive resource (here, the file stream) gets allocated and released inside the function, you don't have expensive members being added to your closures.

The other problem with expensive resources captured in closures is less severe, but it can affect your application's performance metrics. Consider this method:

```
IEnumerable<int> ExpensiveSequence()
{
    int counter = 0;
    IEnumerable<int> numbers = Extensions.Generate(30,
        () => counter++);

    Console.WriteLine("counter: {0}", counter);

    ResourceHog hog = new ResourceHog();
    numbers = numbers.Union(
        hog.SequenceGeneratedFromResourceHog(
        (val) => val < counter));
    return numbers;
}
```

Like the other closures I've shown, this algorithm produces code that will be executed later, using the deferred execution model. This means that ResourceHog lives beyond the end of this method to whenever client code enumerates the sequence. Furthermore, if ResourceHog is not disposable, it will live on until all roots to it are unreachable and the garbage collector frees it.

If this is a bottleneck, you can restructure the query so that the numbers generated from ResourceHog get evaluated eagerly and thus Resource-Hog can be cleaned up immediately:

```
IEnumerable<int> ExpensiveSequence()
{
    int counter = 0;
    IEnumerable<int> numbers = Extensions.Generate(30,
        () => counter++);

    Console.WriteLine("counter: {0}", counter);

    ResourceHog hog = new ResourceHog();
    IEnumerable<int> mergeSequence =
        hog.SequenceGeneratedFromResourceHog(
            (val) => val < counter).ToList();
```

```
    numbers = numbers.Union(mergeSequence);
    return numbers;
}
```

This sample is pretty clear, because the code isn't very complicated. If you have more-complicated algorithms, it can be quite a bit more difficult to separate the inexpensive resources from the expensive resources. Depending on how complicated your algorithms are in methods that create closures, it may be quite a bit more difficult to unwind different resources that are captured inside bound variables of the closure. The following method uses three different local variables captured in a closure.

```
private static IEnumerable<int> LeakingClosure(int mod)
{
    ResourceHogFilter filter = new ResourceHogFilter();
    CheapNumberGenerator source = new CheapNumberGenerator();
    CheapNumberGenerator results = new CheapNumberGenerator();

    double importantStatistic = (from num in
                                    source.GetNumbers(50)
                                 where
                                     filter.PassesFilter(num)
                                 select num).Average();

    return from num in results.GetNumbers(100)
           where num > importantStatistic
           select num;
}
```

At first examination, it appears fine. `ResourceHog` generates the important statistic. It's scoped to the method, and it becomes garbage as soon as the method exits.

Unfortunately, this method is not as fine as it appears to be.

Here's why. The C# compiler creates one nested class per scope to implement a closure. The final query statement—which returns the numbers that are greater than the important statistic—needs a closure to contain the bound variable, the important statistic. Earlier in the method, the filter needs to be used in a closure to create the important statistic. This means that the filter gets copied into the nested class that implements the closure. The return statement returns a type that uses an instance of the nested class to implement the `where` clause. The instance of the nested class implementing the closure has leaked out of this method. Normally you wouldn't care. But if `ResourceHogFilter` really uses expensive resources, this would be a drain on your application.

To fix this problem, you need to split the method into two parts and get the compiler to create two closure classes:

```
private static IEnumerable<int> NotLeakingClosure(int mod)
{
    var importantStatistic = GenerateImportantStatistic();

    CheapNumberGenerator results = new CheapNumberGenerator();
    return from num in results.GetNumbers(100)
           where num > importantStatistic
           select num;
}

private static double GenerateImportantStatistic()
{
    ResourceHogFilter filter = new ResourceHogFilter();
    CheapNumberGenerator source = new CheapNumberGenerator();

    return (from num in source.GetNumbers(50)
                where filter.PassesFilter(num)
                select num).Average();
}
```

"But wait," you say. "That return statement in `GenerateImportantSta-tistic` contains the query that generates the statistic. The closure still leaks." No, it doesn't. The `Average` method requires the entire sequence (see Item 40, earlier in this chapter). The enumeration happens inside the scope of `GenerateImportantStatistic`, and the average value is returned. The closure containing the `ResourceHogFilter` object can be garbage-collected as soon as this method returns.

I chose to rework the method in this way because even more issues arise when you write methods that have multiple logical closures. Even though you think that the compiler should create multiple closures, the compiler creates only one closure, which handles all the underlying lambdas in each scope. You care in cases when one of the expressions can be returned from your method, and you think that the other expression doesn't really matter. But it does matter. Because the compiler creates one class to handle all the closures created by a single scope, all members used in any closures are injected into that class. Examine this short method:

```
public IEnumerable<int> MakeAnotherSequence()
{
    int counter = 0;

    IEnumerable<int> interim = Extensions.Generate(30,
        () => counter++);
    Random gen = new Random();

    IEnumerable<int> numbers = from n in interim
                               select gen.Next() - n;
    return numbers;
}
```

`MakeAnotherSequence()` contains two queries. The first one generates a sequence of integers from 0 through 29. The second modifies that sequence using a random number generator. The C# compiler generates one private class to implement the closure that contains both `counter` and `gen`. The code that calls `MakeAnotherSequence()` will access an instance of the generated class containing both local variables. The compiler does not create two nested classes, only one. The instances of that one nested class will be passed to callers.

There's one final issue relating to when operations happen inside a closure. Here's a sample.

```
private static void SomeMethod(ref int i)
{
    //...
}
private static void DoSomethingInBackground()
{
    int i = 0;
    Thread thread = new Thread(delegate()
        { SomeMethod(ref i); });
    thread.Start();
}
```

In this sample, you've captured a variable and examined it in two threads. Furthermore, you've structured it such that both threads are accessing it by reference. I'd explain more in a sample as to what happens to the value of i when you run this sample, but the truth is that it's not possible to know what's going to happen. Both threads can examine or modify the value of i, but, depending on which thread works faster, either thread could change the value at any time.

When you use query expressions in your algorithms, the compiler creates a single closure for all expressions in the entire method. An object of that type may be returned from your method, possibly as a member of the type implementing the enumeration. That object will live in the system until all users of it have been removed. That may create many issues. If any of the fields copied into the closure implements IDisposable, it can cause problems with correctness. If any of the fields is expensive to carry, it can cause performance problems. Either way, you need to understand that when objects created by a closure are returned from methods, the closure contains all the variables used to perform the calculations. You must ensure that you need those variables, or, if you can't do that, ensure that the closure can clean them up for you.

Item 42: Distinguish Between IEnumerable and IQueryable Data Sources

IQueryable<T> and IEnumerable<T> have very similar API signatures. IQueryable<T> derives from IEnumerable<T>. You might think that these two interfaces are interchangeable. In many cases, they are, and that's by design. In contrast, a sequence is a sequence, but sequences are not always interchangeable. Their behaviors are different, and their performance metrics can be very, very different. The following two query statements are quite different:

```
var q =
    from c in dbContext.Customers
    where c.City == "London"
    select c;
var finalAnswer = from c in q
                  orderby c.Name
                  select c;
// Code to iterate the final Answer sequence elided
var q =
    (from c in dbContext.Customers
    where c.City == "London"
    select c).AsEnumerable();
```

```
var finalAnswer = from c in q
                    orderby c.Name
                    select c;
```

```
// code to iterate final answer elided.
```

These queries return the same result, but they do their work in very different ways. The first query uses the normal LINQ to SQL version that is built on `IQueryable` functionality. The second version forces the database objects into `IEnumerable` sequences and does more of its work locally. It's a combination of lazy evaluation and `IQueryable<T>` support in LINQ to SQL.

When the results of a query are executed, the LINQ to SQL libraries compose the results from all the query statements. In the example, this means that one call is made to the database. It also means that one SQL query performs both the `where` clause and the `orderby` clause.

In the second case, returning the first query as an `IEnumerable<T>` sequence means that subsequent operations use the LINQ to Objects implementation and are executed using delegates. The first statement causes a call to the database to retrieve all customers in London. The second orders the set returned by the first call by name. That sort operation occurs locally.

You should care about the differences because many queries work quite a bit more efficiently if you use `IQueryable` functionality than if you use `IEnumerable` functionality. Furthermore, because of the differences in how `IQueryable` and `IEnumerable` process query expressions, you'll find that sometimes queries that work in one environment do not work in the other.

The processing is different at every step of the way. That's because the types used are different. `Enumerable<T>` extension methods use delegates for the lambda expressions as well as the function parameters whenever they appear in query expressions. `Queryable<T>`, on the other hand, uses expression trees to process those same function elements. An **expression tree** is a data structure that holds all the logic that makes up the actions in the query. The `Enumerable<T>` version must execute locally. The lambda expressions have been compiled into methods, and they must execute now on the local machine. This means that you need to pull all the data into the local application space from wherever it resides. You'll transfer much more data, and you'll throw away whatever isn't necessary.

In contrast, the `Queryable` version parses the expression tree. After examining the expression tree, this version translates that logic into a format appropriate for the provider and then executes that logic where it is closest to the data location. The result is much less data transfer and better overall system performance. However, there are some restrictions on the code that goes into query expressions when you use the `IQueryable` interface and rely on the `Queryable<T>` implementation of your sequence.

As I show earlier in this chapter in Item 37, `IQueryable` providers don't parse any arbitrary method. That would be an unbounded set of logic. Instead, they understand a set of operators, and possibly a defined set of methods, that are implemented in the .NET Framework. If your queries contain other method calls, you may need to force the query to use the `Enumerable` implementation.

```
private bool isValidProduct(Product p) {
    return p.ProductName.LastIndexOf('C') == 0;
}
// This works:
var q1 =
    from p in dbContext.Products.AsEnumerable()
    where isValidProduct(p)
    select p;
// This throws an exception when you enumerate the collection.
var q2 =
    from p in dbContext.Products
    where isValidProduct(p)
    select p;
```

The first query works, because LINQ to Objects uses delegates to implement queries as method calls. The `AsEnumerable()` call forces the query into the local client space, and the `where` clause executes using LINQ to Objects. The second query throws an exception. The reason is that LINQ to SQL uses an `IQueryable<T>` implementation. LINQ to SQL contains an `IQueryProvider` that translates your queries into T-SQL. That T-SQL then gets remoted to the database engine, and the database engine executes the SQL statements in that context (see Item 38 earlier in this chapter). That approach can give you an advantage, because far less data gets transferred across tiers and possibly across layers.

In a typical tradeoff of performance versus robustness, you can avoid the exception by translating the query result explicitly to an `IEnumerable<T>`.

The downside of that solution is that the LINQ to SQL engine now returns the entire set of dbContext.Products from the database. Furthermore, the remainder of the query is executed locally. Because IQueryable<T> inherits from IEnumerable<T>, this method can be called using either source.

That sounds good, and it can be a simple approach. But it forces any code that uses your method to fall back to the IEnumerable<T> sequence. If your client developer is using a source that supports IQueryable<T>, you have forced her to pull all the source elements into this process's address space, then process all those elements here, and finally return the results.

Even though normally you would be correct to write that method once, and write it to the lowest common class or interface, that's not the case with IEnumerable<T> and IQueryable<T>. Even though they have almost the same external capabilities, the differences in their respective implementations mean that you should use the implementation that matches your data source. In practice, you'll know whether the data source implements IQueryable<T> or only IEnumerable<T>. When your source implements IQueryable, you should make sure that your code uses that type.

However, you may occasionally find that a class must support queries on IEnumerable<T> and IQueryable<T> for the same T:

```
public static IEnumerable<Product>
    ValidProducts(this IEnumerable<Product> products)
{
    return from p in products
           where p.ProductName.LastIndexOf('C') == 0
           select p;
}


// OK, because string.LastIndexOf() is supported
// by LINQ to SQL provider
public static IQueryable<Product>
ValidProducts(this IQueryable<Product> products)
{
    return from p in products
           where p.ProductName.LastIndexOf('C') == 0
           select p;
}
```

Of course, this code reeks of duplicated effort. You can avoid the duplication by using `AsQueryable()` to convert any `IEnumerable<T>` to an `IQueryable<T>`:

```
public static IEnumerable<Product>
    ValidProducts(this IEnumerable<Product> products)
{

    return from p in products.AsQueryable()
           where p.ProductName.LastTndexOf('C') == 0
           select p;
}
```

`AsQueryable()` looks at the runtime type of the sequence. If the sequence is an `IQueryable`, it returns the sequence as an `IQueryable`. In contrast, if the runtime type of the sequence is an `IEnumerable`, then `AsQueryable()` creates a wrapper that implements `IQueryable` using the LINQ to Objects implementation, and it returns that wrapper. You get the `Enumerable` implementation, but it's wrapped in an `IQueryable` reference.

Using `AsQueryable()` gives you the maximum benefit. Sequences that already implement `IQueryable` will use that implementation, and sequences that support only `IEnumerable` will still work. When client code hands you an `IQueryable` sequence, your code will properly use the `Queryable<T>` methods and will support expression trees and foreign execution. And if you are working with a sequence that supports only `IEnumerable<T>`, then the runtime implementation will use the `IEnumerable` implementation.

Notice that this version still uses a method call: `string.LastIndexOf()`. That is one of the methods that are parsed correctly by the LINQ to SQL libraries, and therefore you can use it in your LINQ to SQL queries. However, every provider has unique capabilities, so you should not consider that method available in every `IQueryProvider` implementation.

`IQueryable<T>` and `IEnumerable<T>` might seem to provide the same functionality. All the difference lies in how each implements the query pattern. Make sure to declare query results using the type that matches your data source. Query methods are statically bound, and declaring the proper type of query variables means that you get the correct behavior.

Item 43: Use Single() and First() to Enforce Semantic Expectations on Queries

A quick perusal of the LINQ libraries might lead you to believe that they have been designed to work exclusively with sequences. But there are methods that escape out of a query and return a single element. Each of these methods behaves differently from the others, and those differences help you express your intention and expectations for the results of a query that returns a scalar result.

`Single()` returns exactly one element. If no elements exist, or if multiple elements exist, then `Single()` throws an exception. That's a rather strong statement about your expectations. However, if your assumptions are proven false, you probably want to find out immediately. When you write a query that is supposed to return exactly one element, you should use `Single()`. This method expresses your assumptions most clearly: You expect exactly one element back from the query. Yes, it fails if your assumptions are wrong, but it fails quickly and in a way that doesn't cause any data corruption. That immediate failure helps you make a quick diagnosis and correct the problem. Furthermore, your application data doesn't get corrupted by executing later program logic using faulty data. The query fails immediately, because the assumptions are wrong.

```
var somePeople = new List<Person>{
    new Person {FirstName = "Bill", LastName = "Gates"},
    new Person { FirstName = "Bill", LastName = "Wagner"},
    new Person { FirstName = "Bill", LastName = "Johnson"}};

// Will throw an exception because more than one
// element is in the sequence
var answer = (from p in somePeople
            where p.FirstName == "Bill"
            select p).Single();
```

Furthermore, unlike many of the other queries I've shown you, this one throws an exception even before you examine the result. `Single()` immediately evaluates the query and returns the single element. The following query fails with the same exception (although a different message):

```
var answer = (from p in somePeople
            where p.FirstName == "Larry"
            select p).Single();
```

Again, your code assumes that exactly one result exists. When that assumption is wrong, `Single()` always throws an `InvalidOperationException`.

If your query can return zero or one element, you can use `SingleOr-Default()`. However, remember that `SingleOrDefault()` still throws an exception when more than one value is returned. You are still expecting no more than one value returned from your query expression.

```
var answer = (from p in somePeople
              where p.FirstName == "Larry"
              select p).SingleOrDefault();
```

This query returns `null` (the default value for a reference type) to indicate that there were no values that matched the query.

Of course, there are times when you expect to get more than one value but you want a specific one. The best choice is `First()` or `FirstOrDefault()`. Both methods return the first element in the returned sequence. If the sequence is empty, the default is returned. The following query finds the forward who scored the most goals, but it returns `null` if none of the forwards has scored any goals.

```
// Works. Returns null
var answer = (from p in Forwards
              where p.GoalsScored > 0
              orderby p.GoalsScored
              select p).FirstOrDefault();
// throws an exception if there are no values in the sequence:
var answer2 = (from p in Forwards
               where p.GoalsScored > 0
               orderby p.GoalsScored
               select p).First();
```

Of course, sometimes you don't want the first element. There are quite a few ways to solve this problem. You could reorder the elements so that you do get the correct first element. (You could put them in the other order and grab the last element, but that would take somewhat longer.)

If you know exactly where in the sequence to look, you can use `Skip` and `First` to retrieve the one sought element. Here, we find the third-best goal-scoring forward:

```
var answer = (from p in Forwards
              where p.GoalsScored > 0
```

```
        orderby p.GoalsScored
        select p).Skip(2).First();
```

I chose `First()` rather than `Take()` to emphasize that I wanted exactly one element, and not a sequence containing one element. Note that because I use `First()` instead of `FirstOrDefault()`, the compiler assumes that at least three forwards have scored goals.

However, once you start looking for an element in a specific position, it's likely that there is a better way to construct the query. Are there different properties you should be looking for? Should you look to see whether your sequence supports `IList<T>` and supports index operations? Should you rework the algorithm to find exactly the one item? You may find that other methods of finding results will give you much clearer code.

Many of your queries are designed to return one scalar value. Whenever you query for a single value, it's best to write your query to return a scalar value rather than a sequence of one element. Using `Single()` means that you expect to always find exactly one item. `SingleOrDefault()` means zero or one item. `First` and `Last` mean that you are pulling one item out of a sequence. Using any other method of finding one item likely means that you haven't written your query as well as you should have. It won't be as clear for developers using your code or maintaining it later.

Item 44: Prefer Storing Expression<> to Func<>

In Item 42 (earlier in this chapter) I briefly discuss how query providers such as LINQ to SQL examine queries before execution and translate them into their native format. LINQ to Objects, in contrast, implements queries by compiling lambda expressions into methods and creating delegates that access those methods. It's plain old code, but the access is implemented through delegates.

LINQ to SQL (and any other query provider) performs this magic by asking for query expressions in the form of a `System.Linq.Expressions.Expression` object. `Expression` is an abstract base class that represents an expression. One of the classes derived from `Expression` is `System.Linq.Expressions.Expression<TDelegate>`, where `TDelegate` is a delegate type. `Expression<TDelegate>` represents a lambda expression as a data structure. You can analyze it by using the `Body`, `NodeType`, and `Parameters` properties. Furthermore, you can compile it into a delegate by using the `Expression<TDelegate>.Compile()` method.

That makes `Expression<TDelegate>` more general than `Func<T>`. Simply put, `Func<T>` is a delegate that can be invoked. `Expression<TDelegate>` can be examined, or it can be compiled and then invoked in the normal way.

When your design includes the storage of lambda expressions, you'll have more options if you store them using `Expression<T>`. You don't lose any features; you simply have to compile the expression before invoking it:

```
Expression<Func<int, bool>> compound = val =>
    (val % 2 == 1) && (val > 300);
Func<int, bool> compiled = compound.Compile();
Console.WriteLine(compiled(501));
```

The `Expression` class provides methods that allow you to examine the logic of an expression. You can examine an expression tree and see the exact logic that makes up the expression. The C# team provides a reference implementation for examining an expression with the C# samples delivered with Visual Studio 2008. The Expression Tree Visualizer sample, which includes source code, provides code that examines each node type in an expression tree and displays the contents of that node. It recursively visits each subnode in the tree; this is how you would examine each node in a tree in an algorithm to visit and modify each node.

Working with expressions and expression trees instead of functions and delegates can be a better choice, because expressions have quite a bit more functionality: You can convert an `Expression` to a `Func`, and you can traverse expression trees, meaning that you can create modified versions of the expressions. You can use `Expression` to build new algorithms at runtime, something that is much harder to do with `Func`.

This habit helps you by letting you later combine expressions using code. In this way, you build an expression tree that contains multiple clauses. After building the code, you can call `Compile()` and create the delegate when you need it.

Here is one way to combine two expressions to form a larger expression:

```
Expression<Func<int, bool>> IsOdd = val => val % 2 == 1;
Expression<Func<int, bool>> IsLargeNumber = val => val > 300;

InvocationExpression callLeft = Expression.Invoke(IsOdd,
Expression.Constant(5));
InvocationExpression callRight = Expression.Invoke(
    IsLargeNumber,
    Expression.Constant(5));
```

```
BinaryExpression Combined =
    Expression.MakeBinary(ExpressionType.And,
    callLeft, callRight);

// Convert to a typed expression:
Expression<Func<bool>> typeCombined =
    Expression.Lambda<Func<bool>>(Combined);

Func<bool> compiled = typeCombined.Compile();
bool answer = compiled();
```

This code creates two small expressions and combines them into a single expression. Then it compiles the larger expression and executes it. If you're familiar with either CodeDom or Reflection.Emit, the `Expression` APIs can provide similar metaprogramming capabilities. You can visit expressions, create new expressions, compile them to delegates, and finally execute them.

Working with expression trees is far from simple. Because expressions are immutable, it's a rather extensive undertaking to create a modified version of an expression. You need to traverse every node in the tree and either (1) copy it to the new tree or (2) replace the existing node with a different expression that produces the same kind of result. Several implementations of expression tree visitors have been written, as samples and as open source projects. I don't add yet another version here. A Web search for "expression tree visitor" will find several implementations.

The `System.Linq.Expressions` namespace contains a rich grammar that you can use to build algorithms at runtime. You can construct your own expressions by building the complete expression from its components. The following code executes the same logic as the previous example, but here I build the lambda expression in code:

```
// The lambda expression has one parameter:
ParameterExpression parm = Expression.Parameter(
    typeof(int), "val");
// We'll use a few integer constants:
ConstantExpression threeHundred = Expression.Constant(300,
    typeof(int));
ConstantExpression one = Expression.Constant(1, typeof(int));
ConstantExpression two = Expression.Constant(2, typeof(int));
```

```
// Creates (val > 300)
BinaryExpression largeNumbers =
    Expression.MakeBinary(ExpressionType.GreaterThan,
    parm, threeHundred);

// creates (val % 2)
BinaryExpression modulo = Expression.MakeBinary(
    ExpressionType.Modulo,
    parm, two);
// builds ((val % 2) == 1), using modulo
BinaryExpression isOdd = Expression.MakeBinary(
    ExpressionType.Equal,
    modulo, one);
// creates ((val % 2) == 1) && (val > 300),
// using isOdd and largeNumbers
BinaryExpression lambdaBody =
    Expression.MakeBinary(ExpressionType.AndAlso,
    isOdd, largeNumbers);

// creates val => (val % 2 == 1) && (val > 300)
// from lambda body and parameter.
LambdaExpression lambda = Expression.Lambda(lambdaBody, parm);

// Compile it:
Func<int, bool> compiled = lambda.Compile() as
    Func<int, bool>;
// Run it:
Console.WriteLine(compiled(501));
```

Yes, using `Expression` to build your own logic is certainly more complicated than creating the expression from the `Func<>` definitions shown earlier. This kind of metaprogramming is an advanced topic. It's not the first tool you should reach for in your toolbox.

Even if you don't build and modify expressions, libraries you use might do so. You should consider using `Expression<>` instead of `Func<>` when your lambda expressions are passed to unknown libraries whose implementations might use the expression tree logic to translate your algorithms into a different format. Any `IQueryProvider`, such as LINQ to SQL, would perform that translation.

Also, you might create your own additions to your type that would be better served by expressions than by delegates. The justification is the same: You can always convert expressions into delegates, but you can't go the other way.

You may find that delegates are an easier way to represent lambda expressions, and conceptually they are. Delegates can be executed. Most C# developers understand them, and often they provide all the functionality you need. However, if your type will store expressions and passing those expressions to other objects is not under your control, or if you will compose expressions into more-complex constructs, then you should consider using expressions instead of funcs. You'll have a richer set of APIs that will enable you to modify those expressions at runtime and invoke them after you have examined them for your own internal purposes.

6 | Miscellaneous

No matter how much you try, some advice doesn't fit neatly into a category. Even so, this miscellaneous advice is important. It involves practices you'll use every day, and following it will make your code easier to use, easier to understand, and easier to extend in the future.

Item 45: Minimize the Visibility of Nullable Values

Nullable types require more checks than non-nullable types. It makes more sense to use non-nullable structs whenever you can and to limit nullable types to those algorithms that require the nullable abstraction. Nullable types add a missing, or unavailable, value to a non-nullable struct. In many ways, this makes using nullable types similar to older designs that used a marker value for a missing value.

Programming against nullable types is more complicated than programming against the corresponding non-nullable value. Nullables mean extra checking: What should happen when the value is missing? The answer will vary, but for every algorithm, the missing value should be interpreted in some known way. Your goal should be to isolate the extra work required for nullable values to the smallest set of code. Then client code can assume that your libraries have already accounted for any missing values.

Nullables are an important way to standardize algorithms built on sentinel values for missing data. Earlier, in Item 34 (Chapter 4), I show an extension method that attempts to parse a string and returns a nullable value for the output:

```
public static int? DefaultParse(this string input)
{
    int answer;
    return (int.TryParse(input, out answer))
        ? answer : default(int?);
}
```

An input string that cannot be parsed as an integer value returns a nullable `int` that does not contain a value. From the context of this method, there is no better answer. The input string—whether typed by a user, read from a file, or coming from an unknown source—isn't what was expected. However, somewhere up the call chain, some logic exists that knows the correct behavior when the input string cannot be parsed. It is at that location in the code that you should replace the nullable integer with the correct default value. Or if there is no default value and if a missing value means a hard failure, that's the point where your code should throw an exception. In that way, you limit the scope of the nullable type to those portions of your code where the correct behavior for the nullable value isn't known. External code should not see the extra complications introduced by the nullable type.

Nullable types add semantics to everyday operations on value types. As an example, nullable numeric types provide semantics similar to those defined for floating-point numbers and NaN values. Any order comparison involving a NaN returns false:

```
double d = 0;
Console.WriteLine(d > double.NaN);          // false
Console.WriteLine(d < double.NaN);          // false
Console.WriteLine(double.NaN < double.NaN); // false
Console.WriteLine(double.NaN == double.NaN); // false
```

Nullables behave in almost the same way. Unlike NaN, nullables support equality even in the case of a missing value.

Furthermore, any nullable having no value trumps any other value on calculations, just as NaN does for floating-point values:

```
// Working with nullable values:
int? nullableOne = default(int?);
int? nullableTwo = 0;
int? nullableThree = default(int?);

Console.WriteLine(nullableOne < nullableTwo);     // false
Console.WriteLine(nullableOne > nullableTwo);     // false
Console.WriteLine(nullableOne == nullableThree);  // true

// Working with NaNs:
double d = 0;
```

```
Console.WriteLine(d + double.NaN);   // NaN
Console.WriteLine(d - double.NaN);   // NaN
Console.WriteLine(d * double.NaN);   // NaN
Console.WriteLine(d / double.NaN);   // NaN
```

Operations on nullable numeric types work in exactly the same way as do numeric operations with NaN. Any numeric operation involving a nullable numeric type with no value results in a nullable type with no value:

```
int? nullableOne = default(int?);
int? nullableTwo = default(int);
int? nullableThree = default(int?);

Console.WriteLine((
    nullableOne + nullableTwo).HasValue);   // false
Console.WriteLine(
    (nullableOne - nullableTwo).HasValue);   // false
Console.WriteLine(
    (nullableOne * nullableThree).HasValue); // false
```

This property—that any null in an expression causes the result of that expression to be null—means that you often must define default values for those operations. You could use the `Nullable<T>.GetValueOrDefault()` method, but the C# language provides a simpler way to use this idiom: the null coalescing operator (`??`). The **null coalescing operator** returns the value stored in the nullable object on the left of the coalescing operator if that object has a value. Otherwise, it returns the value on the right side of the operator. The first line here performs the same action as the second line:

```
var result1 = NullableObject ?? 0;
var result2 = NullableObject.GetValueOrDefault(0);
```

You can use this operator in any expression using nullable objects:

```
int? nullableOne = default(int?);
int? nullableTwo = default(int);
int? nullableThree = default(int?);

int answer1 = (nullableOne ?? 0) + (nullableTwo ?? 0);
Console.WriteLine(answer1); // output is 0

int answer2 = (nullableOne ?? 0) - (nullableTwo ?? 0);
Console.WriteLine(answer2); // output is 0
```

```
int answer3 = (nullableOne ?? 1) * (nullableThree ?? 1);
Console.WriteLine(answer3); // output is 1
```

Nullable types have a few other issues when they permeate further through your code. Serializing nullables can be very dangerous. Consider this snippet of code:

```
int? f = default(int?);


XmlSerializer x = new XmlSerializer(typeof(int?));
StringWriter t = new StringWriter();
x.Serialize(t, f);
Console.WriteLine(t.ToString());
```

It produces this XML document:

```
<int xmlns:xsi="http://www.w3.org/2001/XMLSchema-instance"
    xmlns:xsd="http://www.w3.org/2001/XMLSchema"
    xsi:nil="true" />
```

Notice that the type of the XML element is `int`. The XML element does not contain any indication that the integer may be missing. Yet, as you can see from the node, it is missing.

That missing value causes this seemingly correct code to throw a `Null-ReferenceException`:

```
string storage = t.ToString();
StringReader s = new StringReader(storage);
int f2 = (int)x.Deserialize(s); // f2 can't be null
Console.WriteLine(f2);
```

This makes sense when you think about it. You saved a nullable `int`, which could contain every integer value as well as the null value. When you read that value back in, you implicitly converted the `int?` to an `int`. The null value was no longer valid, so your code generated an exception.

This same problem occurs in production environments that include serializing XML documents. Types that contain nullable values may have the same problem. Those member elements appear to be typed as value types, and yet the value itself is null. Tools that build classes from XML documents create `int`s, rather than nullable `int`s. Deserialization using those tools would produce the same errors when your program encounters null values.

Nullable types also introduce complicated behavior when you work with virtual methods defined in `System.Object` or with interfaces implemented by the underlying value type. Those operations will cause a boxing conversion of the enclosed value type to `System.Object` or to the interface pointer. Consider these two conversions of a nullable `int` into a `string`:

```
int? defaultNullable = default(int?);
string s = defaultNullable.ToString();
Console.WriteLine(s);
string s2 = ((object)defaultNullable).ToString();
Console.WriteLine(s2);
```

`defaultNullable.ToString()` produces the empty string, `""`, as its string representation. That makes sense: If the string has no value, it produces no string representation. However, the second conversion throws a `NullReferenceException`. That's because the conversion to object tries to box the value type contained in the nullable object. There is no value, so the conversion returns `null`, typed as `System.Object`. It's expected. It's the right behavior, but it takes some time to get accustomed to it. It's different behavior from that of the first call, because the first version calls `nullable<int>.ToString()`. The second version boxes the contained value, which is a `null`, and then calls `object.ToString()` on a null object.

Similar problems occur because every nullable type can be implicitly converted to any interface that is implemented on the contained non-nullable type. For example, you can use the `IComparable<T>` interface with any numeric nullable type:

```
int? one = 1;
int? two = 2;

IComparable<int> oneIC = one;
if (oneIC.CompareTo(two.Value) > 0)
    Console.WriteLine("Greater");
else
    Console.WriteLine("Not Greater");
```

But a boxing conversion is being performed, so if you convert a nullable object containing a null value into an interface and then use that interface reference, you'll throw a `NullReferenceException`:

```
int? empty = default(int?);

IComparable<int> emptyIC = empty;
// throws NullReferenceException
if (emptyIC.CompareTo(two.Value) > 0)
    Console.WriteLine("Greater");
else
    Console.WriteLine("Not Greater");
```

It makes sense. The empty nullable object has no value, so any operation that relies on that value must fail. There's nothing there.

All the examples I've shown use nullable counterparts to numeric types. That's not because numbers are special but because the semantics are simple, and less code is necessary around the core numeric values compared with some other structure you have created. However, every example I've shown will occur on any struct you've created when you use the nullable counterpart of the struct. Of course, the numeric operators aren't automatically defined on your structures, but other methods are. Accessing the value in a nullable struct without ensuring that the value exists causes a `NullReferenceException`. That conversion is implicit, so the compiler doesn't warn you of the potential danger.

As an API designer, you need to create an API that's easy to use and hard to misuse. Nullable types complicate your task somewhat. If you can avoid exposing the nullable types in your public interface or your storage model, your type is easier to use. That's not to say that nullable types should never be a part of your API. The very first example in this item shows a parsing method that returns a `nullable<int>` when it tries to convert an input string to an integer. If the nullable type really is the proper representation of the types you're working with, then you should use it. Internally, a nullable struct is often the proper storage model for your algorithms. However, minimizing the scope of those nullable objects makes your types easier to use and harder to misuse.

Thus, when you work with nullable types, you need to carefully examine any conversions between the nullable object and its non-nullable counterpart. When you expose those nullable types as part of your public interface, you force your users to understand all those rules as much as you do. That may be the correct behavior. But you should make it an explicit choice, and not an implicit choice.

Item 46: Give Partial Classes Partial Methods for Constructors, Mutators, and Event Handlers

The C# language team added partial classes so that code generators can create their part of the classes, and human developers can augment the generated code in another file. Unfortunately, that separation is not sufficient for sophisticated usage patterns. Often, the human developers need to add code in members created by the code generator. Those members might include constructors, event handlers defined in the generated code, and any mutator methods defined in the generated code.

Your purpose is to free developers who use your code generator from feeling that they should modify your generated code. If you are on the other side, using code created by a tool, you should never modify the generated code. Doing so breaks the relationship with the code generator tool and makes it much more difficult for you to continue to use it.

In some ways, writing partial classes is like API design. You, as the human developer or as the author of a code generation tool, are creating code that must be used by some other developer (either the person or the code generation tool). In other ways, it's like having two developers work on the same class, but with serious restrictions. The two developers can't talk to each other, and neither developer can modify the code written by the other. This means that you need to provide plenty of hooks for those other developers. You should implement those hooks in the form of partial methods. Partial methods let you provide hooks that another developer may, or may not, need to implement.

Your code generator defines partial methods for those extension points. Partial methods provide a way for you to declare methods that may be defined in another source file in a partial class. The compiler looks at the full class definition, and, if partial methods have been defined, the compiler generates calls to those methods. If no class author has written the partial method, then the compiler removes any calls to it.

Because partial methods may or may not be part of the class, the language imposes several restrictions on the method signatures of partial methods: The return type must be `void`, partial methods cannot be abstract or virtual, and they cannot implement interface methods. The parameters cannot include any `out` parameters, because the compiler cannot initialize `out` parameters. Nor can it create the return value if the method body has not been defined. Implicitly, all partial methods are private.

For three class member types, you should add partial methods that enable users to monitor or modify the class behavior: mutator methods, event handlers, and constructors.

Mutator methods are any methods that change the observable state of the class. From the standpoint of partial methods and partial classes, you should interpret that as any change in state. The other source files that make up a partial class implementation are part of the class and therefore have complete access to your class internals.

Mutator methods should provide the other class authors with two partial methods. The first method should be called before the change that provides validation hooks and before the other class author has a chance to reject the change. The second method would be called after changing state and allows the other class author to respond to the state change.

Your tool's core code would be something like this:

```
// Consider this the portion generated by your tool
public partial class GeneratedStuff
{
    private int storage = 0;

    public void UpdateValue(int newValue)
    {
        storage = newValue;
    }
}
```

You should add hooks both before and after the change. In this way, you let other class authors modify or respond to the change:

```
// Consider this the portion generated by your tool
public partial class GeneratedStuff
{
    private struct ReportChange
    {
        public readonly int OldValue;
        public readonly int NewValue;

        public ReportChange(int oldValue, int newValue)
        {
            OldValue = oldValue;
```

```csharp
            NewValue = newValue;
        }
    }

    private class RequestChange
    {
        public ReportChange Values
        {
            get;
            set;
        }
        public bool Cancel
        {
            get;
            set;
        }
    }

    partial void ReportValueChanging(RequestChange args);
    partial void ReportValueChanged(ReportChange values);

    private int storage = 0;

    public void UpdateValue(int newValue)
    {
        // Precheck the change
        RequestChange updateArgs = new RequestChange
        {
            Values = new ReportChange(storage, newValue)
        };
        ReportValueChanging(updateArgs);
        if (!updateArgs.Cancel) // if OK,
        {
            storage = newValue; // change
            // and report:
            ReportValueChanged(new ReportChange(
                storage, newValue));
        }
    }
}
```

If no one has written bodies for either partial method, then Update-Value() compiles down to this:

```
public void UpdateValue(int newValue)
{
    RequestChange updateArgs = new RequestChange {
        Values = new ReportChange(this.storage, newValue)
    };
    if (!updateArgs.Cancel)
    {
        this.storage = newValue;
    }
}
```

The hooks allow the developer to validate or respond to any change:

```
// This represents the hand-edited portion.
public partial class GeneratedStuff
{
    partial void ReportValueChanging(
        GeneratedStuff.RequestChange args)
    {
        if (args.Values.NewValue < 0)
        {
            Console.WriteLine("Invalid value: {0}, canceling",
                args.Values.NewValue);
            args.Cancel = true;
        }
        else
            Console.WriteLine("Changing {0} to {1}",
                args.Values.OldValue,
                args.Values.NewValue);

    }
    partial void ReportValueChanged(
        GeneratedStuff.ReportChange values)
    {
        Console.WriteLine("Changed {0} to {1}",
            values.OldValue, values.NewValue);
    }
}
```

Here, I show a protocol with a cancel flag that lets developers cancel any mutator operation. Your class may prefer a protocol in which the user-defined code can throw an exception to cancel an operation. Throwing the exception is better if the cancel operation should be propagated up to the calling code. Otherwise, the Boolean cancel flag should be used because it's lightweight.

Furthermore, notice that the RequestChange object gets created even when ReportValueChanged() will not be called. You can have any code execute in that constructor, and the compiler cannot assume that the constructor call can be removed without changing the semantics of the UpdateValue() method. You should strive to require minimal work for client developers to create those extra objects needed for validating and requesting changes.

It's fairly easy to spot all the public mutator methods in a class, but remember to include all the public set accessors for properties. If you don't remember those, other class authors can't validate or respond to property changes.

You next need to make sure to provide hooks for user-generated code in constructors. Neither the generated code nor the user-written code can control which constructor gets called. Therefore, your code generator must provide a hook to call user-defined code when one of the generated constructors gets called. Here is an extension to the GeneratedStuff class shown earlier:

```
// Hook for user-defined code:
partial void Initialize();

public GeneratedStuff() :
    this(0)
{
}

public GeneratedStuff(int someValue)
{
    this.storage = someValue;
    Initialize();
}
```

Notice that I make Initialize()the last method called during construction. That enables the hand-written code to examine the current object state and possibly make any modifications or throw exceptions if the developer finds something invalid for his problem domain. You want to make sure that you don't call `Initialize()` twice, and you must make sure it is called from every constructor defined in the generated code. The human developer must not call his own `Initialize()` routine from any constructor he adds. Instead, he should explicitly call one of the constructors defined in the generated class to ensure that any initialization necessary in the generated code takes place.

Finally, if the generated code subscribes to any events, you should consider providing partial method hooks during the processing of that event. This is especially important if the event is one of the events that request status or cancel notifications from the generated class. The user-defined code may want to modify the status or change the cancel flag.

Partial classes and partial methods provide the mechanisms you need to completely separate generated code from user-written code in the same class. With the extensions I show here, you should never need to modify code generated by a tool. You are probably using code generated by Visual Studio or other tools. Before you consider modifying any of the code written by the tool, you must examine the interface provided by the generated code in hopes that it has provided partial method declarations that you can use to accomplish your goal. More importantly, if you are the author of the code generator, you must provide a complete set of hooks in the form of partial methods to support any desired extensions to your generated code. Doing anything less will lead developers down a dangerous path and will encourage them to abandon your code generator.

Item 47: Limit Array Parameters to Params Arrays

Using array parameters can expose your code to several unexpected problems. It's much better to create method signatures that use alternative representations to pass collections or variable-size arguments to methods.

Arrays have special properties that allow you to write methods that appear to have strict type checking but fail at runtime. The following small program compiles just fine. It passes all the compile-time type checking. However, it throws an `ArrayTypeMismatchException` when you assign a value to the first object in the `parms` array in `ReplaceIndices`:

```
static void Main(string[] args)
{
    string[] labels = new string[] { "one", "two",
        "three", "four", "five" };
```

```
        ReplaceIndices(labels);
}


static private void ReplaceIndices(object[] parms)
{
    for (int index = 0; index < parms.Length; index++)
        parms[index] = index;
}
```

The problem arises because arrays are covariant as input parameters. You don't have to pass the exact type of the array into the method. Furthermore, even though the array is passed by value, the contents of the array can be references to reference types. Your method can change members of the array in ways that will not work with some valid types. Of course, the foregoing example is a bit obvious, and you probably think you'll never write code like that. But examine this small class hierarchy:

```
class B
{
    public static B Factory()
    {
        return new B();
    }

    public virtual void WriteType()
    {
        Console.WriteLine("B");
    }
}


class D1 : B
{
    public static new B Factory()
    {
        return new D1();
    }

    public override void WriteType()
    {
        Console.WriteLine("D1");
    }
}
```

```
class D2 : B
{
    public static new B Factory()
    {
        return new D2();
    }

    public override void WriteType()
    {
        Console.WriteLine("D2");
    }
}
```

If you use this correctly, everything is fine:

```
static private void FillArray(B[] array, Func<B> generator)
{
    for (int i = 0; i < array.Length; i++)
        array[i] = generator();
}


// elsewhere:
B[] storage = new B[10];
FillArray(storage, () => B.Factory());
FillArray(storage, () => D1.Factory());
FillArray(storage, () => D2.Factory());
```

But any mismatch between the derived types will throw the same `Array-TypeMismatchException`:

```
B[] storage = new D1[10];
// All three calls will throw exceptions:
FillArray(storage, () => B.Factory());
FillArray(storage, () => D1.Factory());
FillArray(storage, () => D2.Factory());
```

Furthermore, because arrays don't support contravariance, when you write array members, your code will fail to compile even though it should work:

```
static void FillArray(D1[] array)
{
    for (int i = 0; i < array.Length; i++)
        array[i] = new D1();
}
```

```
B[] storage = new B[10];
// generates compiler error CS1503 (argument mismatch)
// even though D objects can be placed in a B array
FillArray(storage);
```

Things become even more complicated if you want to pass arrays as ref parameters. You'll end up being able to create a derived class, but not a base class, inside the method. However, the objects in the array can still be the wrong type.

You can avoid those problems by typing parameters as interface types that create a type-safe sequence to use. Input parameters should be typed as IEnumerable<T> for some T. This strategy ensures that you can't modify the input sequence, because IEnumerable<T> does not provide any methods to modify the collection. Another alternative is to pass types as base classes, a practice that may also avoid APIs that support modifying the collection.

When you need to modify the sequence, it's best to use an input parameter of one sequence and return the modified sequence (see Item 17, Chapter 3). When you want to generate the sequence, return the sequence as an IEnumerable<T> for some T.

And yet there are times when you want to pass arbitrary options in methods. That's when you can reach for an array of arguments. But make sure to use a params array. The params array allows the user of your method to simply place those elements as other parameters. Contrast these two methods:

```
// regular array
private static void WriteOutput1(object[] stuffToWrite)
{
    foreach (object o in stuffToWrite)
        Console.WriteLine(o);
}
// Params array
private static void WriteOutput2(params object[]
    stuffToWrite)
{
    foreach (object o in stuffToWrite)
        Console.WriteLine(o);
}
```

You can see that there is very little difference in how you create the method or how you test for the members of the array. However, note the difference in the calling sequence:

```
WriteOutput1(new string[]
    { "one", "two", "three", "four", "five" });
WriteOutput2("one", "two", "three", "four", "five");
```

The trouble for your users gets worse if they don't want to specify any of the optional parameters. The `params` array version can be called with no parameters:

```
WriteOutput2();
```

The version with a regular array presents your users with some painful options. This won't compile:

```
WriteOutput1(); // won't compile
```

Trying `null` will throw a null exception:

```
WriteOutput1(null); // throws a null argument exception
```

Your users are stuck with all this extra typing:

```
WriteOutput1(new object[] { });
```

This alternative is still not perfect. Even `params` arrays can have the same problems with covariant argument types. However, you're less likely to run into the problem. First, the compiler generates the storage for the array passed to your method. It doesn't make sense to try to change the elements of a compiler-generated array. The calling method won't see any of the changes anyway. Furthermore, the compiler automatically generates the correct type of array. To create the exception, the developer using your code needs to write truly pathological constructs. She would need to create an actual array of a different type. Then she would have to use that array as the argument in place of the `params` array. Although it is possible, the system has already done quite a bit to protect against this kind of error.

Arrays are not universally wrong method parameters, but they can cause two types of errors. The array's covariance behavior causes runtime errors, and array aliasing can mean the callee can replace the callers' objects. Even when your method doesn't exhibit those problems, the method signature implies that it might. That will raise concerns among developers using your code. Is it safe? Should they create temporary storage? Whenever you use an array as a parameter to a method, there is almost always a better alternative. If the parameter represents a sequence, use `IEnumerable<T>` or a constructed `IEnumerable<T>` for the proper type. If the parameter represents a mutable collection, then rework the signature to mutate an input sequence and create the output sequence. If the parameter represents a set of options, use a `params` array. In all those cases, you'll end up with a better, safer interface.

Item 48: Avoid Calling Virtual Functions in Constructors

Virtual functions exhibit strange behaviors during the construction of an object. An object is not completely created until all constructors have executed. In the meantime, virtual functions may not behave the way you'd like or expect. Examine the following simple program:

```
class B
{
    protected B()
    {
        VFunc();
    }

    protected virtual void VFunc()
    {
        Console.WriteLine("VFunc in B");
    }
}

class Derived : B
{
    private readonly string msg = "Set by initializer";

    public Derived(string msg)
    {
        this.msg = msg;
    }

    protected override void VFunc()
    {
        Console.WriteLine(msg);
    }
}
```

```
class Program
{
    static void Main(string[] args)
    {
        Derived d = new Derived("Constructed in main");
    }
}
```

What do you suppose gets printed—"Constructed in main," "VFunc in B," or "Set by initializer"? Experienced C++ programmers would say, "VFunc in B." Some C# programmers would say, "Constructed in main." But the correct answer is, "Set by initializer."

The base class constructor calls a virtual function that is defined in its class but overridden in the derived class. At runtime, the derived class version gets called. After all, the object's runtime type is `Derived`. The C# language definition considers the derived object completely available, because all the member variables have been initialized by the time any constructor body is entered. After all, all the variable initializers have executed. You had your chance to initialize all variables. But this doesn't mean that you have necessarily initialized all your member variables to the value you want. Only the variable initializers have executed; none of the code in any derived class constructor body has had the chance to do its work.

No matter what, some inconsistency occurs when you call virtual functions while constructing an object. The C++ language designers decided that virtual functions should resolve to the runtime type of the object being constructed. They decided that an object's runtime type should be determined as soon as the object is created.

There is logic behind this. For one thing, the object being created is a `Derived` object; every function should call the correct override for a `Derived` object. C++ is inconsistent here: The runtime type of an object changes as each class's constructor begins execution. Second, this language feature avoids the problem of a having null method pointer in the underlying implementation of virtual methods while the current type is an abstract base class. Consider this variant base class:

```
abstract class B
{
    protected B()
    {
        VFunc();
    }
```

```
    protected abstract void VFunc();
}

class Derived : B
{
  private readonly string msg = "Set by initializer";

  public Derived( string msg )
  {
    this.msg = msg;
  }

  protected override void VFunc()
  {
    Console.WriteLine( msg );
  }

  static void Main()
  {
    Derived d = new Derived( "Constructed in main" );
  }

}
```

The sample compiles, because B objects aren't created, and any concrete derived object must supply an implementation for VFunc(). The C# strategy of calling the version of VFunc() matching the actual runtime type is the only possibility of getting anything except a runtime exception when an abstract function is called in a constructor. Experienced C++ programmers will recognize the potential runtime error if you use the same construct in that language. In C++, the call to VFunc() in the B constructor would crash.

Still, this simple example shows the pitfalls of the C# strategy. The msg variable is immutable. It should have the same value for the entire life of the object. Because of the small window of opportunity when the constructor has not yet finished its work, you can have different values for this variable: one set in the initializer, and one set in the body of the constructor. In the general case, any number of derived class variables may remain in the default state, as set by the initializer or by the system. They certainly don't have the values you thought, because your derived class's constructor has not executed.

Calling virtual functions in constructors works only under the strictest of conditions. The derived class must initialize all instance variables properly in variable initializers. That rules out quite a few objects: Most constructors take some parameters that are used to set the internal state properly. So you could say that calling a virtual function in a constructor mandates that all derived classes define a default constructor, and no other constructor. But that's a heavy burden to place on all derived classes. Do you really expect everyone who ever uses your code to play by those rules? I didn't think so. There is very little gain, and lots of possible future pain, from playing this game. In fact, this situation will work so rarely that it's included in the FxCop and Static Code Analyzer tools bundled with Visual Studio.

Item 49: Consider Weak References for Large Objects

No matter how much you try to avoid it, sometimes you need large blocks of memory for certain algorithms. And sometimes those blocks of memory are needed only occasionally. Maybe you need to read large files to find certain values, or maybe one of your algorithms requires large lookup tables. It seems that you are stuck between two bad alternatives: You could create a local variable, thereby generating a huge heap of garbage every time you run that algorithm. Or you could create a member variable and lock up a large amount of memory for long periods. There are times when neither of those options feels correct.

There is a third option: Create a weak reference. Weak references are almost garbage. You tell the garbage collector that an object is ready to be collected, but you keep a handle to it just in case you want it back before it's collected. When you do it correctly, using a weak reference lets you work with the garbage collector, instead of fighting it, to optimize memory usage.

Suppose you have an algorithm that sometimes needs a 1,000×1,000 array. You've created a class that holds the large array:

```
class MyLargeClass
{
    private int[,] matrix = new int[1000, 1000];
    private int matrixXDimension;
    private int matrixYDimension;

    // elided
}
```

Well, having 1,000,000 element arrays is expensive in any environment. After benchmarking, you see that even though you need one of these arrays only occasionally, allocating and releasing the occasional `MyLarge-Class` object is costing you time. That's when you should create a weak reference to a single `MyLargeClass` object in the hopes that you can reuse it whenever you need it.

Using a weak reference is simple. You create a new weak reference, telling it to hold on to an object that you are finished using, and then you set the strong reference to `null`:

```
WeakReference w = new WeakReference (myLargeObject);
myLargeObject = null;
```

Now the object referred to by `myLargeObject` is considered garbage by the system. If the garbage collector runs, it will collect it. However, suppose you need a `myLargeObject` again before the garbage collector runs. You simply ask `WeakReference` for the object:

```
myLargeObject = w.Target as MyLargeClass;
if (myLargeObject == null)
    myLargeObject = new MyLargeClass();
```

The target property returns `null` if the object has already been garbage-collected. Then you have no choice except to create a new object. You've off-loaded a very hard optimization problem to the runtime. You get to reuse objects when they are still around, but you let the system reclaim the memory resources when necessary. If the weak reference is reclaimed as a strong reference, it has the same contents and state that it had before. But that's not the reason to use a weak reference. If creating the state is what's expensive, then you should keep a strong reference. A `WeakReference` is for the case when allocating the memory is expensive.

That's the simplest scenario. But in many cases this simple scenario isn't what happens. Objects rarely live in complete isolation. Any large object undoubtedly contains references to other objects. The garbage collector needs to be careful about items that are owned by objects that still have weak references outstanding. Suppose `MyLargeClass` contained more member variables:

```
class MyLargeClass
{
    private int[,] matrix;
```

```
    private string reallyLongMessage;
    private int matrixXDimension;
    private int matrixYDimension;

    // elided
}
```

This definition contains an array of value types, a reference type, and two value types. If a MyLargeClassObject becomes garbage, then both the string and the array are candidates for garbage collection. That makes sense. But this code needs to be modified a bit if there are weak references to the MyLargeClass object. Chances are very good that if the garbage collector freed the matrix and the message from the object, something would break. It's just not the kind of eventuality we usually take into consideration. The GC ensures that you never get into this situation, but that takes some work. This discussion is a gross simplification of what really goes on inside the GC, but it is sufficient. You're not writing the GC, only using it.

When you make a weak reference to an object, you really make a weak reference tree: Every reference that is reachable from the target object is marked as being a weak reference. The GC adds an extra step when it marks the in-use objects: After marking all strongly referenced objects, it marks all weakly referenced objects. Then it cleans up. If that does not free enough memory, then the GC reclaims *everything* that is reachable only through weak references.

From your perspective, two things happen when you add weak references. First, the garbage collector takes an extra step to find all memory that might be in use. Second, those objects that can be referenced from objects that are findable using weak references are a better class of garbage. These objects are less likely to be collected than garbage that is completely unreachable. The result is that a weak reference is either completely recoverable or completely lost.

There are other considerations regarding weak references and objects that implement IDisposable. These objects are not good candidates for weak references. You have no way of knowing when to call Dispose() on those objects. You can't very well reuse an object that has been disposed of; its essential elements have been reclaimed. On the other hand, you can't call Dispose() on a weak reference. In short, you cannot know when you should call Dispose() on an object that you turn into a weak reference.

But wait—there is still the finalizer. This causes even more problems. It even introduces the concept of "long" and "short" weak references. A **short weak reference** returns `null` as its target value as soon as it is no longer alive. This means that it has either been collected or finalized. A **long weak reference** continues to return its target value as long as that object is in memory. Even after the object has been finalized, it is still in memory. A long weak reference returns a pointer to an object that has already been finalized. There is very little that you can do with an object after it has been finalized, so I have never run into a situation in practice where I would use a long weak reference.

In practice, weak references help you when you have objects that are very large and are needed only intermittently by an algorithm in your application. Weak references work best for objects that do not need to support `IDisposable`. Almost by definition, these classes do not have finalizers. Within those constraints, weak references work well to let the garbage collector efficiently manage your memory needs. But if you stray outside those bounds, you need to work very carefully.

This advice must come with a considerable caution and warning: Weak references may make your algorithm work faster, but they also have a large impact on the performance of the garbage collector. Because of that impact, adding weak references to your program may make it much slower. Before you consider weak references, optimize your algorithms. Try to rework them to create less memory pressure overall (see Item 37, Chapter 5). Only after those approaches have been exhausted should you consider using weak references. Then benchmark your application with and without weak references, and carefully measure the difference.

Item 50: Prefer Implicit Properties for Mutable, Nonserializable Data

Additions to the property syntax mean that you can express your design intent clearly using properties. Starting with C# 2.0, you can provide different access rights for property getters and setters. In C# 3.0, you can add implicit properties, which complement property access modifiers rather well.

When you add accessible data to a class, often the property accessors are simple wrappers around your data fields. When that's the case, you can increase the readability of your code by using implicit properties:

```
public string Name
{
    get;
    set;
}
```

The compiler creates the backing field using a compiler-generated name. You can even use the property setter to modify the value of the backing field. Because the name of the backing field is compiler generated, even inside your own class you need to call the property accessor rather than modify the backing field directly. That's not a problem. Calling the property accessor does the same work, and because the generated property accessor is a single assignment statement, it will likely be inlined. The runtime behavior of the implicit property is the same as the runtime behavior of accessing the backing field, even in terms of performance.

Implicit properties support the same property access specifiers as do their explicit counterparts. You can define any more-restrictive set accessor you need:

```
public string Name
{
    get;
    protected set;
}
// Or
public string Name
{
    get;
    internal set;
}
// Or
public string Name
{
    get;
    protected internal set;
}
// Or
public string Name
{
    get;
    private set;
}
```

Implicit properties create the same pattern of a property with a backing field that you would have typed yourself in previous versions of the language. The advantage is that you are more productive, and your classes are more readable. An implicit property declaration shows anyone reading your code exactly what you intended to produce, and it doesn't clutter the file with extra information that only obscures the real meaning.

Of course, because implicit properties generate the same code as explicit properties, you can use implicit properties to define virtual properties, override virtual properties, or implement a property defined in an interface.

When you create a virtual implicit property, derived classes do not have access to the compiler-generated backing store. However, overrides can access the base property get and set methods just as they can with any other virtual method:

```
public class BaseType
{
    public virtual string Name
    {
        get;
        protected set;
    }
}


public class DerivedType : BaseType
{
    public override string Name
    {
        get { return base.Name; }
        protected set
        {
            if (!string.IsNullOrEmpty(value))
                base.Name = value;
        }
    }
}
```

You gain two additional advantages by using implicit properties. When the time comes to replace the implicit property with a concrete implementation because of data validation or other actions, you are making binary-compatible changes to your class, and your validation will be in only one location.

In earlier versions of the C# language, most developers directly accessed the backing field to modify it in their own class. That practice produces code that distributes the validation and error checking throughout the file. Every change to an implicit property's backing field calls the (possibly private) property accessor. You transform the implicit property accessor to an explicit property accessor, and then you write all the validation logic in the new accessor:

```
// original version
public class Person
{
    public string FirstName
    {
        get;
        set;
    }
    public string LastName
    {
        get;
        set;
    }
    public override string ToString()
    {
        return string.Format("{0} {1}", FirstName, LastName);
    }
}


// Later updated for validation
public class Person
{
    private string firstName;
    public string FirstName
    {
        get
        {
            return firstName;
        }
        set
        {
            if (string.IsNullOrEmpty(value))
                throw new ArgumentException(
                    "First name cannot be null or empty");
```

```
            firstName = value;
        }
    }
    private string lastName;
    public string LastName
    {
        get
        {
            return lastName;
        }
        private set
        {
            if (string.IsNullOrEmpty(value))
                throw new ArgumentException(
                    "Last name cannot be null or empty");
            lastName = value;
        }
    }
    public override string ToString()
    {
        return string.Format("{0} {1}", FirstName, LastName);
    }
}
```

You've created all the validation in one place. If you can continue to use your accessor rather than directly access the backing field, then you can continue to keep all the field validation in one location.

All this might make you think that implicit properties are always the best choice, but implicit properties have some limitations when it comes to creating immutable types. Even inside your constructor, you must use the property accessor to set the values of your properties. The backing field must support changes, no matter when you call the set accessor. It can't tell the difference between setting the value during construction and setting the value from some other method. This means that your type does not have the initonly flag on the backing field. Furthermore, you could write any mutator methods (subject to access modifiers) and have mutator methods sneak into your type. Thus, when you create immutable types, you should use explicit member variables.

The only way to create a true immutable type is to write the properties and backing fields yourself using a concrete implementation. Implicit properties do not support true immutable types at the JIT level. A type may appear immutable from the perspective of client code, but the runtime cannot verify that the backing field does not change after construction.

There is one other important limitation of implicit properties. You cannot use implicit properties on types that are decorated with the `Serializable` attribute. The persistent file storage format depends on the name of the compiler-generated field used for the backing store. That field name is not guaranteed to remain constant. It may change at any time when you modify the class.

In spite of those two limitations, implicit properties save developer time, produce readable code, and promote a style of development in which all your field modification validation code happens in one location. If you create clearer code, it helps you maintain that code in a better way.

Index

X

Y

Other Great Books on C#

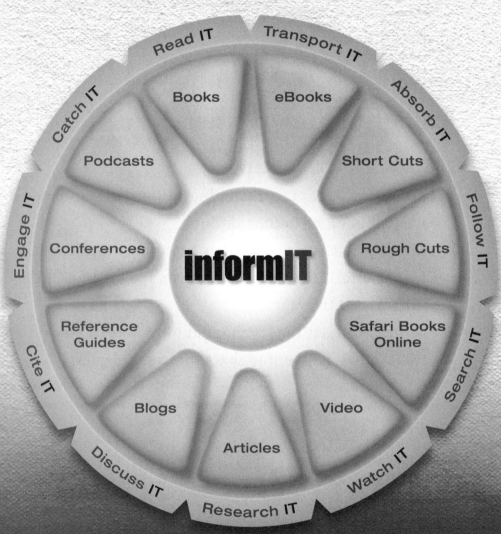

FREE Online Edition

Your purchase of **More Effective C#: 50 Specific Ways to Improve Your C#** includes access to a free online edition for 45 days through the Safari Books Online subscription service. Nearly every Addison-Wesley Professional book is available online through Safari Books Online, along with more than 5,000 other technical books and videos from publishers such as Cisco Press, Exam Cram, IBM Press, O'Reilly, Prentice Hall, Que, and Sams.

SAFARI BOOKS ONLINE allows you to search for a specific answer, cut and paste code, download chapters, and stay current with emerging technologies.

Activate your FREE Online Edition at www.informit.com/safarifree

> **STEP 1:** Enter the coupon code: 1ILP-SCZJ-4HL2-SBJQ-RKWI.

> **STEP 2:** New Safari users, complete the brief registration form.
> Safari subscribers, just log in.

If you have difficulty registering on Safari or accessing the online edition, please e-mail customer-service@safaribooksonline.com